HUBERT RICHARDS

Clare Richards

A Voice Crying in the Wilderness
Hubert Richards:What Really Happened?

the columba press

First published in 2011 by
the columba press
55A Spruce Avenue, Stillorgan Industrial Park,
Blackrock, Co Dublin

Cover by Bill Bolger
Origination by The Columba Press
Printed in Ireland by Gemini International Ltd

ISBN 978 1 85607 746 0

Contents

This book is for
Blanca and Pedro
who
with their beloved Dad
have made my life complete.

Acknowledgments

I must thank Bert's sister Margaret, and friend Nadine, for reading my first manuscript, offering ideas and support. Thanks also to Bert's niece, Ingrid, for her warm encouragement. I want to thank my friend Anne Jackson for correcting typing errors and spelling mistakes!

I am grateful to the hundreds of Bert's former students and colleagues who have shared their love and appreciation of Bert with me. The messages I received on his death inspired me to write this book, as did a re-reading of his extraordinary diaries.

I want to thank the family and friends of Bert who have contributed to a memorial in his name, made possible by Mgr Nicholas Hudson in Rome, Fr Alan Williams in Walsingham, the Walsingham Russian community and Helen McIldowie-Jenkins. Helen, an iconographer, is writing a copy of the icon of Our Lady of Walsingham which Mgr Hudson is receiving at the English College. I am deeply grateful to them. A reading of the book will reveal its significance.

Foreword

'What will happen to my diaries when I die?' my husband asked me. It was only after his death, on 24 March 2010, that I realised I could share his vision through them. For 29 years he was an influential, much loved Roman Catholic priest of Westminster Diocese. For 35 years he was my husband, more than much loved, by me and by our children.

His life tells the story of the Catholic Church in England, from 1939 when he went to the English College, and the Gregorian University in Rome, to the present day. He started his diary in that year, recording not only seminary life, but also the Second World War seen through the eyes of the students. Bert was a brilliant student with a warm heart. He had a great sense of fun, and endless energy that he channelled into building up communities wherever he was. He recorded, with letters, programmes, reports and photographs, the life of the church before Vatican II, during the Council and after. They give us a glimpse behind the scenes of the struggles between the 'Guardians of the Faith and the Prophets'.

Bert, with his love of Greek, Latin and Hebrew, responded to Pope Pius XII's call, in his 1943 encyclical *Divino Afflante Spiritu* to study scripture at the Pontifical Biblical Institute in Rome. As Professor of Scripture at the Westminster Seminary, at Corpus Christi College, in lectures at home and abroad, later in Norwich, and in his writings, Bert has been an inspiration to many people. He was a 'prophet' and as one bishop wrote to me on his death: 'He was a great man and made a massive contribution which was not always recognised and welcomed.' It was the English hierarchy, the 'Guardians', who did not welcome his scholarship, and finally forbade him to 'teach or preach to teachers or students'. He resigned from the priesthood, remaining a Catholic. A priest wrote to him at the time: 'It is you that have the courage and the rest of us who have not.' Bert was readily accepted by other Christians.

The hundreds of letters I received at his death testify to the influence he had on others. An Anglican priest wrote that he was 'a remarkable person, one of the few who was as close to an embodiment of the "Good man, Jesus" as you will get.' A former student reading the eulogy at his Memorial Service, ended with the words: 'He was a humble man, loved by so many. The words of Saint Irenaeus "The Glory of God is a man fully alive" inspired Bert and he passed this on to all of us. Many will have recognised that in him the Glory of God did indeed shine.'

Bert lived what he taught. He put the gospels into a few words: 'Jesus says, God is love, so go and be like him.'

CHAPTER ONE

Early Years
1921-1939

'The Richards', wrote Bert, 'are a strange mixture. My parents were born and bred in parts of Germany so distant from each other that when they first met, they could not understand each other. Worse, when they eventually succeeded in communicating with each other, they both had to learn English, since England was where they had both emigrated to, he at 16, she at 18. This *Englisch* was pretty basic, and remained so for the rest of their lives, punctuated throughout with dozens of *Schwabische* loanwords like *butzlumpa, brilla, nudlunbona*.'

Hubert's father, Richard, was from Broich, near Aachen in the Rheinland. His mother, Bertha, was a southerner, a Schwebischer from Württenberg. In 1905, 16 year-old Richard and his older brother Cornel, emigrated to England to work as butchers in Camberwell. In 1908 Bertha, age 18, came to England to find work as a housemaid. Richard and Bertha met at the Catholic Church of St Boniface in Whitechapel. They married there 18 January 1914 when Richard was 26 years old and Bertha a year younger. There had been a growing German immigrant population in London since the start of the 19th century. By 1875 German Catholics had not only their own large church in Whitechapel, but also their own primary school. Both suffered damage in 1917, and in the second war, complete destruction in a 1940 Zeppelin raid. After the war there was another Catholic influx from Germany, students, hospital workers, domestic workers, au pairs. The church was rebuilt and today there is a German hostel, Wynfrid House, next door.

Just six months after the young couple's wedding, war broke out. Hubert was to describe his parents' anguish in his family history diary. 'German butchers and bakers were attacked. Every night Papa sat on the top step of the stairs in his shop, with a bag of pepper ready to throw at invaders.' Baby Bertha was born in December 1914. By May 1915 Security Forces had decided that all Germans should be interned in the Isle of Man.

Richard and Cornel both had to go. Much later Hubert wrote: 'Mamma and baby Bertha went back to Nagelsberg for the duration. A photo of Richard and Cornel, and a finely fashioned box, that we still use in Norwich for medicines, are the only record we have of this era.' He didn't mention that there is also an envelope, stamped Broich 20.7.15, sent to his father at n. 10300, Camp 7, Comp 5, Hut 3.

The two brothers were not released from the Isle of Man until 1919. Richard returned to Germany, and took his wife and daughter to Weilderstadt where he worked for Daimler cars. 'Then', as Hubert wrote, 'making up for lost time, they produced Cecilia in 1920, me in 1921, Franz in 1923, and Therese in 1925. Hubert, born on Christmas Day, was baptised Johannes Cornelius Hubert on 6 January 1922 in Sts Peter & Paul's Church, Weilderstadt, best known as the birthplace of astronomer Johannes Kepler.

Hubert could only remember watching the trains go by in Weilderstadt. He had better memories of Gailingen where the family moved in 1926 to take over the Gasthaus zum Schwert, which was also the local slaughter-house. He would recall walking uphill to church, and in winter sledging all the way down. He remembered pram journeys over the wooden bridge into Switzerland to smuggle home untaxed tea, and passing the imposing Rothchild mansion near the river. One memory stood out. The day when the two young brothers, blindfolded, dared each other to get nearest to the sewage dump at the back of the house. They both fell in. Running the guest-house was hard work for Richard who was required nightly to sit up with his guests into the early hours, as they played cards. The venture was not very successful and the memory of pre-war London, with streets paved with gold, was enough to persuade Richard and Bertha to leave their homeland and return to seek their fortune in England. In 1928 the family of seven said goodbye to countless relatives and set sail for Dover. It was a brave step because the former years in London had not been easy, with nine moves in seven years.

The return to England years later was just as difficult for immigrants. There were moves and more moves across London as Richard looked for enough work to support his family. His first job was as manager for a butcher in Hoxton, then another move to lodge with relatives in Woodford. In 1930 the family celebrated the birth of a fourth daughter, Margaret. There were two more moves, to Crouch Hill and Kilburn, from where he cycled daily down Cambridge Road to work for his brother Cornel. The family were on the move again in 1933, this time to Cricklewood. Richard commuted daily to work for Schweitzer in Stoke Newington.

Hubert was just seven when they arrived in England and his education was also marked by several moves. In four years he had been to four schools, beginning at St Gildas Convent where he learnt to sing *'Bon jour, ma mère, merci'* whenever the superior turned up. He recalls those school days in his diary. 'My most miserable day was spent with a boy who taught me how to play truant, but had no idea of what to do with ourselves. A better friend taught me the joys to be found in a penn'orth of chips. We went to church at St Peter in Chains, where I made my first communion in 1932.' He recalls, at this time, many happy holidays at his great uncle Lievertz in Southall, with his cousin Gertrud newly arrived from Germany. They explored the canal that ran through the back garden and the fields beyond, vowing eventually to marry each other.

There followed schooling in Salisbury Road, Kilburn, then at the Catholic school in Granville Road. On the move to Cricklewood the younger children attended St Agnes Catholic School, and the two boys joined the scouts. Finally, at the age of 12, Hubert won a scholarship to Finchley Catholic Grammar School, some achievement for a boy who spoke German until he was 7, and who had a disturbed primary education in England. However, it was soon to prove that he was a serious and outstanding scholar.

Hubert travelled the long distance to Finchley on a series of trams, after serving Mass each morning at St Agnes Church. He dutifully raised his cap at the four Catholic churches he passed, referring to them as 'lid stations'. He was allowed a hot meal at school on Mondays when he had carried 2 heavy bags of his Pa's sausages to school. He wrote of these days: 'I have hazy memories of our fleapit cinema in the High Street and of continued nightmares after a horror film; dragging Frank out of the treach-

erous mud at the Welsh Harp where he was being dragged
under; helping on a milk-round, and later a Dollis Hill green-
grocer who failed to pick us up to visit Covent Garden at 5 am,
and walking home sobbing, tailed by a police car; walks on
Hampstead Heath after evening Benediction, for which Papa
would leave his cigar stump on railings; faggots and pease-pud-
ding served hot out front until late on Saturdays.'

In September 1935 the family received their naturalisation
papers. They felt that they had finally become fully 'Englisch'. A
year later Hubert's father bought another shop, this time in
Portobello Rd W11. It was the last move, with the family living
over the shop. The children bussed in their different directions
to school, two girls to the Convent of Jesus and Mary, Frank to St
Ignatius, Stamford Hill, and Hubert on the long journey out to
Finchley. The shop, on the edge of the market, was very busy on
Saturdays when the boys had to help, either at the back, 'where
Papa would make sausages and say a Hail Mary on each one as
he divided them up,' or taking out orders on the shop bike.
Sometimes they had a penny for this service from a customer
and the boys took out a floorboard in the bedroom to keep their
savings in an Oxo tin. From those days Hubert's memories were
of serving Mass at the Dominican Convent up the road; accompanying Papa to Smithfield Market at 6 am and having breakfast there; and the year he carried off 4 prizes at the school
Speech Day. One of these was a prize presented by St Michael's
Convent, the school in Finchley that I was to attend some years
later.

In 1939 when the family officially changed their name by
deed poll to Richards, Hubert gained his Higher Certificate of
Education in Latin and English (with distinction), and in Greek
and French as subsidiary subjects. Hubert's old school, now
Finchley Catholic High School, on reading an obituary in the
Catholic press, researched his school life and wrote their own
obituary for their website. They record that Hubert 'proved
himself to be a brilliant scholar.' He won his Form prize along
with his General Average prize year by year. The latter was
awarded to pupils who gained high average marks in the annual
school exams. It would seem that young Hubert was a serious
academic student with his head always in books. But he was

already showing that he had the remarkable gift of being much more than an academic. He took part in all the social and community activities of the school with enthusiasm. He was treasurer of *Le Cercle Français*, was a regular player in the school dramatic productions on prizegiving evenings, and was the student Tuck Shop Monitor. He took part in all school sports, later to become a daring rock climber and an enthusiastic skier.

Hubert's headmaster was Canon Parsons, affectionately known as Pop Parsons, a formidable and much respected priest. He must have been proud of his bright pupil and overjoyed when he realised that Hubert's parents had instilled a great love of the Catholic faith in their son. He was probably not surprised when his perceptive sixth-form student asked him why very little was ever said about the scriptures. Religion lessons were always about the church. This was, of course, the 1930s when the Catholic Church still imposed upon Catholics a prohibition to read the scriptures without the guidance of a priest to give it the 'true interpretation'. Hubert thought, years ahead of the time, that the four gospels, and an understanding of their Jewish background in the Old Testament, should be more central than the church as an institution that came later. Pop Parsons advised him that the only way he could pursue a deeper understanding of scripture would be to train for the priesthood in Rome where he could move on to the Pontifical Biblical Institute (The Biblicum). Hubert was prepared and ready to take up this advice. His love of the Classics, of Latin and Greek, made him the ideal student to study for the priesthood in Rome.

CHAPTER TWO

And So to Rome
1939

Hubert left school in July 1939 and a few months later left home for Rome. He starts his diary: 'I went to study, at the age of seventeen, at the Venerable English College in Rome. I started keeping a daily diary in January 1940, but have no record of anything before that, except the script of the speech I had to give (along with all the other first-year philosophers) on the feast of St Alexandria, patron of philosophy. A cruel sport.' His speech was short; a simple description of the journey to the college and his impression on entering the fine building, and his obvious delight in what he saw. He had arrived on 2 November and a week later was enrolled in the Pontifical Gregorian University. Students from all the national seminaries in Rome studied there together, with the lectures held in Latin.

During the 1930s William Godfrey, a former brilliant Roman student, was Rector of the English College. It was during this time that the standard of academic teaching at the Gregorian and other colleges reached the highest scholarship. It was also Godfrey who imposed the strictest of rules on the students, which he insisted moulded their character. In November 1938 it was announced that Godfrey was to become Archbishop and return to London. His replacement was Monsignor John Macmillan. Notes in the Senior Student's Diary in 1939 reported that the new Rector was strict, but more approachable and rather less dogmatic about rules. The students were happy.

This was not the best time to be in Rome, with war approaching. Hubert was not to know that the Munich crisis in August 1938 had already made the English hierarchy anxious about the future of the college, with war a possibility. The Fascist government was putting a strain on the church and this seemed to lead the Congregation of Seminaries and Studies to instruct College Rectors to put ever more restrictions on students' behaviour. Rules were severe and there were serious consequences for those who broke them. Michael Williams, in his history of the

English College, commented that '... an attitude to the rule can add to the complications of a life already plagued by customs and traditions.' Hubert, however, seemed to take all this in his stride and entered whole-heartedly into his new life and his studies. He quickly fell in love with Rome and the *Venerabile*. In fact he embraced those customs and traditions with enormous enthusiasm and often with humour.

Pope Pius XI died early in 1939 and the conclave elected Cardinal Pacelli as Pius XII. At the same time the political situation was becoming critical and by August the new Rector was making plans to protect the Venerabile from impending war. The college archives and treasures were removed to the Vatican for safe keeping. Money was transferred to the Vatican Bank. There was the distinct possibility that the college would be transferred to England, and even that students would be mobilised for war. How fortunate for Hubert that following the invasion of Poland and the declaration of war by Chamberlain on 3 September, the immediate danger for the college subsided as it became clear that Italy would not enter into the war at this stage. There followed an eight-month period of calm, with very little military action between Germany, France and Britain, known as the 'phoney war'. It was during those eight months that Hubert left for Rome and became absorbed in his Roman life. His future would have been very different had he started his seminary training in England.

Hubert's diaries are a great witness to his deep faith and his desire to serve God in the church. He commented on every aspect of his priestly formation and from his writings I have been able to understand why he always looked back with such affection for Rome and why the memories of his Venerabile days never left him. From the diaries, I have been able to reconstruct the customs, traditions and daily routine of his student life. His reflections describe prayer life, lectures, meals, walks, and gitas (longer expeditions). He writes with eagerness of the Feast Days celebrated with extra wine and cigarettes, of sporting events, of the many play performances and Gilbert and Sullivan productions. He reports the war news, with anxiety about home, and describes the evening talks, sermon practices and debates that gave these young men the opportunity to explore ideas and appreciate differing views. Not least, Hubert describes the student friendships, their pranks and common room exuberances. He was often at the centre of these youthful escapades, and many a time he had to report to the 'Boss' for oversleeping. His constant tiredness was hardly surprising as he gave himself so entirely to every situation. But let his writing speak for him.

Hubert had arrived in Rome 'in company with one monsignor, two new priests and five youths, sent to study (the youths, that is to say,) in the Venerable English College, the Venerabile, in that City.' Their stay was to be short for Mussolini took Italy into the war in June, and the college evacuation plans were quickly put into action as that became inevitable. Those few months had been enough for the 'youths' to become absorbed into seminarian life of the Roman type.

The first Diary notes in January 1940, set the pattern for the nine hand made volumes that record the next nine years of study, family, and recreation. They are typed pages (originally written by hand) on A4 sheets, illustrated throughout with photographs, drawings, and ticket or programme reminders of concerts and ceremonies.

Mon Jan 1 VEC
New Year's Day
No time yet for any resolutions: too preoccupied with tonight's play. Spent the morning practising Acts II and III, apart from High Mass, where I was thurifer.
After lunch, coffee and liqus, with free tabs for Buxton's 21st birthday. Bed at 2.40, and up at 2.55 for Benediction. Then changed for the play, *Youth at the Helm*, and was made up by Flick (Auchinleck) marvellously, with whiskers and bushy eyebrows (with Tolkien, I was one of the members of the Board). Play went off wonderfully. Not very pleased with self, but the others were really good. Dozens of 'Prosits' after.
Must write some letters.

Tue Jan 2 VEC
We all got up at 6.00 instead of 5.30.
Larry Smith (Vice Rector) has the weird idea we should not

use our zimarra capes as scarves, and telling everyone off.
New Year Resolutions:

>   Make better meditation.
>   Say rosary with more devotion.
>   Act more like a gentleman.
>   Stop using bad language.

Stayed in all morning writing letters and clearing up room.
The Boss gave a talk on bad language, and threatens to chuck
out anyone using it.
Afternoon to S. Benedetto and S. Paulo Fuori di Mure, both
marvellous places, though didn't like Stations of the Cross in
Benedette, Joan Morris or something, too modern. Paul's is a
wonderful place, more impressive at first sight than Peter's.
Tram back 40 cents.
*(I should report that in our 35-year marriage I never heard one
swear word from Bert's lips. Well done Boss!)*

Wed Jan 3 VEC
We return to 5.30 rise. Very cold.
Made better meditation and communion, and at last learnt
the prayer after the Angelus. Disgusting not knowing it be-
fore.
Back to the Gregorian. Three morning lectures.
Mordandini awfully boring, even though a new subject.
Slept.
Soccorsi, realising we don't get what he means, is going
slower.
Arnou is a marvellous chap, the most interesting. His book is
good too.
No lectures this afternoon, so siesta till 3.45.
Then to Pam (Pamphilj Gardens). Nice fresh air.
Couldn't smoke though, because I promised to stop for 3
days if my parcel came. Nuisance. Have locked my cigarettes
away till Saturday.
Main roads clear of snow now.
Evening, did some work on Minor Logic notes. Must get fin-
ished.

Thu Jan 4 VEC

Overslept and got up at 6.15.

Worked on Logic notes till 10.00, then shopping with Tolkien and Lavery. Bought an *Ordo* for 3.50, terribly dear but still. Jewellers to ask cost of new wheel. 15-20 lire 'vairee cheap'. But I could buy a new one for that money. Pity, I like the watch.

Home at 11.30, and worked on notes. Have started reading my Greek New Testament at Spiritual Reading, as well as *Quadragesimo Anno* and *Ave Maria*.

Afternoon it rained so stayed in. Got up at 4.30 for more work. At tea, controversy over the word Chancellor. Looked it up. From Latin'cancer' (lattice). Diminutive 'cancelli' was the fence around the tribunals.

Finished Minor Logic notes, and did some Italian verbs. Forgot to report to the Boss for oversleeping.

Fri Jan 5 VEC

After breakfast looked over my Metaphysics notes.

9.30 lecture quite interesting for Morandini. He explained the purpose of Critica.

Looked at my Guide Book map, and after dinner discussed a good walk with Tyler. Decided on Monte Testaccio, if we could get a camerata together. (Students were only allowed to go on such walks in small groups). All refused except Mark Swaby, game for anything. Dragooned Duck Killeen to come along as well. Set out on a brisk walk. Found it: a small hill with a cross on top. Returned via Trastevere, marvelling how we found our way through this maze of slums.

After tea, choir practice. Then blackened my slippers to look like house shoes. Put a brusher on my cassock. Confession – first time in 3 weeks.

No time to reply to a letter from home. Bed at 10.30.

As the months went by the new students learnt that main Feast Days meant no lectures, good food and drink (binges), extra cigarettes and regular productions of Gilbert and Sullivan. The first one in this year was *The Mikado*. Hubert was to become a big part of productions: acting in many, but always organising and even sewing costumes, building stage sets, as well as putting on performers' make-up. He was always there to tidy up afterwards. He overslept again after the *Mikado*. Already on January 7th he is writing: 'Overslept till 8.00! Almost last one out at breakfast. Shall have to stay up when I am up in future. Disgusting. This is the 4th time. Told the Boss, who was very nice about it, but says I must get up whatever happens.' Hubert was obviously trying to have a quick nap after meditation, before breakfast.

The new men were introduced to the evening programmes. Sometimes they had priests, especially the Vice Rector, visitors or students giving talks or reading papers to them, with very mixed receptions.

'A correspondent from the *Daily Mail* arrived – Ward-Price – and gave us a wonderful talk on "People I have Met" including Hitler, Goering and Ribbentrop. Marvellous description of Goering's castle 7 miles outside Berlin. He likes Goering, but loathes Hitler and Ribbentrop. Very interesting talk, arousing at least 20 questions afterwards. Prosit.'

'Fr Rope gave a paper to the Wiseman Society on "English Literature and the Martyrs". Dreary readings: 3 of the lads near me fell asleep.' Father Rope was a hero a few days later, providing an 'English tea' to celebrate his anniversary. 'The English tea was terrific: bombe, cakes, butter, jam, sugar. Good old Rope! Tyler was last out of the ref, finishing off all the small cakes left over.' This was in March, when rations had been cut, with 'no jam, little sugar, and a scraping of butter'.

They had debates on interesting, even absurd, topics. They also had to listen to 'practice' sermons, knowing that their turns would come one day.

Debate after supper: 'That fanatics have produced greater results than men of clear and calm reasoning'. Some quite good speeches. Some very good summing up speeches for the motion, but the clear calm reasoners won 13-8.

Later in the evenings they retired to the common room for songs around the piano or what they called 'roughhouses' – wild, physical games that often ended in chairs broken or buttons flying off cassocks. On other evenings they watched films.

Three films this evening. *Action for Slander* with Clive Brook
and Ann Todd. Two Charlie Chaplins. Both pre-war, custard
pies. Finished 10.45. Bed at 11.00, with splitting headache.

In fact the splitting headache was due to a bad throat infection that was developing. There was often sickness amongst the
students and staff, no doubt due to tiring long hours – 5.30 am to
11.00 pm on average, with days packed with activities, and low
rations. Hubert, out of action for a week, was well looked after,
but to his great disappointment missed his first gita. On 3
February he wrote: 'Communion in bed. Felt awful, even with
loads of "bloods" to read. Had to sell my Adriano ticket, and
told Meldan not to buy me a ticket for the gita. What a life, to
miss my first gita! Dad Hulme kindly came up to give me St
Blaise's blessing with candles.' He continued the following day:
'Throat worse in spite of gargling and drinking a sort of cough
varnish. A rumour that the gita may be off tomorrow: felt cal-
lously glad.' But the gita went ahead, and Hubert's consolation
was sharing a refectory table with the staff and having 'breakfast with tea (!) and jam (!)'. Fr Harry Martindale spent time with
him during the day, finishing with a walk together and 'tea out
at Watts'. A week later, on the Rector's suggestion, the 'sick
men' had their own gita, led by Fr Martindale. It included a
magnificent meal laid on by a local convent. The diaries suggest
that there was always a warm, respectful relationship between
staff and students.

The gita was an essential part of the Venerabile experience,
the days off when all the students went out for the whole day in
'camerata' groups, to explore their surroundings. They were always energetic journeys, mostly by foot, and often well over 20
miles. They became an enthusiastic part of Hubert's life for
many years.

Behind the scenes the Rector and Vice were keeping their
eyes and ears on the war. As the months went by the students
became more aware of the situation, but life went on as normal.
Hubert was in the unusual position of a kind of neutrality. As
early as January he writes: 'Long letter home. They have asked
me to stop sending on the post I'm getting from Germany.'
Clearly his parents in London were anxious about the political

situation that was emerging, and fearful that their mail could be opened. Meanwhile, Hubert was happily in regular touch with the relations in Germany, and friendly with the German students at the Gregorian. It was a tricky situation, as it became clear that Mussolini was making moves to support Hitler. Hubert was as English as his fellow students, just as his parents were now British citizens and totally loyal to the country that had adopted them. Later, Hubert's brother Frank and cousin Dick Bradley were to join the British army.

An entry on 24 February reads: 'Soccorsi didn't turn up for his lecture, so we turned on the wireless and listened to the English news. Germans and Russians weren't too pleased.' From March Hubert was recording the war news as it came through. 'News in Italian papers that two Jerry planes got over London yesterday. Bad news if its true: our defence must be poor.' Two weeks later: 'News of peace in Finland, where Voborg, the Carelia Isthmus and all the islands in the Gulf have been ceded to Russia for 30 years. Everyone up in arms against England for not intervening.' In March Rector Macmillan returned to England to make preparations in case an evacuation became necessary.

But war was far from the students' minds as the Easter holiday came. Hubert and three others, with only two tickets between them, managed to find excellent places in St Peter's for the Papal Mass on Easter Sunday. 'A 3-hour service, well worth every minute of it. We were bang opposite the papal altar. Cardinals Caccia Dominioni and Heard were there, also D'Arcy Osborne resplendent in uniform. The marvellous Papal March, the Papal Chair, the crowds cheering like mad. Then outside for the *Urbi et Orbi*. The Italians going crazy. Terrific binge for supper, with Easter eggs.'

The next day the college moved out to the Villa, their summer residence at Palazzola, outside Rome, overlooking Lake Albano. They had six glorious days of rest, walks, climbs, swims and their own versions of billiards, 'with enormous balls, and rods of wood for cues.' They tried golf as well, 'But could only find one hole, so we played it from four different angles.' They visited local trattorias and clearly made up for the poor rations at the college. On a gita day, fourteen of them climbed the nearby

Monte Algido. 'At the binge we had the best spaghetti I've ever
tasted, sugo, steak, potatoes, fruit, 2 wines, cheese, coffee and
liqus. 15 lire (3/-) each, the best ever.' As they walked back to
the Villa they recited the rosary, and later that evening had hot
vino and campfire songs. When the holiday was over Hubert
wrote that 'Everyone is pretty miserable coming back to Rome,'
and 'To think it is another 13 weeks before we go back there
again.' It was, in fact, another 6 years and 10 months before he
returned.

In April and May 1940 there are frequent references to the war
in the diary, as everyone was getting anxious about the future. On
7 April the students had a talk from a Dr Fredericsson on
'Finland and the Scandinavian Countries'. He believed that the
Finns were the best soldiers in the world. Hubert noted down
points the speaker made: '1. No chance of a battle on the
Western Front because the fortifications of both sides are im-
pregnable. 2. Our leaflet raids do no good because the people
believe in Hitler whatever he does. 3. Catholics are quite free to
practise their religion. 4. Hitler and Goebbels put themselves
down as Catholics in the Who's Who. 5. Goering isn't the fanatic
he's made out to be, he's got some sense.'

On 9 April news came through of Germany's invasion of
Norway. 'We are said to have sent troops and sunk a German
destroyer off the coast, with air battles all day. But Germany
seems to be winning hands down. Gloom.' News the next day
was different. 'News that the Norway battle is over. We have
sunk 10 German ships, including the Bremen with 10,000 troops
aboard, and landed on the Cattegat. Blimey! Surely an exaggera-
tion. All the chaps enthusiastic that something is finally happening. We all sang Rule Brittania.'

With more news in the Italian newspapers over the next
days, Hubert reports: 'The Italian newspapers are saying that
our navy has withdrawn, leaving Hitler the winner. If this is
true, I believe Churchill has something up his sleeve. I was right.
In the evening news it came through that our navy has laid a
belt of mines 1200 miles long from Holland to Bergen, and also
round the Skaggerak and Cattegat, leaving only a 20 mile gap
for Sweden. We've imprisoned the Germans! Up the British
Navy!' In the same entry he writes: 'An Italian woman is said to

have been thrown into prison for going up to a newspaper stall and asking for 30 cents worth of lies.' On 13 April the stall where the students read the morning paper featured a copy of the day's *Marc' Aurelio* with caricatures of Chamberlain and Churchill on the front. One of the students tore it down and threw it inside the booth.

The Italian lady may have been right about newspaper lies. On 15 April, Reynolds, the *Daily Telegraph*'s Rome Correspondent, visited the college to talk in the Common Room. The Italian papers that day wrote of German success in Norway, and England's failure. Reynolds, who had been in Berlin for 18 years ... 'told us of Germany paying Italy to put this propaganda into their papers, in order to get the Allies worried about Italy's intentions.' Hubert was not sure about this. He continued, 'His paper didn't strike me as being too good: it almost contradicted what Fredericsson told us last week. Catholics (*sic* Reynolds) are undergoing a terrible persecution. Many stories of Jew baiting. He linked the two: Nazis hate Catholicism because it has a Jewish origin! Rather feeble.' On 19 April, it was reported that Italian papers were slackening off the German propaganda, but still said the English were being wiped out. A few days later Hubert reflected that 'All are talking about the likelihood of us having to go back to England soon. They say that the Vice has already got our tickets. I say tripe.'

For the rest of April, and the first 9 days of May, life at the Venerabile went on as usual. Hubert played tennis, swam, and shopped for roses for the Feast of St George, a day when rectors from the Scots, American and Irish Colleges, and the British Consul, joined the 'marvellous binge'. An operetta, written and composed by the Vice, was performed. It was, according to Hubert, 'An absolutely smashing production, with marvellous acting and surprisingly fine costumes.' That same week the students had revision exams, a debate, and went shopping, where Hubert bought a good German anthology to help him keep up his German. They also had a 'Marvellous Common Room roughhouse'.

Hubert only hints at the prayer and priestly life he was embracing but the glimpses are enough to see how seriously he approached it. He mentions that he made a 'marvellous meditation', and that he was beginning to prefer Compline to Vespers. He describes a walk on the Pincio with Shelton, when they had a conversation on prayer. The seminarian life was a healthy mix of serious spiritual preparation and secular, academic and social student life. Hubert liked the ceremonies in St Peter's and had a *specialissimo* ticket, which allowed three others to accompany him for the canonisation of Gemma Galgani and Maria Pelletier. With typical enthusiasm he 'tried the sacristy and the Cardinals' Quarters for a better entrance, but got nowhere. Finally I tagged on to a bishop and walked down the aisle with him, stopping at the Confessio with no one in front of me. Denis Fahy had done even better: he had brought a cotta and walked in with the choir.'

On 3 May news came through of a complete defeat in Norway. 'We have evacuated all our positions, holding on only to Narvik. We have totally underrated the strength of the Germans. It seems more likely now that Italy will enter.' For a few days college life went on as normal, with visits to churches, gita lists being prepared, thesis notes distributed, study, evening walk to St Peter's to see the illuminations, second performance of the operetta, choir practices, many swims, a cricket match, and Hubert playing one of his jokes – as usual. 'Woke Shelton up at 5.30, to remind him we get up at 6.00 today.'

9 May was the last carefree Roman entry where war was not mentioned.

'Catacombs Mass today. Most set off at 6.10 for Low Mass there. I had to serve here. Shelton served with me. We set off at 8.00, walking, and got there at 9.00. (5 miles?). Many interruptions by groups. "O Roma Felix" at the Offertory, bursting into polyphony. I put in a bass part. Photos after, and a Birra Peroni. Walked back to Paul's, tram, tank. 16 of us.' The next day changed everything when news came through that Germany had 'taken over the protection' of Holland, Belgium and Luxembourg. All the Belgian students left. Hubert reported: 'This evening Chamberlain spoke on the wireless, having handed over to that horrible Churchill! The old man sounded in tears as he spoke of his weary endeavours to establish a just peace, and of his miserable failure. He was bitter about "the cause of all this misery in the world – Hitler – a wild beast who has come out of his lair to threaten all of us." He wished Churchill well.'

On 11 May, the Whit holiday, Hubert's group walked miles
to the Piazza di Spagna, to Castel S. Angelo, through Trastevere
and back, looking for strawberries for the gita, but the stallhold-
ers only 'gave us raspberries'. They returned home for the news
to discover that Germany had taken over Luxembourg, but the
Dutch and Belgians were holding the enemy back. The diary
records that 'The Pope has sent messages of sympathy to the
three neutrals. Churchill is forming a Coalition Government,
but we didn't get the names. If it includes Eden and Duff-
Cooper, there's little hope of us staying on here. Mussolini
today said, "You'll have to get used to my silence; deeds will
speak for me" – another of his cryptic remarks which could
mean anything.' Hundreds of placards now appeared all over
Rome about the failure of the Allies. Hubert wondered if that
could mean Italy was ready to join the war. He wrote that 'Three
of our chaps tore one down, and a dago sneaked on them. A
carabiniere called at the College. The Vice stood bail for our
good conduct, but warned us to keep calm and put up with in-
sults ... Shelton told me of a dream he had of us both being med-
ically examined for the army. Tripe. I'm still convinced we'll
stay on.' But he was clearly concerned and his remaining diary
entries for his short stay in Rome simply describe the build up to
their exit and the journey back to England. It is an interesting
read, which follows (abridged).

May 12th VEC
More placards today, but the Italians themselves have been
tearing them down. The Blackshirts are mobilising. The Vice
is worried that the Boss is still in England.
The Italian King is said they have been pressed to rise with
the army against Mussolini. Civil War? When the *Osservatore*
came out last night, the Fascists bought up all the copies.
They know the way the wind is blowing. The Pope has built
a gasproof air-raid shelter in the Vatican, but is preparing to
leave for Portugal.
The Belgians haven't in fact gone home, because they don't
know where to go. Arnou is pleading to go as Chaplain to the
French Army.
A bombshell at supper as the Vice told us that the gita is off.

He's been to the French and British Embassies, who expect
the worst. We must prepare our passports and make arrange-
ments for clothés.
There is only one train, and he's not sure we'll all get on it.
Meanwhile we must keep calm, as it might blow over. Amen.
The rowdiest Common Room ever, everyone singing like stink.
The Vice looks very ill. All passports handed in to him.

May 13th VEC
Public meeting after breakfast. Say nothing to anyone, keep
calm, take with you what you need. Binge for dinner:
Antipasto, meat, sausages, lettuce, radishes, crisps, ham,
fruit, salad, vino, and smoking! Terrific nightmare after, and
slept until 4.00.
Shopping. Bought a rucksack. Said it was for a gita, because I
was looked at suspiciously. Also bought a *Summa Theologica*.
An American stopped us and asked us if we were going. I
told him to suck lemons: we hadn't even thought of it.
The Vice is more optimistic. We're not going tomorrow, and
he doesn't see why we should ever go. In a lovely speech at
supper he prayed for the success of our army against 'that
damned devil, blast him'.

Tue May 14 VEC
Public meeting after breakfast. We had expected to go to the
Villa for the day, but it's been cancelled so that we can fill in
forms for French visas (5 each) and get photos taken.
Student demonstration outside the French Embassy flopped.
Another demonstration at the Palazzo Venezia, where Musso
came out to salute the Nazi flag. Behind it came a coffin with
the Union Jack painted underneath.
At Rosary, the Vice told us that we were definitely going, on
the advice of D'Arcy Osborne. He was in tears. We said the
rosary to ourselves but I couldn't concentrate.
Out immediately to the photograph machine, German
Officers parading in the Piazza Colonna. 5 photos, 5 lire.
Over to the Fagiano to toast coffins to Hitler and Musso in
lager and Orvieto. Back via Peter's for the last time.
Helped store stuff not being taken with us in the organ loft,

which is to be bricked up. All entrances to the Farnase now blocked.

Wed May 15 VEC
Up at 6.00. Communion before Mass.
To the Gregorian to see Arnou. He told us physical and moral force was necessary, and was sure he'd see us back again next November.
Went on to see Morandini, smoking, to say goodbye.
In front of the Gregorian, 300-400 students were shouting 'Down with the English and French'. Came home to pack. All schools closed till September. Holland has capitulated.
We were all given £1 each at dinner. Coffee and liqus to get rid of stocks.
After, with Meldan C. and Tyler to Watts to have a good feed. Then Mary Major's and the Doge for a beer. Guards stopped us and a soldier escorted us to the door.
The *Osservatore* was publicly burnt in front of Mary Major's. Finished packing. Another £1 distributed at supper, plus visas, passports and identity cards. The boss finally returned, to huge cheers.
We're definitely off tomorrow, only one train available. Forbidden to make any demonstrations. Packed and talked till midnight.

Thu May 16 VAC TRAIN
Up at 4.15, Mass at 5.00. Breakfast.
I was in the second taxi to the Station. Dreary waiting. Neville Henderson and all the diplomatic staff to see us off. Also a couple of German students, in black cassocks. Decent.
Train, crowded, started off at 8.30. Journey uneventful till Turin, where Fallon, Hannon, Fraser and Auchinleck got off to buy tabs, and missed the train. Vice beserk, since they had no tickets.
Posh dinner with Shelton, though had to push.
Modane at 10-00 pm ... singing the *Marseillaise* & cheering the Frogs.
In the 2 hours delay the delinquents caught us up, fruited by Vice.

Fri May 17 PARIS

Horrible journey. What is more uncomfortable than a French 3rd class carriage overnight with 6 other people round you? Troop movements slowed us up considerably. We arrived in Paris at 1.00 pm, 5 hours late, dead tired. Dragged our cases and rucksacks across from St Lazare Station to the Hotel Anglo-Americain. Rooms, a wash, and out to find food with Swaby, Tolkien, Wall and Shelton.

Walked up the Champ Elysées, examining the cinemas.

Good dinner at hotel with vino and ice cream. Then with Shelton and Wall to see *Hunchback of Notre Dame* in English with French subtitles. Very good, but a bit creepy. Could find no beer, nor would the hotel serve us. Went to bed thirsty.

Sat May 18 TRAIN

Up at 6.30 for Mass across the road in a pretty poor church. Continental breakfast, and off on the Metro to see 'Notre Dame', heavily sandbagged. PM with Shelton to see Ginger Rogers and David Nixen in *Bachelor Mother*, a good film. High tea at 5.00, but an air-raid warning cleared all the cars off the streets and closed the shops. Guns in the distance. Tea delayed. Bought a beret, and took bags over to the station, and grabbed seats. Another dreary journey to Le Havre, with an air-raid on the way stopping us for an hour. Reached the port, a filthy hole, at 11 pm, and then dragged my cases around for 2 hours to get my passport stamped.

A woman threatened to throw herself into the sea, and I felt like doing the same. Very cold. Got some beer and coffee with Shell who had managed to get on an hour earlier.

Sun May 19 CHANNEL

Found a deckchair and rug. Tried to sleep, but it was too cold. Sailed at 4.00 am. Eventually got some breakfast, but no eggs and bacon, which had to be ordered beforehand! Due in Southampton at 6.00, but didn't reach there till 11.00. I had my bags all ready on the top deck, only to find we were landing from downstairs. The language! Most of us decided to stay on board till everyone else was off. It took one and a half hours. Customs very suspicious, and asked about letters.

Luckily I had hidden the German ones inside an English envelope.

Arrived in London about 6.00 pm. Papa, Mamma, Cecilia, Frank and Margaret came to meet me in a taxi. (I had managed to phone them in Southampton). Lovely to ride through the London streets again. In the evening to Hyde Park to listen to the band. Cecilia and Teresa very interested in Rome.'

CHAPTER THREE

'Rome' in England
1940-1946

To the family Hubert was, of course, always 'Hubert'. In Rome he was first called Bert, that is how all his future friends, fellow priests and students came to know him. Bert reported that he had a good holiday, during which time he also helped his father in the shop. He wrote: 'I went to see Cardinal Hindsley, who told me I was too thin (jealous of me I imagine). Kelly, Brown and the Boss were also there. The Boss told us he'd found a place for us all on Lake Windermere, but it was very small, and 2 or 3 of us would have to share a room. Later we heard from the Vice that we were all to come to Ambleside on 17 June. No library, so to bring plenty of books. Opportunity for swimming and tennis. The news delighted me.'

In the first week of June, Bert reported the Retreat to Dunkirk, and a week later he comments: 'The evacuation of Dunkirk draws to a close. 98% of our men are saved. It is being acclaimed as a miracle. Every seaworthy ship in England underwent bombing and machine gunning to ferry our men home.' Two days later Italy finally declared war, with Mussolini clearly thinking it would come to an end sooner rather than later. In a memo to the Army Chief-of Staff, Marshall Badoglio, he wrote: 'I only need a few thousand dead so that I can sit at the peace conference as a man who has fought.' The Italian people, and even the soldiers, did not really know what they were fighting for, and many saw little justification for it. Bert made no comment on hearing the news, merely stating 'Italy finally declares war.'

There was determination that the England 'exile' would not harm the special character of the Venerabile. The intention was to preserve the spirit and traditions of Rome and to keep the students together as the already formed community before returning to Rome after the war. The Vice Rector, Monsignor Smith, was responsible for making the arrangements for a temporary stay in Croft Lodge, a large house with good grounds overlooking the river Brathay. A Miss Cobbe owned the house and let it out to the Catholic Holiday Guild. The students saw themselves as her holiday guests, although during the six-week stay there were lectures, exams and the usual routines. The students enjoyed the river and had use of two boats, Hubert having a swim and a row on the very evening of his arrival.

A shock awaited the students. At first it was the sleeping arrangements: 'The bedroom was a bit of a shock: ten of us in one room, with only 2 washing places, one wardrobe and one chest of drawers. We shall just have to manage.' This simple acceptance of the situation, without grumble or complaint, is an early indication of Bert's ability throughout his life, to cope with anything thrown at him however disturbing, with a humble dignity and amazing self control. But a bigger shock was to come, when they discovered that in England there were to be no servants as in Rome. They would have to make their own beds and help in the kitchen. A public meeting was called to discuss 'What is and what is not in a programme of a seminary.' A motion was passed 'That this house repudiates potato peeling and looks upon it as a purely voluntary effort. Either the Vice must get maids or a mechanical potato peeler'.

The young seminarian students were not unaware that other men of their age were going to be in far greater hardship, with their lives in danger, fighting for their country. It caused much soul-searching about 'vocation', and the diaries suggest that Bert and his friends needed reassurance from their spititual director that they were in the right place.

During the short stay at Croft Lodge the students studied hard but enjoyed hours on or in the river, exploring the magnificent countryside with long walks and climbs on gita days. They swam in Windermere, Loughrigg Tarn, Grasmere and Grisedale Tarn. They walked the 3 miles daily into Ambleside and 3 miles back for the 'Stations of the Cross'. Bert helped the local parish priest in his garden to make a rose bower, and 'swotted hard, at least for the last three days, and got 85% on the thesis *Voluntas potest movere intellectum.*' He enjoyed the final concert as the best he had ever attended at the college. The Roman experience was still alive.

Their stay ended on 27 July. They had a long summer holiday until the Jesuit College at Stonyhurst in Lancashire was ready to take them in. This meant that Bert was in London when the bombing of the capital began.

It was during these holidays that the Battle of London started. The first air raid warning was very scary after there had been nothing for nearly a year. Then came the bombs, first on the East End, which I went across to see, a smoking mass of wreckage (our shopman Fred was made homeless); and then of the West End, all the big stores and hospitals; and then nearer home. Then came the night raids, the siren going with clockwork regularly every evening at 9.00. At first the raid used to last till about 1.00 am, but this later stretched to 5.00, then 6.00, then 7.00.

For safety's sake we all eventually decided to sleep in the corridor on the ground floor, between the shop and the meat safe, taking pillows and blankets down every evening. I managed to sleep well after a time. The screaming bombs were the most frightening, and we resigned ourselves to our last moment. The invasion never came of course, but we're all expecting anything to happen.

On 25 September Stonyhurst was ready to receive the English College. It was a Jesuit place of study, which meant a link with the Jesuit Gregorian University in Rome. The move was into St Mary's Hall, but its acquisition had not been easy. Stonyhurst had been built in 1794 to house English Jesuit semi-narians returning from Europe because of the expulsion of the unpopular Religious Order. St Mary's Hall was added in the 19th century as the house of study for philosophy. It was left empty and neglected when the Jesuits moved their seminary to Heythrop in 1926. Thanks to the persistence of Cardinal Hinsley and Monsignor Smith, the Jesuits offered the Hall to the college. There was work to be done before it could be made their home, but it was ideal, having a chapel, kitchens and enough rooms for the students and staff.

Furniture was found and stored, and priests everywhere were asked to lend or give books. They responded well, including Canon Parsons from Bert's old school in Finchley. An advance party cleaned and painted some of the building, before it was left to the arriving body of students to claim 'piled up furniture crammed in the chapel', to make their rooms habitable. Bert had a great time 'snooping stuff and cleaning up my barn of a room,' walking the next day the 5 miles to Clitheroe for paint, whitewash, yellow ochre, distemper, cloth, nails, and lino. Between the resumed daily routine he decorated his room, finding odd pieces of old furniture to make into useful additions to the room. Auchinleck gave him a washstand on which he put shelves to serve as a 'tallboy-cum-bookstand'. He got hold of an old toilet seat to make into his new washstand, and rigged up a board on brackets he had found for a wardrobe. He planned to put curtains around his bed and extend the lighting. His parents helped by sending him lengths of material. He made a candle-extinguisher out of a tin and a lid. A few weeks later he made himself an armchair!

All the students had to be inventive, but the diary reveals that many would go to Bert when they needed DIY jobs. It continued over the years. He also helped out staff, decorating rooms and chopping logs for their fires. The large rooms had inviting fireplaces, and throughout the cold months in Stonyhurst Bert and friends would search the woods for fallen logs, chop them up and portion them out to staff and students. It supplemented their weekly ration of coal. It may be this enthusiastic willingness to 'get stuck in' to help the community that endeared Bert to the Rector and staff. He was sometimes reprimanded for his exuberance, talkativeness in lectures, breaking of small rules, and especially for oversleeping and arriving late for meditation. Yet the reprimands were usually gentle and understanding. 'Overslept again till 7.45. Reported I was late to the Boss. He said "Was you?" in an octave.'

On 16 October Mass of the Holy Spirit was said for the 'Solemn Inauguration of Studies'. The students were urged to keep up all the good things of the Roman tradition. That was not difficult for Bert who always longed for Rome. On the Feast of Quattre Coronati, three weeks later, he writes: 'I remembered the beautiful little church where I had first experienced bay leaves underfoot. *O Roma Felix*. Oh to be back there.' It was a full five months since they had left Rome. After the first lecture Bert wrote that there was a 'fight for the back bench. I got a place, and intend to stick to it so that I can sleep in peace.' His friend, Tyler, was probably there too, as it seems he slept through many a lecture. It is interesting that the two of them got consistently high marks in all the exams, quite especially Tyler.

The two of them also spent time exploring everything around them. Within days they had discovered the underground tunnel leading across to a priest's hiding hole in Stonyhurst College. They could see the other end, but were cut off by the mud. Jesuits were so used to persecution that they built priests' hiding holes in their houses as late as the eighteenth century, when Stonyhurst was built.

In these very early days at St Mary's Hall there were many headaches for the Cardinal and the Rector, behind the scenes. They had to ensure a good staff to deliver the high standard expected of the Venerabile. Several came over to England with the students, including the Jesuits, Fr Bernard Leeming and Fr Bob Dyson. The Stoneyhurst Jesuits were able to give talks, take retreats and hear confessions, or occasionally teach an individual thesis. Another anxiety was to find nuns to take over the kitchen. However, the students still had to live without servants, keeping their rooms clean and generally helping around the house. Bert became chapel sacristan.

With lectures in place, four on some days, life settled down to normal: prayer dispersed throughout the day, the obligatory camerata walks, with occasional gitas, debates, papers, concerts, the G&S Operas, swims over at the school, plenty of sport, choir practice, songs around the piano in the common room, and those boisterous roughhouses where cassocks were torn and buttons were lost. Thursdays were free days which meant shopping trips, time to read, time to draw breath, to work on the pantomimes or sew the costumes, and even time to hatch new tricks on each other. It also gave time to swat for the exams, with Bert sometimes wondering why it was so difficult to get down to it. He would surely have been depressed if he had realised that it would take years before the journey back to Rome. Later he writes: 'New Stations of the Cross have arrived, in white terracotta, originally designed for the Villa chapel. The best I've ever seen, except for the ones in S. Girolamo. *O Roma, nostris cordibus.* Stonyhurst invited us to a *March of Time* film of Vatican

City, Peter's, the City, the Greg. Made me homesick.' Three days later: 'p.m. The Boss caught me in the house and gave me a fruit (a reprimand) for not being out. But where can you go day after day? It's not like Rome.'

It was September 1946 before that return to Italy. Like Mussolini, Bert got it wrong, always thinking that the war would end soon. He was nervous about the situation, especially because his family were in London. At times he wrote with anxiety that his parents' letters were late in arriving. They faithfully kept in touch, often sending wonderful parcels of chocolate, tabs, Mama's cakes, and anything he asked for; once that included a bicycle! There were high times and low times during those long years of study and exams, with Bert never losing that desire for Rome. He was an 'international' student with a love of languages and music, of classics and of art. He had all that in Italy. He could already speak French and German, warmed immediately to Italian, and Latin came very easily to him, so that he was comfortable with the Roman lectures given in Latin. He was a Venerabile student through and through when many of his fellow students lost interest in the past; they enjoyed Stonyhurst to the extent that they did not wish to return to Italy. They were perhaps delighted that, in time, some lectures in St Mary's Hall were delivered in English. In November 1940 Hubert reported that the 'Boss's lecture began in Latin – but only for 5 minutes, it beat him too.'

Early in 1941 Bert went on a walk with a small group, including one of the lecturers, Fr Ekbery. The diary entry reads: 'We got into so much mud, Ekbery refused to go further. We had a tab and walked back. Interesting conversation with E. about those who are so happy here they don't want to return to Rome, those who want to go back because they are not happy here, and those who are happy here and also want to go back.' Bert comments further, 'If the college was composed entirely of the last, this place would be less dead and more alive than it is.'

Later annual diaries are shorter than the 1940 one. Bert had already set the scene and given a very accurate picture of the daily life of a seminarian at the Venerabile. Further glimpses into the seminary diaries illustrate the richness of his experience, which profoundly influenced the rest of his life. The acad-

emic courses were rigorous. He preferred some lecturers to others, as any student would. 'Ekbery very dry, even Kileen went
to sleep.' Probably not surprising as Bert found one of his lectures 'totally unintelligible. It was on psychophysical paral-
lelism.' Years later he was to become a lively lecturer and
teacher, widely acclaimed for his attractive style, which caught
the admiration of his students. He could always make them
relax and laugh. Perhaps he learnt this from the Rector, reporting
good lectures 'from the Boss, with some really funny remarks.'
When Bert had difficulties he would seek help. 'Went to see
Leeming about difficulties on the divinity of Christ. He explained the matter well, but was annoyed that none of the theologians had solved my difficulties.'

As exams approached he noted that the daily 5½ hours of
study expected, with 2¼ hours for a walk 'just about right'. He
found that he preferred to 'swot' using all Latin texts rather than
suggested English ones, and it enabled him to report in July
1941, 'My exam was at 9.30. I got '*intellectus agens*', and quan-
tites' as an accident really distinct. I got a 10. Much relieved.' A
year later students had to lead the class (in Latin) on difficult
theses. Bert reports that he had to lead 'the *Disputatio* next
Monday on the first of St Thomas's Five Ways, and defend the
difficulties.' It went well. He wrote: 'Ought I to find these Ways
more convincing than I do?' On another occasion he reported:
'Lectures today on the Simplicity of God. Never heard anything
more complex!'

In July 1942 he took his first important exams. His entry in
the diary was simple: 'My exam on 100 Theses of Philosophy. I
became PhL.' On return to Stonyhurst after the holidays Hubert
wrote: 'I am glad to have finished with all the abstruse philosophy we have had over the last three years, and to get down to
some theology.' A new Jesuit professor joined the staff from
Innsbruck University, Fr Engelbert Gutwenger. 'He has already
become known variously as Fr Finknockle, Fr Luftwaffe, Fr
Lebensraum, and Fr Knuckleduster.' Bert found him a good
lecturer, with a fine command of English and Latin, although
'his pronunciation (*tsolum* for *caelum*) causes laughter'.

In 1943 Bert did well in his Canon Law exam, which he had
been dreading. Meanwhile he was enjoying Church History and

finding his study of *De Deo Trino* (the Trinity) getting himself into 'deep water'. Later he is still finding it very 'tough going'. He was taking the lead in giving the *difficultates* in a lecture, and was reported that it went well, 'I gave my *difficultates* today in 3rd lecture. They were apparently very good, because Clark couldn't answer them.' Clark was one of the best students, later to become Bishop of East Anglia. As the term ended Bert was happy to gain a 9 in both History and Morals. In his 1944 and 1945 diaries he made little mention of his lectures, fretting more over his sermons, which had to be given to the students for criticism, and over his solo parts in the chapel: 'I made a terrible hash of cantor at Vespers: first couldn't reach the note for the Alleluia, then made the Boss and the whole side stand up for their antiphon, only to realise there wasn't one (I nearly made one up to save face).'

In July 1944 Bert took more final exams. He wrote: 'The many activities during the year, and the many minor subjects to be taken (Canon Law, Hebrew, Prophecy, Church History, Morals) meant that I was very far behind in my swat. But I did quite well, taking the main exam in Latin, and got a 9. After the Morals exam, Graser even said there could be a post-grad place in Rome for me, doing Canon Law. No, the subject doesn't appeal to me, but it's one way of ensuring a return to Rome!' After the holidays Bert talked with Fr Dyson about going back to Rome to take the biblical degree, which he really wanted. Fr Dyson was to recommend him to Cardinal Griffin. The final exams for theology were in 1946, after ordination. Bert makes no mention at all of his studies during this time; he simply pasted the 100 theses sheets into the diary and a copy of his Gregorian degree –*Licentiam in S. Theologica, cum laude probates*. (With praise).

The evening talks and debates were a way of ensuring the students would look at church, social and world issues, in a more relaxed way. The list of visiting lecturers or personalities was impressive. Some were better speakers than others. Bert found Christopher Hollis' talk to the Literary Society on 'The Situation in America' 'dry and uninteresting'. He praised Fr George Burns SJ who addressed the same group on 'English Catholics and Catholicism in Europe'; and enjoyed Fr Dyson's evening lantern lecture on 'Egypt and Tutankhamen'. Bert had much praise for Fr D'arcy talking on 'Belief': 'The real goods! Kept presenting problems, and just leaving them open. He wound up with some beautiful remarks on the Philosophy of History.'

Robert Speaight, the actor, spoke one evening about 'The Sword of the Spirit', 'without making it any clearer to me what it's all about. In a vote of thanks, Fooks finished: "The last time I saw Mr Speaight he was pretending to be St Thomas of Canterbury in *Murder in the Cathedral*. I must say I preferred him tonight. Then I saw St Thomas. Tonight I have seen Mr Speaight".' Bert found Fr Agnellus Andrew OFM inspiring in his talk on 'Social Action', and enjoyed the stories told by a Passionist priest, 'the legendary Dr Garvin,' who, during a Mission in Willesden, London, visited a cockney woman. 'Are you a Catholic?' 'Yus.' 'Did you go to church last Sunday?' 'Nah.' 'I'm sorry, I thought you were a Catholic'. 'Yus.' 'Well, did you go to church the Sunday before?' 'Nah.' 'Oh, I thought you were a Catholic.' Yus.' 'Well, have you ever been to church?' 'Nah.' 'Well, do you realise that you are in a state of mortal sin, and that if you died now, you would go to hell and burn for all eternity?' 'Blimey, you aint arf got up cheerful this morning, aintcha?'

The students were impressed by Arnold Lunn, who spoke on his reminiscences of America and Spain, especially enjoying his stories about Churchill. 'He told his son Randolph to kneel for the Pope's blessing, being unable as Head of State to do so himself, but "snuggling up behind Randolph to get the back-wash".' Lunn told of Churchill in a Russian Hotel 'telling Cripps how he disliked the Russians, and Cripps warning him of hidden microphones. Churchill replied, 'I called them bloody baboons before this war, and shall continue calling them bloody baboons after the war. At the moment I am in a position where I can't call them bloody baboons. But if there's a secret microphone in this room, I hope the bloody baboons at the other end like to hear themselves called bloody baboons, because bloody baboons are what they are.'

At one talk, on 'The Catholic Missionary Society', Bert bet a tab with Tyler, who was giving the vote of thanks, that he wouldn't introduce the 'Cappadocian Cloverleaf' from the Boss's notes on Church History into his speech. 'He said that for another tab he'd even bring in the "Angel of Meaux". And he did. I snorted half way through in my struggle to keep a straight face, and it nearly made him burst as well. The Boss meanwhile buried his face in his hands.' Bert saved his greatest praise for one of the Jesuits, without any explanation. 'Early supper, and a talk from Fr Broderick, the best speaker I have ever heard, a great man and a great priest.' The students had to contribute to these evenings by presenting papers. Bert's talk was on the 'The Problem of Pain'. Tolkien, a student in his year, gave his on 'Lewis Carroll'. Tolkien's father was J. J. R. Tolkien, who wrote some chapters of *The Lord of the Rings* at Stonyhurst. He enjoyed staying there and occasionally spoke to the students during his long stays. The famous book is set on Pendle Hill, a favourite location for Bert's gitas.

Evening debates were always lively and pleasant introductions to a wide variety of issues and opinions. They were as varied as 'Professionalising Sport', and 'Modern Literature is Degenerate'. Bert enjoyed one debate in particular. 'A debate: "That the commercialisation of the Press is increasing and ought to be diminished".' Cotter was Prime Minister and Fr Leeming led the Opposition. I thought every speech the best ever made in our debates, until I heard the next one! It finished, the next day, in a galaxy of more wonderful speeches, to which I wanted to add mine, but time was up. Motion won by 1 vote.' In this debate it was a student who won the motion, the staff member who lost. Bert wrote how concerned he was over a debate he was asked to lead: 'That women should be excluded from the professions.' He writes: 'The blasted debate looms ahead. Can find hardly any arguments to support the motion, least of all from Johnson who is supposed to be seconding me.' (I hope Bert 'happily' lost the motion.) Unfortunately, he was so occupied at that time writing an article for the Venerabile College Diary, that he makes no comment on the result.

I suspect that it would be difficult to find a better academic and cultural education for the priesthood anywhere. The balance between prayer, study, and healthy recreation was unique. The relationship between staff and students was remarkable,

with the former readily taking active part with students in recreation hours, yet remaining respected and dignified because of
their genuine affection and concern for the young seminarians;
and this in spite of the rigid application of rules and discipline.
Perhaps it was possible because of them. The students had a
voice, and were able to express concerns, and offer suggestions
at the regular Public Meeting. What was missing, as it had always been in Catholic seminaries, was an adequate study of
psychology, sexuality and sociology. A change would be introduced later with the Vatican Council and encyclicals, like Pope
Paul VI's *Populorum Progressio*.

Each new academic year started with a tradition in the
Common Room, called 'Premiations'. Students took on roles of
the staff, giving speeches and presenting appropriate mock
'prizes'. In 1945 Bert took the part of the Rector of the Gregorian,
another student was the Cardinal, Spud was a Cockney
Prosecuting Counsel, and a new professor Rea (Bert was later to
find his 'rolling and eloquent Latin a sheer delight') a comic
character. Bert's Latin speech introduced two professors, 'Dns
Gulielmus Butterfield and Dns Georgius Ekbery' before 'Spud
appealed to "My Lord, gentlemen of the Jury, gentlemen, and
Mr Killeen" in a most atrocious Cockney voice, and proceeded
to accuse Ekbery of murdering Mendelsohn, and Butterfield of
742 crimes, reduced to 10 charges.' The charges included:
spending too long preparing lectures, of being himself, of
singing in public, and of singing at all. Bert added: 'Any inter-
ruption in Spud's flow, or even any attempted answer to his
questions, was answered with a rasping "Shaddup". Farrow as
Cardinal Protector welcomed the new professors, Lynch and
Rea, the first "volunteering to go from one prisoners' camp to
another, and Rea for being the sort of person who might hope-
fully give us many *dies non*".' (Free days).

Bert entered into these community activities with enormous
enthusiasm, and he never lost the opportunity in later life to
bring people together and create harmony in the groups he
taught, and the pilgrimages he led. He had a natural gift of making everyone feel comfortable, and even important, in any
group. He often achieved this through his love of music, which
he was to express in his song writing and guitar playing. The

College seemed to give every student the invitation to explore their own gifts and to share them in the wider community. Bert, quick to respond, was happy to comply with any request. He always loved art and found himself drawing and painting throughout his years of study. At first it was the drawings of Rome, requested in his first year at Stonyhurst, to decorate the common room. Later requests came from the Rector, who asked Bert to sign them, and had them framed. The students had a satirical magazine *Chi Lo Sa?* (Who are you?). Bert was asked to provide a dozen or so cartoons of staff and students for each issue. No doubt he had been spotted drawing cartoons of students in class. There are some in his diaries.

One edition caused quite a stir. The new German professor was showing his visitors around, and in the Common Room they picked up the Christmas issue with a comic article and cartoon about him. 'He flew in a rage, and went straight to the Boss to offer resignation! The Senior Student was called, and had to explain it was the students' sense of humour, not the superiors. When G. was assured that it hadn't had the 'imprimatur' from the beaks, he relaxed. But of course it had! The Boss called me in, bewailed the German sense of humour, (!) and told me to make sure the magazine was left in the cupboard in future.' Later Bert was to become editor of the magazine, staying up all hours to get it out.

His artistic skills were again called upon when scenery for the plays and operas was needed. He painted Gilbert and Sullivan characters on the theatre back wall, with Tolkien and Johnson. In October 1943, Bert reports: 'Tolkien and I have graduated from the Theatre murals to another in the main entrance, of Ralph Sherwin and Thomas of Canterbury.' The accompanying photo shows the students, in their cassocks, painting a very fine mural. A week earlier Bert had entered into his diary that: 'It rained all day, so wrote several letters, and started framing my pictures again, the Villa and Croft Lodge for the common room, and one for Swan and one for Clark. I have a translation to type, some drawings to do for a Venerabile Romanesqe, and a Panto to write.' Was it any wonder that his last entry for that year reports: 'The fact that I did only one drawing for *Chi Lo Sa?* is indicative. I went to bed on 26 December for 2 days, and so missed the CR sessions, where the panto songs were yelled for again and again.'

Bert was able to relax. He somehow found time to read. This included Shakespeare (which he tried to translate into Latin), *Pride and Prejudice*, P. G. Wodehouse, murder mysteries ('bloods'), German novels, and Graham Greene. He criticised Greene's *The Power and the Glory*: 'A powerful book, but completely off the lines. These authors ought to learn some dogma before writing such books about the faith. The characters are nebulous, and the main figure is quite inconsistent.' It was *Wuthering Heights* that completely caught his attention. 'I have hardly put it down.' He opted to give a paper on the Bronte Sisters which came to 20 typewritten pages, and he could only give half of it on the first evening. 'It went very well, and by popular request I finished it yesterday, with only time for one question at the end. Everyone keen on the Brontes, and wanting to borrow *Wuthering Heights*.' This was in 1942. Two years later Bert lead a gita to the Bronte country, writing it up with unusual detail, and Tyler suggested that it should appear in the Venerabile magazine. In the November 1943 edition William Purdy had written an article suggesting gitas were not for export to England. Tyler and Bert were anxious to prove Fr Purdy wrong. Bert's article, in the November 1944 edition was well received. The two articles are stapled into the diary and a short note follows, sent from Carlisle. It read:

> Dear Hubert,
> Bravissimo! You are more
> than a *Venerabilino* – you are a
> Roman *et le saluto*.
> *Romanamente*
> Richard L. Smith.

What pleasure this must have given Bert, a note from the former Vice Rector, who had passed on to his student his own deep love and appreciation of The English College, Rome.

Bert was also able to relax by listening to music, writing it or playing it. He appreciated all kinds of music, as one person later wrote, 'from Beethoven to the Beatles'. As a student he took violin lessons from another student, and later taught himself to play the guitar, which he took everywhere. On one occasion, passing through the checkout at Heathrow, he was asked, 'What have you in there?' 'Oh, it's packed with cigars', he replied with a smile. He was waved through. It was indeed packed with cigars for Papa! In those first months in Rome he was able to go to a few concerts at the Adriano. 'Made our way to the Adriano, George Pitt having paid for my ticket when he heard I wasn't going to go. Wonderful programme: Mozart's Symphany in G minor, Lalo's Spanish symphony, some Greek dances, Wagner's Tannhauser Overture – this last especially striking. Good seats too. Really enjoyed the whole thing. All of us (about 30) got home late.' A week later he was at the Adriano for another concert: 'On the whole, not so good as last week, but the Mozart (*Eine Kleine Nacht Musik*) I enjoyed as I have never enjoyed music before.' The students were able to listen to records on the 'gramophone', and Hubert took full advantage of it, especially enjoying Beethoven. In his holidays he went to BBC Promenade Concerts conducted by Sir Adrian Bolt. At Stonyhurst, the college hosted concerts, including the Halle Orchestra, conducted by Malcolm Sargent. Of one concert in 1941, which included Dvorak's *Carnival* Overture, and Handel's *Water Music*, he writes: 'Better than anything we heard at the Adriano in Rome. He (Sargent) just flung himself at the orchestra, and played every instrument with them. Superb.'

Another recreational enjoyment in Stonyhurst, which Bert clearly liked, was the films, shown regularly in the common room. Later, when one of these 'old' films was shown on television, he enjoyed the memory of seeing it that first time. Some were better than others: 'This evening a film, Edgar Wallace's *The Squeaker*, rather poor, but a good supporting programme of a *Micky Mouse*, Reg Forte on the organ, and an advert for *Spillers Shapes*.' A better one was: *The Lady Vanishes*, a great film, with Margaret Lockwood, Michael Redgrave, Paul Lukas and the 2 comedians from *Night Train to Munich*. A good thriller, with many laughs.

Bert never lost his love for the Gilbert and Sullivan musicals. He produced many of them as a seminarian, organised the costumes, sang the choruses, did the sound effects and made up the artists. His triumph was taking the role, with trepidation, of the

Major General in *The Pirates of Penzance*. Hugh Lavery reviewed
the production for the Venerabile Diary. He was full of praise
and wrote: 'The entrance of the Major General, a truly Gilbertian
figure, was faultless both in idea and execution; an immediate
encore was called for, and the Major General (who was also the
producer) never belied the excellence of his entry. His song of
accomplishments was a delight; he made the most of the sheer
swank of the rhyme, nor did we miss a consonant in the delivery.' Bert had spent the Christmas holiday worrying whether he
was right for the part, whether he had the right voice and the
acting ability. 'Won't I have my hands full enough with producing?' he asked himself. He need not have worried. It was Vice
Rector Smith who had enthused Bert for G&S when he had spoken to the literary society on 'The Craftsmanship of Gilbert &
Sullivan', illustrating it on the piano. Bert, finding it 'beautifully
done', was captivated, and well into old age he could still sing
songs from all the shows.

Reading through these diaries leaves me quite breathless at
times. So much was packed into each day, including physical
and sporting activities. It is clear that 'the chaps', as Bert called
them, were expected to give a hand with digging the garden;
and alongside the compulsory daily walks, there were a variety
of sports. Not unexpectedly, Bert threw himself into these. He
favoured tennis and handball, representing 'Westminster' in the
handball contests. He played some 'rugger', and football, occasionally turning out as referee or linesman in matches.
'Volunteered to ref a football match. Was shouted at throughout
the whole match, but thanked after.' He was also one of those
who painted the white lines on the pitches, and who mowed the
cricket field. Students not playing were expected to support
team matches, and Bert clearly found this less attractive.
'Watched the North *v*. South rugger match in wonderful weather. Read some Chaucer there. South lost 20-3 or something.' He
recorded all matches, with photographs.

Bert enjoyed, most of all, swimming in the Hodder River in
the hot summers, ice-skating on frozen lakes and tobogganing
in the deep snows that occurred every winter in the North West.
There were many accidents with the hand-made toboggans. On
2 February 1942, he describes how, after High Mass, he helped

'Sowerby finish making a new toboggan. A day of fun and jollity on the slopes, 16 of us with the 3 toboggans. The new one, with paint still on the runners, suddenly stopped at high speed, and I (having jumped on the back) went flying over the others, landing on my shoulder, but OK. The Stonyhurst cads laughed at the monstrous machine we had built, but although the bump at the bottom threw us off again and again, we did manage to stay on twice. Very cold.' With freezing winters, Bert was able to become a good ice-skater, and took to the slopes to become an adventurous skier. In 1945 he was still enjoying the sledging, and still getting injuries. 'A lot of skating on the reservoir, and loads of tobogganing, with me cutting my knee open and Spud Murphy O'Connor, twisting his badly enough to be in bed for a few days.'

There must have been quite a number of such injuries at the college. There was also, especially during these winter months, a good deal of sickness passing from student to student. On 25 June 1942, Bert reports that he 'inherited McCann's job as infirmarian, and began by bringing meals up for Campbell.' By October he is reporting that 'An infirmarian's lot is not a happy one; fetching coal for Roche, and doing 2 poultices a day for Fallon.' Later more were laid up, including the Boss and Fr Dyson, and he was writing that it is 'a fulltime job washing things, and taking temperatures and trays up and down. Harrison is in bed with mumps, Tyler went down with flu, and Peters with biliousness. Many others feel lousy.' A year later Bert explains why he was 'Too tired, lazy and busy to keep this diary for a week. Much coming and going in the infirmary – Groakes with boils on his forehead, Jones in his ear (plus wicklows on his fingers), Scantlebury and Gallagher on the neck, and me on the knee, back and forehead. Is it the wartime food?' There was more than one infirmarian, each having his own group of students to care for.

Throughout 1944 and 1945 Bert was still tending the sick, and had several severe cases to face. He was so worried by the anxious state of a new student, who had daily asthma attacks, and who even talked to him of suicide, that he called in the doctor and referred everything to the Rector. The young man returned home. Bert's friend, Tyler, had a severe case of flu, which

developed into jaundice. Bert put it down to overworking. After
ten days in bed, 'The boss told me to take him to Mount St
Hospital, Preston, by taxi, for a week's rest.' Two weeks later he
reports that 'Tyler and Devaney in bed. More work'; and then
'Peters is in bed too now, though Tyler has arisen.' The war
years were certainly tough for everyone. It is a far cry from students' lives today.

The diary seems to suggest that Bert took on more than most
of his companions, although this is difficult to tell. He reports
putting up the 14 crosses over the new 'Stations of the Cross' in
the chapel; frequently mending the blackout curtains round the
building; painting the figures in the nuns' Christmas crib; end-
lessly typing out lists, prayers, public notices, and lecture notes
for students. He was even typing for the Boss. He organised the
auction of books, which took place at the end of terms; he translated French notes for the Catholic Action Group; fixed up a
music stand for the Common Room; helped cut down holly and
decorate for Christmas; did a fair amount of shopping for
others, and made and hung up the 'letter box' for the African
student, adopted by the college.

Bert had an invitation from the Rector to help him out with
his galleon kit. 'The boss has asked me to take over the galleon
kit of the *Santa Maria* he has bought, but never got down to. A
long but interesting job.' Only three weeks later he can report,
'Took the galleon to the boss today. He was bucked and paid me
the 2/6 I had spent on paints. I may keep the tools. He wants to
shift the furniture in the Superiors' Common Room so that it
will form a focus.' He had a rather more important request, from
the Vice Rector, to use his skills for Holy Week. 'Started making
a baldachino for Maundy, the Vice appealing to my ingenuity as
props man. The aspidistra stand upside down will make a good
base for the Paschal Candle. Now for the Lumen Christi stand
and holder.'

The domestic jobs were shared out, with frequent changes.
Bert found it 'a sweat' arranging the end of term taxis, with their
many different departures. But there was one task, towards the
end of the war, he thoroughly enjoyed. A local Stonyhurst
farmer had asked for help with the threshing, and Bert was 'appointed *capo di lavoro* over four Italian prisoners. My Italian

lessons are coming in very useful, and they love chatting with me, especially one who used to be a comedian. They get pitifully little to eat, and I have bought them a loaf of bread and some chocolate. Charlie Rae (the new Dogma lecturer) shared out some tabs with them. They were deeply grateful.' A few days later Bert helped them with the threshing, and reported that he could not understand how the prisoners 'claim to be non-cooperating yet continue to work, and even produced a £1 note asking me to buy them tabs. I threw in 40 Capstan of my own. They showed me their day's ration – a thick slice of bread, a small sausage, and an uncooked inch square piece of bacon. Today we brought them some "V2 pies", chocolate and cheese. Frost added some soap and razor blades.' These men, separated from their wives and children through war, must have made Bert think of his father's internment and separation during the First World War.

CHAPTER FOUR

War and Ordination
1941-1946

Five years of study were now completed. During all this time the war had hovered in the background. Bert had been sheltered from its horrors by studying for the priesthood. The whole student body, about 90 young men, received the tonsure in October 1941 to gain exemption from conscription to military service, causing so much soul searching for the students, as to where their loyalties lay – to their country or to the church. The college kept up with the war news through the daily bulletins. Bert wrote frequently to his parents, and waited anxiously for their news. He was worried because they worked in the heart of London, and this anxiety increased when his brother, Frank, enlisted in June 1942. For a German born family, with many loving relatives in Germany, it must have been particularly difficult for all of them.

Bert wrote occasional comments about the war news as it came through. He began to praise Churchill's speeches, having once called him that 'terrible' man. In May 1941 he reported that it was 'Great news that Rudolf Hess, 3rd bigwig in Germany, has fled in a Messerschmidt and landed in Scotland', and he records the sinking of the *Bismarck*. The students presumed there would be no air raids in the north. There were a few, one causing damage to the college building. In June Bert writes of his Fire Watching duty. 'Stayed up till 2.35. Wrote a letter to Baily, rhinosoled my slippers, read a blood, painted some plaster casts, cleaned my shoes, and mended my windjacket. Nothing happened.' He was convinced that the war would be over quickly, so was worried months later, with 'Bad news that the Germans are within 65 miles of Moscow.'

Bert was alarmed when, in April 1942, he heard that his cousin Dick Bradley was reported missing after the St Nazaire raid; and then shortly afterwards when he wrote: 'Churchill spoke on the wireless. Moving. But he warns gas may soon be used. Blimey!' A month later he was probably more worried when he had news that Frank 'has been in an airplane! News that we've been sending 1000 bombers over Cologne and Essen, losing 35-40 at a time.' Frank had enlisted in the Paratroop Regiment. An interesting debate was held about this time, which deserves reporting in full.

It was over two evenings, on the motion: "When we have won the war, that Germany be disarmed and made a weak nation." A good speech from Campbell about Germany's history of crime persuaded Peters and me to speak on behalf of Germany tonight, P. speaking as correspondent of Berlin Paper *Voelkischer Beobachter*. He asked the audience to balance against the German War of 1850-1900 the unscrupulous British exploitation of India; against the war of 1870 the French attempt at world conquest by Napoleon; against the Great War of 1914 the British theft of S. Africa from the Dutch, on the plea of civilising it; and against the World War of 1939 the British treatment of Ireland at the siege of Wexford and Drogheda. Against Nietzsche's servility to the State he quoted Hobbes and Rousseau. Against German glorification of arms he put the English songs which glorify the brigands Raleigh and Drake, thieves of Spanish gold. The 1939 war was started by England and France to protect their world market. Germany's invasion of Poland was only an attempt to right the balance. England and France are whited sepulchres, sitting in judgement on Germany in order to hang on to their ill-gotten gains. No Englishman or Frenchman at this Conference Table is honest enough to admit this.

My own contribution began, *"Herr Richter, Hiereingestellten Delegaten! Heute Nacht bin ich in Bratwuerste und Ver ploetzden bei Splitzung und Verdammerung Deutschlands."* I claimed that the cause of the War was the raw deal given to Germany at Versailles, and the breaking of many promises over the colonies and the Saar made there. Germany as a world power has always risen again when pushed under. Another Versailles now will raise another Hitler in 25 years.

Jones made a good reply, blaming the War on Germany's landed gentry, the Junker class. Which England doesn't possess?

Alexander made a fine speech in French.

The vote was a draw.

10 October 1943 was a day that Bert never forgot. Frank had written to tell him that he was stationed with the Paratroops near Manchester. They were able to meet up. They had tea at Smiths, joined by Peters, Sowerby and Hannon. 'When the others went home, I stayed to show him Stonyhurst, St Mary's Hall from the drive, and the Hodder, and put him on the 6.15 bus from Preston. Entering stealthily from the back, whom should I meet at the back door but the Boss, worried about the draught coming in! I didn't want to explain in front of Swaby, so he told me to see him later. He welcomed me with a smile, "Now you rascal, let's hear all about it." I told him the truth. Why hadn't I asked permission? Because I was afraid he might have refused. "Do you mean you would have gone even if I forbade it?" "No, the very opposite".' The Rector said he would easily have given him permission, even for a whole afternoon in Preston. But Bert had broken a strict rule by coming in late. 'His first reaction had been to expel me, but now realised this was a grace sent to me to turn over a new leaf. He would be keeping his eyes on me to ensure I was keeping all the rules very strictly. I felt shattered, and very, very stupid.' A former colleague of Bert told me recently that he had never known anyone as honest and up front as him. He would never distort the truth, even slightly, to get out of trouble. 'The rest of us probably would', he said. Perhaps another student would have pretended to go out for a cigarette. Hubert didn't tell a lie to escape punishment, but he was not prepared for the punishment he did receive.

The next day the Rector called 'me up again to say that he'd forgotten to tell me my Orders next February would have to be deferred.' There is a rather sad entry a week later. 'The Boss has seen me again: the stopping of the Orders is definite, not provisional on my behaviour. Can't he think of anything else? What will the fellows think of me?' Bert, heart and soul of his group, must have felt dreadful to be left out of the communal ceremony. It is a sad note in his preparation for the priesthood.

There are only glimpses, in the diaries, of his spiritual and religious preparations. The seriousness with which he prepared is not in doubt. His generous, fun-loving contribution to daily life hid the quiet, serious, indeed contemplative spirit that lay behind the appearance. He could be worried too. Early on, in 1941, when he was suffering from homesickness, a fellow student told him that this was one of the first signs of wanting to leave. He spoke to Fr Leeming about it. 'He put me at my ease as soon as I entered, gave me a tab, and sat me by the fire. He said my homesickness was a sign of a noble spirit, not of an inclination to leave. He then talked about every imaginable thing for half an hour. What a blessing to have such a confessor.'

Bert never learnt his theology just to pass exams. Some students seemed to do so. He clearly thought deeply about how it related to his spiritual development. He writes of having great arguments with one student on 'Free will, confession, miracles, time and knowledge in heaven,' and then asks the question, 'Why do people dismiss such matters as "mere swat", when they obviously affect our lives?' This attitude he carried with him throughout his life. Sitting at his desk puffing his pipe, he would reflect quietly as he paused in his reading, often from his well-thumbed Bible, while preparing a lecture or writing a book. In later years he would share his deep thoughts with me over dinner.

From the first year in Rome and throughout the Stonyhurst years Bert made brief mention of the liturgy, except an occasional few words. 'The Holy Week Ceremonies moved me deeply.' He found Gregorian Chant the most prayerful liturgical music, and later discovered the beauty of the sung Russian liturgy, which gave time and mood for deep reflection. Bert's tiredness worried him as it made prayer and meditation a struggle. Occasionally he writes with relief, 'Today I made a very good meditation.' 'This evening I had a good Holy Hour.' He was serious about his spiritual life and mentions the priests who gave him most inspiration, hoping 'for Fr Broderick as Spiritual Director'.

On 9 February 1944, Bert describes the day: sleeping in his armchair by the fire; getting a good swat in; opera practice and supervising the speaking parts, finishing with: 'Our year went into Retreat for 2nd Minor Orders tonight, without me. News is getting around that I've been blocked. Many think it must be a joke.' Three days later the 2nd Minors ordination took place in the evening, without him. The next day main ordinations took place, Subdiaconate, Diaconate and Priesthood. Bert lined up to receive a blessing from Harrison, one of the Westminster priests. He made no comment about his feelings and was never heard to complain about the harsh rule. But he did write to Frank that day.

On 21 February, the day of the Bronte Country Gita, Papa wrote a long letter to Bert describing recent events. Days later another of the newly ordained Westminster priests, Bernard Chapman, went to the butchers shop to give Bert's family his special blessing. Papa gave him something for his mother, and £1 for himself. Bert's family celebrated with the new priest, Bryan Harrison, at Sunday Mass. Papa writes: 'Bryan came over this evening and I gave him a £1. Have you still got some cash? So you have a fire, yer? Well, I think I can beat that!' He then describes the bombing of Portobello Road with damage to the shop. Hubert's room was burnt out, with phosphorous bombs going right through to the meat safe. The Dominican convent was destroyed, with nine killed. On reading the news Bert writes, 'Typical of Papa to spend all day serving customers, and only at the end assess the damage.' Mama added her note and told that 'the Carmelite Church in Church Street, Kensington, is gone and the monastery.'

The only obvious sign of Bert's approaching priesthood were talks on prayer, ordering a book, *Be Ye Perfect*, from Burns Oates, and the many references to sermon practice which worried him, but he gained approval for his. His praise was for Tyler: 'His sermon on the church was the finest I have heard here.' Aiming high did not stop him getting up to the usual pranks. 1 April was always a competition to better the years before. Johnson and Bert got up at 1.00 am to wrap cloth round all the bells. It didn't work, as everyone got up at the correct time. It got better as the morning went on. 'For the Morals lecture, Tyler and I collected 8 alarm clocks and put them under Butterfield's rostrum. The first went off at 9.30. B. looked straight at Swan and said, "If you do that again you'll go out." I nearly burst thinking of the other 7. They went off in 5 minute intervals, with B. trying to ignore them, and us scraping our feet to drown the ticking noise.

My own come uppance came after lectures, when I just missed a bucket of water balanced over my door, and then found my chair hanging out of the window. I went to rescue it, but the top came off and the rest crashed to the ground, exploding into sticks. I went and bootblacked Hamilton's doorknob.' Bert had also removed the clapper from the table bell in the refectory. It foxed the Boss. He gave 'a public fruit for tricks that disrupt public services, and demanded an apology. I gave it, and he was very nice about it.' A few hours later Bert was sitting his Hebrew exam.

After successful summer exams he took a holiday in the Lake District with some of his year and his sister Teresa. They stayed with Sowerby and then returned to Ambleside, visiting Miss Cobbe at Croft Lodge, remembering their exile from Rome in 1940. She gave them raspberries and cream and lent them the boat for a week. They met up with other Venerabile, all revisiting the usual gitas at Helvellyn and Scafell. Back in Ruislip, Sowerby came to stay, Kelly visited from Ealing and Hannon came across a few times to say a final goodbye. He was to become secretary to Bishop Doubleday of Brentwood.

On returning to Stonyhurst in September 1944, Bert was delighted to hear the Rector's optimism about a return to Rome, though not immediately. Always nostalgic for Rome he had written earlier: 'I hope we get there soon. Yet a spirit is growing up amongst the younger students that doesn't care. They can't be blamed; they've not been there. It's really up to us older students. Perhaps we don't talk of Rome enough? Yet if I were ignorant of Rome, I'd hate to have it rammed down my throat day by day. But it seems we are slowly becoming just another English seminary.' Archbishop Griffin of Westminster had visited the College himself, and was able to bring the good news. 'The Boss spoke after supper about the future: we could be in Rome in the summer of 1945, but there would be difficulties over food, coal & electricity. Farrow bet me we shall start to move by Xmas (2/6), and Swan another 2/6 that the war will be over by July 1945. I say no.'

It was going to be a difficult term as the Jesuit staff were needed elsewhere, and temporary staff had to be employed. Bert was sad to hear that Fr Dyson was going to America. The

scripture professor was himself in tears when the students sang
Ad Multos Annos at a presentation. Fr Alec Jones replaced him,
and impressed the students by his lectures. Many years later
Bert was to collaborate with him in translating the Jerusalem
Bible.

News was coming in from Rome despite the war. A former
Venerabile priest, Fr Redmond, chaplain to the forces, had entered Rome with the Allies in June 1944. He was able to visit the
college with good news. There had been enormous efforts made
by Sir D'Arcy Osborne of the British Legation to the Holy See,
and the Vatican Congregation of Studies to protect the college
and villa buildings. They were partly successful. The college
was taken over by the Knights of Malta as a hospital for civilian
casualties. Fr Redmond reported that it was kept in beautiful
order, where 'the sisters are quite undisturbed and carry on
with the cooking and laundry.' It was different at Palazzola.
Occupied for a short time by the Germans, it was left in some
disorder, with bedroom furniture broken up for firewood. It
was restored later, without much difficulty.

It was in fact two years before the students returned, and
Bert won his bet. Meanwhile, when a new hospital building was
found, the college housed Italian university students and became the offices for the church's relief work for the needy of
Rome. The Venerabile were grateful to the Italian authorities
and the friends of the college who gave their support to its sur-
vival. Meanwhile in England, life went on as usual. Bert reported
a most enjoyable Christmas vacation during January 1945, even
though he did not get to see his brother. Letters arrived from the
'vague places abroad' where he was stationed. Then came a
frightening letter from the War Office, without details, to say
that Frank had been wounded.

On 1 February 1945 Bert writes that: 'Tyler has twisted my
arm to write the College Diary for The Venerabile, starting from
this month. More work.' He concludes the entry with 'My private diary stops here, the public Venerabile diary having taken
over all my energies. A helluva job.' It was a job very well done.
The entries are informative but amusing, with frequent bursts of
Latin, and some references that only the college students and
staff would understand. He was the Diary writer from 1

February until July. His entries show that skill in writing that he developed over the years with such success.

February 28th Wednesday
In the refectory Scott is still going South, and today's instalment told us of the poor ponies the expedition had to kill for food. We stabbed at our sausages and sympathised.

March 4th Sunday
We convened in the Common Room to listen to the Sir Henry Wood Anniversary Concert. Three orchestras were playing, and to celebrate the occasion we had three wirelesses. In spite of the valiant struggles of the electricians, none of the three wirelesses worked properly, and reception varied between a low gurgle and a piercing shriek. However we sat it out, since there was smoking for the whole afternoon. During the interval the electricians decided that it really wasn't worth staying, and they went to hear the rest of the programme in comfort in Fr Ekbery's room.

May 4th Friday. Feast of the English Martyrs
A crowded day. First a visit to St Peter's, then a walk to Pam, pausing to admire the view of Soracte from the top of the steps, the match with the Scots, and across the Fabrizio to spend the evening on the Pincio. And just as we thought the day was over, lo and behold we were whisked away to the Villa by tram. There we found Luigi singing in the garden, Dom ladling out strings of steaming spag, Marietta and piccolo Bill and Febbo ... hot wine in the wiggery ...We saw all this and more tonight on Mgr Smith's films. They whetted the appetite of those who have yet to see them all in the flesh and blood; and I'm afraid they whetted the cheeks of those who feel they have seen the last of them. Still, it is better to have loved and lost ... or as the poet has put it:
> *Pervixi; neque enim fortuna malignior unquam*
> *Eripiet nobis quod prior hora dedit.*

May 7th & 8th Monday, Tuesday
Tonight we heard the announcement of the official V Day to-

morrow and so opened the bottles we had stored for this occasion and drank the King's health in Port ... and naturally V
Day was celebrated with song and feasting. The refectory
was decorated with beech leaves and a huge Union Jack and
Old Glory provided by the props men. Then Solemn
Benediction with *Te Deum* and a film at Stonyhurst in the
evening.

May 10th Thursday
An error in punctuation made today's programme read:
'11.00 a.m. Beda arrive smoking.' They did, of course, and we
joined them. A most enjoyable day with a game of cricket in
the afternoon in which someone won but I forget who and I
don't care either.

May 19th Saturday
You will be sorry to hear that you will be deprived of my
presence for the next few days, so you can take anything you
read until next Saturday *cum grano*. In the bathroom before
the Retreat began, (to be given by Mgr Smith), I overheard
someone say: 'Poor fellows! I'm glad I'm not going into retreat.' 'Faugh', was the reply (the only time I've ever heard
the word actually spoken), 'wouldn't mind if I was getting
the Sub.' And there you have it in a nutshell. You can keep
your Whit holiday, your free time, your extra smoking, your
cards, your Common Room games and even your gita.
I'm going to get the Sub.

May 26th Saturday
The ten members of Third Year Theology received the
Subdiaconate. *Ad maiora!*
*This meant that the Boss had found a way to let Bert catch up with
his year, for this ordination.*

June 1st Friday
Little white bags with numbers on them (don't mistake me –
I mean laundry bags) have appeared, and notices prop up
periodically signed by either the Vice Rector or the Laundry
Man, telling us what to do with them. Also we have each

been provided with a laundry book, so that we can address our remarks directly to Mr Rosehill. Some I hear have already half filled their books. This regimentation is, I suppose, all to the good. At least it will give less bother to number 40, who has regularly found all the size 40 pyjamas in his pigeon-hole.

June 2nd Sunday
And talking of pyjamas, a pair of bright red ones lies unclaimed in the Visitors' room. The last occupant was the Bishop of Nottingham and tongues are wagging.

June 5th Thursday
The room-changing list in the Common Room is giving those who intend to move next year very pensive looks. Weighing up the respective merits of nearness to ash bucket and wear of mattress is a ticklish business. We found a room two yards nearer the stairs than our present one. Decided to move. Those two yards may make all the difference one morning.

June 14th Saturday
Auguri to Top Year who left this morning for Heythrop, where they are taking their Licentiate.

June 15th Sunday
In view of what is going to happen tomorrow, the choice of hymn at tonight's Benediction was not very happy:

    Lord, for tomorrow and its needs

    I do not pray …

However the fourth verse was fitting enough, and we sang the lines:

    Let me no wrong or idle word

    Unthinking say,

with rather more than usual fervour.

The students left for their long summer holidays in July, which Bert enjoyed apart from spending half of it slaving away at the Venerabile Diary. He thought he would put it together from his notes in about a week, but it took him four. He got down to work for the family, 'renovating the new garage, adding an extension, fiddling with the gas pipes to get water out of them, refitting my two model galleons in order to sell them (flop), and helping Herbert to paint the roof of his bakehouse.'

He had a great Proms evening at the Albert Hall with Campbell, and was happiest of all to be at home with Frank, who was on compassionate leave, having been injured in Holland.

He returned to college in September 1945, as a member now of the top year. In October the serious preparations for ordination began. Bert's year were ordained deacons on the Feast of the Holy Rosary, and immediately had their first Mass practices, and sermon classes. The diary suffered. Bert must have been very busy and preoccupied with his preparations as the personal diary ended on 18 October, the last entry being:

'5.30 Talk from Boss on the rules. "swat".'

There had just been time on 17 October for a final gita. In a Venerabile article he had written the year before he had included a crack about frying an onion on the top of Pendle. 'Peters took up this challenge today, and seven of us humped a large laundry bag full of firewood and 3 bottles of water up to the top of the magnificent hill in perfect weather. The onions tasted like nectar. We sang all the way down, attracting an audience in Pendleton; all the way to tea at Mrs Smith's, and then all the way home.'

The term ended after Christmas, but the 2 months are only recorded in photographs, the programme of the *Ruddigore* performance, and the expenses lists for October to December. The last entry is a short letter from his young niece, Anita, to say that she had got 'a lot of Christmas presents. But I have not got yours yet.'

In January 1946 Bert received a warm Christmas letter from Fr Dyson in Rome, telling him that he had not forgotten his promise to recommend him for the scripture degree at the Biblicum. The Jesuit priest described his Christmas Midnight Mass for the British troops in San Silvestro's, commenting on receiving a bottle of Seagar's gin and 50 cigarettes as a stipend. He had afternoon tea, with trifle and plum-cake at the British Military Hospital, and described life in Rome as normal, except for the novelty of clergy on bicycles, since the buses had been removed. He sent best wishes for the New Year and God's blessings at Ordination.

The letter was the first of many that Bert stuck in his diary in memory of his Ordination to the Priesthood by Bishop Myers. It took place on 10 February 1946, in the family parish church in Ruislip. Charlie Barry, from Stonyhurst, was ordained with him. It is a great pity that there are very few written entries throughout this year, the pages are thick with letters, photographs, cards, lists, notices and other memories of his first year as a priest. He was clearly too busy with all the celebrations: the family occasions, including marriages, that Bert could now conduct for his sister Therese and brother Frank; and the final studies back in Stonyhurst, for his theology exams. We have no words from Bert on his Ordination. It is the Ruislip *Catholic Gazette* that records the occasion:

FATHER RICHARDS: Many hundreds crowded the Church of the Most Sacred Heart last Sunday both for the Ordination Ceremony and the evening Benediction, and had the privilege of kissing the hands of the newly ordained priest and receive his blessing. What a joy it must have been to his father and mother as they knelt there for the blessing of their son they have given to God! And again the following morning, when they received Holy Communion from his hands! Father Richards' first Mass, attended by his near relations, was a High Mass. Being a weekday all the clergy were free to assist and the children of the Sacred Heart School were present, and Juniors III sang the plainchant Mass. On Monday afternoon Father Richards visited the school and received a gift of £5 10s from the children and teachers to buy a sick call set.

The celebration dinner menu is signed by the guests, including the Bishop and Canon Parsons from Finchley. The many letters that follow express the joy that the family felt, especially those in Germany who wanted to be in England. Uncle Joseph, as the oldest relative in the family wrote for them all as he expressed how thankful to God they were, to have 'one in our midst, who serves the Lord, at the altar'. A cousin Joe, from Bruehl, asked Bert to remember all the POWs who are still abroad. 'There is Konrad in America, Karl anywhere, my best friend in France, and still millions of others in Russia. Please pray to God that all soon may return to their families. Your parents may be proud of you who is now God's servant and his representative on earth. You may give us his blessing that we remain good Christians up to our death.'

By March Bert was back in Stonyhurst to finish his studies, perform in the Theologians' Concert and go on a gita, which was really a pubcrawl! Fr Richards put the invitation on the notice board:

Early Brekker
    Drink at Pendleton (Swan with 2 Necks)
    Drink at Downham (George & dragon)
    Drink at Rimington (Black Bull)
    Drink at Gisburn (Crown and Anchor)
    Drink at Stainton (White Hart)
    Drink at Hellifield (Black Horse)
    Drink at Bolton by Bouland (Coach & Horses)
    Drunk at Sawley (Spread Eagle)
    Approx. 26 miles
    Alfresco
    Tea at Kemple End 6.30

He had no trouble in finding 5 others to join him.

The next entry is that year's college photograph, followed by the Top Year 1946 photograph of the 10 newly ordained priests, with the Boss, Mgr MacMillan: Barry, Scantlebury, Shelton, Farrow, Tolkien, Tyler, Swaby, Chadwick, Killeen and Richards. Bert pasted in the list of The Hundred Theses (Theology) on which they had been examined. He gained his Theology Licentiate Degree from the Pontificia Universitas Gregoriana. His certificate states:

LICENTIAM IN S. THEOLOGICA
Consecutus est: suffragium ultimum: 'cum laude probatus'.

He returned to Ruislip for the holidays. In September, at last, Bert was back in Rome. He does not write about his feelings, perhaps lost for words, but pastes into the diary pages of post cards of the city, and photographs of the English College. We can only guess at his joy at being back.

CHAPTER FIVE

Back to Rome and the Biblicum
1946-1947

A small piece of notepaper, brown with age, dated 27 October 1946, announces in Latin that Hubertum Johannes Richards has been accepted at the Pontifical Biblical Institute, known as the Biblicum. His acceptance was on the authority of Bernardo Cardinale Griffin, and on the recommendation of R. P. Dyson SJ. This, and the programme of the Venerabile's *Philosophers' Concert for St Catherine's Day 1946*, is the only entry for the rest of the year. There is a red arrow, added later to a photograph, pointing to the name of a student, St John Stevas, eventually to become the Conservative MP.

Father Richards was busy settling into a new regime at the English College. He was still resident there, and enjoying the post lecture time programme, but as a mature student he attended the Biblicum on his own. He rarely wrote about his fellow students and lecturers there, or whether he slept through some lectures. He surely missed Tyler, who was now doing his further degree in Canon Law at the Angelicum University. As Bert settled in there are only 'Jottings from the Desk Diary'. He started lectures, met up with former student friends and lecturers, shopped for pipes and tobacco, not tabs, and visited his favourite churches where he was now able to say Mass. His evenings were back in the Common Room, and preparing the Christmas Concert. He still had to ask the Boss for permission to be away from the college longer than permitted.

Bert was serious about study, and the seventeen hours of lectures a week were taxing, giving him little time to write down his thoughts. The Pontifical Biblical Institute has been the outstanding Catholic University for generations of scripture scholars. In 2008 the Bishops' Synod in Rome debated 'The Word of God in the Life & Mission of the Church'. Eighty of the delegates, cardinals, bishops, and priests, all graduates of the Biblicum, assembled there to celebrate their times at the college, and pointed out that 'The Biblicum has been and continues to be the home of some of the greatest biblical minds and hearts in the church.' (Fr Rosica CSB.) In 2009 Pope Benedict XVI visited the college to celebrate its centenary. He praised some of those 'illustrious' minds, including Cardinal Bea, Rector and lecturer when Bert was a scholar there. Bert's Fr Dyson earned the reputation as one of its 'most brilliant teachers' during the war and post war years, according to Fr M. Gilbert SJ.

In his address Pope Benedict said that: 'One hundred years have gone by since the birth of the Pontifical Biblical Institute. In the course of this century, it has certainly increased interest in the Bible, and thanks to Vatican II, especially the dogmatic constitution *Dei Verbum* ... there is much greater awareness of the importance of the Word of God in the life and mission of the church.' He also pointed out that: 'Your Pontifical Institution has made its own significant contribution to this renewal with scientific biblical research, the teaching of biblical disciplines and the publication of qualified studies and specialised journals.' He seems to sound a warning: 'If exegesis also wishes to be a theology, it must recognise that faith of the church is that form of "sympathy" without which the Bible remains a closed book. Scripture as a unified whole means reading it on the basis of the church, and maintaining faith in the church as the true key for its interpretation.'

If Bert had been well enough to read this document, would he have felt that scripture is still only second to theology? 'If exegesis also wishes to be a theology'. It was the question he pondered while at school, 70 years earlier. It has to be remembered that in 1939 the Bible was a 'closed book' to most Catholics. It was still a time when Catholic families were not supposed to read the scriptures without a priest giving the 'true' interpretation, and therefore most did not possess a Bible. It was only on 30 September 1943 that things changed, with the publication of an encyclical by Pope Pius XII, *Divino Afflante Spiritu*. Some would say that this was the most important statement made by that Pontiff. In it he clearly stated that the last 50 years had seen such changes in research that a development in understanding of scripture was inevitable. Four days later Bert wrote in his diary: 'We have re-introduced the Roman habit of Bible reading every afternoon.'

Pope Pius XII praised Leo XIII for encouraging wider study of scripture, and Pius X, who created the Pontifical Biblical Institute, establishing the academic degrees of Licentiate and Doctorate of Sacred Scripture. He praised Pius XI for ensuring that all seminary professors must have the degree and that it should have the same rights and effects as Theology and Canon Law. Until then it was considered a minor degree. He also asked that bishops should send their most suitable candidates for this study. Bert was soon to be one of them. Pius XII pointed out that when his predecessor was encouraging study of the sacred scriptures 'hardly a single place in Palestine had begun to be explored by means of relevant excavations ... It now gives us information, more abundant and accurate. Ancient codices and letters are now found.' He noted that the early Fathers, especially Augustine, 'recommended the Catholic scholar of scripture to the study of ancient languages and recourse to original texts ... yet not many knew the Hebrew language and by the Middle Ages, when Scholastic Theology was at the height of its vigour, even the Greek language had long since become so rare in the West that even the Greatest Doctors of the time, had recourse only to the Latin version, the Vulgate.'

Pope Pius XII invited scholars to use all these new means of research; but not only in archaeology and knowledge of languages, but also by developing a 'real skill in literary criticism'. He made an important observation that the ancient people of the East, in order to express their ideas, did not always employ those forms or kinds of speech which we use today, but rather those used by men of their times and countries. He asked for understanding of this, and for the need to research and discover 'the literary mode adopted by the sacred writers'.

What a time for Bert to be recommended for the Pontifical Biblical Institute. No doubt Cardinal Griffin would have been pleased that he had a student already in the forefront of this new directive from the Vatican, to bring scripture more into the heart of the church. It should have been an exciting future for the young priest, and in many ways it was. But it was also to prove a painful way. Forerunners, prophets, are often misunderstood, and blamed for heresy. Such a change of attitude to biblical 'criticism' in the Catholic Church only became more widely accepted at the end of Bert's life. As one bishop wrote to me recently, 'Bert was a great man, and made a massive contribution to the church which was not always recognised or welcomed.'

As the new term began in January 1947, Bert settled into his 3 or 4 lectures a day. It seems from his brief diary entries that he relaxed by visiting a different church each day. He went to Slavonic and Armenian churches, and the German church for Mass. He already had a love for the calm, prayerfulness of the Russian liturgy. On 17 January, after visiting an Orthodox Archbishop from Turkey, he took part in an evening debate at the English College, on 'Mass in the Vernacular'. He found himself in favour of the vernacular, after 'no-one in the house could provide a single valid argument for it.' Bert wrote down his arguments for it:

1. Everyone has pleaded for unity.
   But unity does not depend on language of the Eastern Rites. We do the same thing.
2. Mr Rickards pleaded for occasional travellers.
   But will they be worse off not understanding German than not understanding Latin?
3. Mr Walmesley wants to keep Latin for its beauty & sense of mystery.
   I can imagine a Mass shrouded in all the mystery of Egyptian hieroglyphs. But the Mass is there to be understood, to dispel the 'mystery', not to deepen it.
4. 'They can use their Missals' say many.
   What with the English of *vouchsafery* and *spousemostchastery*?
5. Mr Rossiter says the action of the Mass is intelligible without words.
   Ask the people!
6. Many appealed to the value of the unchangeable dead language.
   Then why didn't the first Christians use Sanscrit?
7. Mr McManus said if people won't listen to the Latin, they will not listen to the English.
   Of course they won't if it's in Jacobean English.
   Let's have the Mass out loud, and in intelligible modern English.
   Let's share the treasure we appreciate with others.

This is unexpected as Bert had such a love for Latin; but he was already wise enough to know that it made more sense for people to understand the meaning of the words. It took another twenty years before Mass could be said in the vernacular.

Later in January he celebrated his first High Mass in Rome, visited the catacombs of S Sebastian, and led a gita to the villa at Palazzola. The whole college went out there for the day in groups. Bert led his camerata of 8, leaving at 5.15 am and walking all the way, with Mass at the catacomb of St Domitilla. The pages are filled with photographs of this 'magnificient day out'. On the anniversary of his first Mass, he went to the Teatro Argentina for Tchaikovsky's Fifth, and afterwards spoke with John Barbirolli and his wife. He continued to visit the German church and the basilicas, met up with many priests, joined the carnival in the Piazza Navona and finished his first Semester with a geography exam at the Biblical Institute. Later that day he had a Papal Audience. On the holiday of St Thomas in March, Bert had a frightening experience. Visiting the Callisto catacombs he asked a guide to lead him to the solitary Hebrew inscription there. 'He found it with difficulty, and I took a copy. But then he couldn't find his way back! We spent an hour traipsing round and round the vast corridors, and only finally escaped by leaving bits of taper burning on corners and working our way backwards. On returning to the college, one of the students asked me, "Did you finally get out?"'

As in his first year in Rome, Bert was keen to take part in all the traditions of Lent in the City, visiting the 'station' churches, 'doing' the Holy Stairs, and attending Tenebrae traditionally sung all over Rome by some of the best choirs. He went to a Benedictine monastery where it was sung, 'just plain chant, but the most beautiful music in the world'. He attended Handel's *Messiah* at the Argentina, and was happy that he was chosen to sing *Christus* at the college passion reading. He was worried, as always, about his sermons, especially one that he was to broadcast on Vatican Radio. Now that he was a priest he was able to celebrate Mass at his favourite churches, but less able to take an active part in the college dramas. He still attended talks and debates, and never missed a Common Room 'roughouse'.

At Easter Bert typed a 19 page letter (A4) home to describe

'the maddest, craziest and most glorious adventure of my life: my Easter gita. Typing it will make it easier to get it around all the family; I want all of them to share it.' First he described the Lenten and Easter ceremonies that he found 'a great joy'. Holy Saturday started his 'week of madness', which he introduced with 'Sit down in a comfortable chair, take your teeth out, and prepare to laugh your head off and your sides out, because this is going to be an immortal letter.'

He had a crazy morning creating mad ideas and doing funny drawings for *Chi Lo Sa?*, and was then told that the parish priest wanted all college priests to help out with the 'Blessing of the Houses'. He thought it would be a half an hour's interesting experience, 'so off I toddled'. He was put in charge of a small altar boy in a white cassock and a bucket of water, and given a list of houses on one side of a street that was not very long. It was to take him four hours, solid going. He wrote:

> You have simply no idea how the houses in our area are crowded one on top of the other. Each family had to be visited, and each room blessed with holy water and long prayers. You didn't dare miss anyone out: for these people that would be worse than excommunication. And each family demanded the full works. So, down an incredibly filthy street, with dozens of kids hanging on to your cotta and trying to dip their hands into the holy water and asking for a special blessing and for holy pictures and for anything else you might have, and enter through a dirty door to face miles of stairs in the dark, some stone, some wood worn right through, some merely a ladder stuck against a wall leading to a tiny attic in the loft. Everyone was expecting us, most of them with a fresh tablecloth on the table and an Easter cake and a couple of eggs, all demanding a special blessing. They talked to you while you were reading the prayers – no stand-offishness here – you might even have to hold the baby while the mother got the cake out of the larder to be blessed. And what a lot of babies there were! The whole place seemed to consist of babies, beds and dirt. Thousands and thousands of rooms, one leading to another like a rabbit warren.

Most surprising of all, now and again you would suddenly

come across really posh people, with beautiful furniture, stuck right in the middle of slums the like of which you can't imagine. The altar boy carried a small sack, and by the time we'd finished it was stuffed tight with lire notes. A lot of people asked for an extra blessing because the children were so naughty, and one old lady made me come back to sprinkle her house again because she thought once wasn't enough. As you can imagine I pretty soon ran out of holy water. About a dozen times I managed to carry on by adding less than half ordinary water (which we are allowed to do). But once, after a very demanding blessing, I simply ran out altogether, so there I was in a dirty old kitchen blessing the salt barrel and making some fresh holy water. The poverty of these people is simply incredible. Some just one room, containing all their worldly goods; an old mattress slung in a corner for a bed, a couple of coats for cover, and a small fireplace. An experience I shall never forget.'

The main purpose of this long letter was to share, with his family, every detail of a most exciting, six-day holiday gita. Bert went with Spud, and Jim Lowry to join the Club Alpino Italiano for climbing the Gran Sasso. It began after Sunday High Mass with a mad rush to get packed:

I could only carry one rucksack, and into it had to fit not only a change of clothes, and dozens of socks, but also my heavy mountain boots, lots of sweaters for the snow, an ice-axe, climbing irons, and lots of tins and bread and food for the week. We had a colossal binge for dinner, coffee and liqueurs after (I had saved a cigar for that), then Solemn Benediction, then a quick visit to the refectory to pour down a scalding hot cup of tea and shove a hunk of bread into our pocket, and then we picked up the sacks, ice-axes and skis to bundle them into the taxi that was taking the three of us to the bus station.

The taxi driver was as mad as a hatter, a fitting start for this mad adventure. He didn't seem to have any teeth. Or they didn't fit him properly. He nearly collapsed when he saw the amount of baggage we were bringing into his decrepit taxi. He said 'gnoughghffing' when he saw the first pair of skis, and kept on with more 'gnoughffhghffhghffs' as we hit him in the neck with the other two. By the time we had everything on board, all the boys were standing at the door to see us off, tying old boots to the taxi and shouting rude remarks. Eventually the driver put the clutch in, there was a terrific explosion, the driver said 'gbnjkfgfgffgfg' and we moved off amid the howls of the bystanders, Except for the steering giving way once or twice, and just missing a tram on the way, this journey was uneventful.

On the next bus the driver raced along the bendy road at 60 mph, and on coming to hairpins just hooted a little longer than usual. Hubert commented, 'After a time I couldn't stand the strain any more, put my hat on me head to stop me hair standing on end, curled up on the back seat, and read my breviary.' Arriving in Aquila, 'All the population turned out to see us. We must have made quite a sight, three clerics in cassocks, huge mountain boots, with rucksacks you could almost fit a house into, ice-axes and skis. We had the same population turn-out in every village and town we passed through later.' The three adventurers got quite a shock when they discovered that they had been booked into the Alberge Grande by the Alpino Club, which to Bert, resembled the Dorchester, not the small town boarding house they had expected. 'We stumbled through swing doors and slid ten yards on the polished floor. Pages and footmen scampered around to appropriate our enormous bundles of luggage. Then along plush carpets to our separate rooms. It was so posh, we hardly knew how to cope.'

Having tired of phoning one another from their rooms, they went out to the local church to say their rosary, only to find a sermon in progress. Then 'everyone fell on their knees, and extempore prayer went on for 10 minutes, concluding with a sung Litany in fullthroated harmony, Abruzzi style. We caught the drift quickly and joined in some interesting bass lines.' Back at the hotel the Club had arrived, looking 'fighting fit in boots, skiing kit, icicles on moustaches, and making us look rather idiotic in our cassocks. We made plenty of show of the mountain boots we wore underneath, but they tended to snigger when they were told we were climbing the Sasse with them tomorrow.' The evening meal was uncomfortable as the three clerics were ignored by the Club members. With the arrival of another Alpine Club a band entertained between courses, much wine was drunk, and guests left the table to 'jitterbug around'. The three, happy with all the wine, dragged themselves off to their rooms, 'where we sat on the bed and got rid of all our laughter, and slapped our thighs saying, "If only our mums could see us now!"'

The Club had early breakfast, but our three fasted in order to say Mass for them half way up the mountain. They took sandwiches and a thermos for breakfast and lunch. The funicular railway took them up 5,000ft to the Hotel Campo Imperatore, the hotel where British soldiers kept Mussolini prisoner, before '(how clumsy can you get?) they lost him when German paratroops flew in and hoicked him off to Germany.' Bert said Mass on a billiard table in the huge ballroom, and only had time to 'whip off my cassock and chase after them, breathless,' as they left for the climb, chewing their dry rolls as they walked across the blinding snow, with 25 Alpine climbers. The cloudless sky, deep snow and warm sun had invited half of the Club to stay behind to ski. At the first Refuge Hut half of the climbers turned back when they needed to dig their way in. Bert was anxious when the remaining 'rough thugs' decided to avoid the *via normale*, and opt for the *via direttissima*, which he described as 'walking up a brick wall'. The climb would have horrified his family!

They trekked along ridges of snow with the ground sloping away thousands of feet on either side. They passed the second Refuge Hut but could only see the chimney above the snow. At one point Spud wandered of the track, to be yelled urgently back as he was walking on an overhang of snow. For two hours, roped together, they climbed breathlessly, higher and higher until two rocks appeared just above the snow. It invited a rest for a sandwich and a coffee. 'I was parked very precariously and needed considerable contortion to reach my sandwich in the rucksack. The thermos came out first, and as I parked it on the snow it slid off and gathered speed to crash thousands of feet below.'

At this point more of the group, but not the clerics, turned back, leaving only nine to complete the climb. They had reached

almost vertical rock which the brave leader climbed and invited
the others to follow, one by one. Bert recognised the Italian 'ripe
language' as each made their slow ascent. When it was his turn,
Bert slipped halfway up, going swinging into space on the safe
rope. 'I laughed like hell, and swarmed up the rest of the rope
like a two year old.' It took four hours to the top when they
shook hands all round as they marvelled at the glorious, 'but
terrifying' view. They could see across Italy from East to West,
and even as far as Greece. They sang the *Gran Sasso* song in its
Abruzzo dialect.

> *Son sajito agliu Gran Sasso, so'remasto ammutolito*
> *Me parea che passu passu je sajesse agl'infinitu.*
> *Che turchinu, guannu mare, che silenzu, che belleza*
> *Pure Roma e glialtru mare se vedea da quell'altezza.*
> *Oooo ooo ooo ooo.*

Bert commented: 'The harmonies turn it into an infinitely
haunting song, and already the whole VEC has taken it up.'

They were knee deep in snow, and needing an immediate
descent, chose the *via direttissima* again. It was not easy but they
made good progress, stopping once to admire the sight of a
golden eagle above them, 'stretched out in the sky, absolutely
still, with the sun shining through his wings, looking absolutely
transparent. It was a kind of vindication of our success.' When
they reached the hotel there were handshakes and kissing all
round, with the 'yesterday's sniggerers' greeting Bert, Spud and
Lowry with respect. The Alpine Cub left later on the funicular,
given a fond farewell from the clerics who recognised that they
had made good friends. The threesome intended to spend another day on the mountain. 'More madness.'

Remo, who ran the funicular, had a small house at the top
station and generously told the three that they could make the
place their own, *casa sua*. They changed into dry clothes, cooked
an enormous supper of spaghetti, meat, coffee and biscuits, and
finally sang until midnight, with Remo putting in harmonies.
He requested again and again Loch Lomond, learnt from the
English soldiers guarding Mussolini. They had also scribbled a
map of London on the wall, marking out Peckham and Barnet.
There were electric fires everywhere, alarmingly wired up, es-

pecially in the bathroom. Not that they washed very much, being far too sore to strip off their shirts over their 'beetroot red, sunburned faces, in spite of pounds of cream applied'. They each had the luxury of a bed, but with only rough army blankets for cover.

Bert describes a morning of skiing on good slopes, being fed by the delightful Remo, who offered to send their skiis back to Rome, so that they could make a more comfortable walk down the 5,000ft to the bottom of the mountain. Another memorable meeting awaited them that afternoon. They walked miles on mountain paths, through small villages almost deserted. The few farmers they met were 'absolutely mesmerised by these three becassocked and rucksacked giants (everyone in these hills is small)'. They were directed to the top of a village, Aragne, for a place to drink wine, but never got there. As they sat on the roadside to rest, 'a small middle-aged man, unshaven, with a battered hat and a motheaten old cloak and pince-nez glasses asked us to take a glass of wine with him. It was the Parish Priest.' The wine was good, but the house was 'an experience', dirt everywhere, pigeons in every corner, logs scattered on the floor around the fireplace, soot all over the walls. The priest was worried that he could not offer them a comfortable stay, but was relieved when they gratefully accepted the two beds upstairs. 'I was ashamed afterwards of accepting such a generous offer, and would have preferred to sleep in a field; the old saint had turned himself out of his own room to doss in the corridor on a straw mattress.'

That evening they went to the little church for Benediction. Bert wrote: 'You never saw such a sight. Men, women and children straight back from the fields packed the church. The priest sat facing them, leaning on the back of his chair, and we all said the rosary in Latin, the children grouping themselves round the strange foreigners. Then a Litany, again all in harmony, all singing their heads off. One kid dashed off in the middle, and came back as we finished with a thurible full of flaming coal. He swung it round and round, enjoying himself immensely. All the servers in ordinary clothes, no cassocks or cottas. Even the MC kept his hands in his pockets all the time, and only took one out to hoick the humeral veil across to the priest at the appropriate time, not batting an eye. During the whole ceremony the sacristan, also one hand in pocket, leaned with the other on the altar staring down the church. Everything was dusty, dirty and crooked, but it was one of the most memorable Benedictions I've ever been at.'

A housekeeper had prepared a supper for them, and breakfast the next morning after an early meditation and Mass. They invited the priest to share their butter, and asked for something to cover the tin of condensed milk they had opened. 'He gave us a piece of paper. Some string? He looked worried, and chased upstairs. We heard a sound of tearing, and down he came with a colossal length of gold braid. I don't know if it was a curtain or a precious vestment, but he'd sacrificed it for our dirty little tin.' This poor country priest refused to accept money for their stay, calling them 'Fratres in Christo', and accompanied them the 'biblical' two miles to see them on their way. He embraced them and stood watching as they crossed over the hills. 'Our last view of him was half an hour later, still on the brow of the hill, a tiny figure in a motheaten cassock, waving goodbye. I shall never forget this old saint in a hurry.'

They followed the mountain paths, often losing their way, but given directions by the farm workers. Bert writes of the joy of a great gita feeling of freedom, with no timetable to keep, and with nowhere particular they had to reach. They took a bus to a larger village, Montereale. 'It was crowded with farmers and pigs and sacks of potatoes and chickens, but they readily made room for these weird foreign clerics, and we soon had the whole busload talking to us. The women at the back gave us saucy looks, asking how three such fine young men could ever want to be priests.' Again they had the proverbial gita good luck. A priest at the bus stop, Dom Pietro, said they should come to stay at his Augustinian monastery. It was a community of three: Dom Pietro, Fra Luigi, the lay brother, and Dom Marianne, the elderly superior. 'They were the most glorious people we met all week.' They were offered amazing hospitality, sharing what Bert described as 'an immortal meal' of bean and rice soup, colossal omelettes with 'mountains of lyonnaise spuds', with the corned beef they provided. They finished the meal with a giant Easter cake, with red wine being served throughout. A good fire had been lit on their arrival with 'dear old Dom Marianne bustling in and out of the rain bringing in wood, while Spud piled it on the fire.' They sat around it after the meal, 'smoking our pipes and talking of Rome (another continent for these people), the war, and the atom bombs, and God knows what. We warmed most to Dom Marianne, who told us of a Polish priest he used to write to, and who stopped writing when the Russians entered Poland. He cried as he told us this story.' The monks had never seen a map before and Dom Pietro was still pouring over it when the visitors were taken next door to a neighbour's house to sleep in 'glorious sprung beds'. They celebrated Mass early the next day, ready to leave after breakfast. But feeling embarrassed to leave while Dom Marianne was celebrating High Mass, they waited for him over another coffee. 'We were hardly into our coffee when they were back, panting, after 20 minutes, so heaven knows what that High Mass was like; but they knew we needed to go, and so hurried! They walked us down the road to say goodbye. Dom Marianne refused to take any money, simply asking for prayers and extending an invitation to any VEC student to visit. He cried again as he said goodbye. Marvellous man.'

That day they walked about 30 miles to reach Leonessa, being advised to seek beds for the night with the Capuchin friars. They were welcomed by 'Father Christmas himself', with the community of five eyeing them rather suspiciously. They became more affable as they talked around the fire. Breakfast was poor black coffee and dry bread, before they set off again, over the mountains to Ferentillo. At the top of the ridge they were invited by a 'big, fat jolly woman' into her cottage kitchen, 'where chickens and pigs and dogs wandered about, and five year old Angelo kept trying to shoo them out. We sat right in the fireplace, and helped her cook, and we had a magnificent meal amid the smoke while she told us about the English and American soldiers she had sheltered up here in the hills during the war. She would take no money, but asked me to send some old clothes from Rome, even old cassocks, from which she could make jackets and pants for the children. I shall certainly do so.'

On reaching the town they sought out the parish priest 'to cadge another cheap night'. This time it was disappointing as he was unhelpful, but they were offered a double bed at the *osteria* where they ate a large supper. 'By the third glass of wine we were into an argument with our neighbours about Communism. They started banging the table, so we banged it too to show how tough we were, and from the Communists went on to Royalists, Garibaldists, Monarchists, Fascists and Democrats. The argumentation and shouting was ferocious, but typically everyone finished by coming up and shaking our hands.' After much singing and the famous cork and match tricks, they went to bed feeling very merry. Unfortunately three in a bed was most uncomfortable and desperately hot, which meant no sleep at all. They had learnt from the host that the other two beds in the room were for himself and friend, who would retire after a coffee or two. But by 3.00 am Spud had had enough. 'Blast it', he said, turning on the lights, 'they're not coming up, and I'm using that bed.' Which he did. As they were drifting off to sleep the two staggered in, blind drunk and still talking about Garibaldi. 'Sitting on the floor, they clearly wished, amid belches and hiccups, to continue the argument we had started hours ago downstairs. We finally cajoled Spud out of the spare bed, and them to undress and take their rightful rest. But the snoring that began immediately made further sleep impossible for us.'

Returning from Mass in the morning to cook a good breakfast, they found they were charged an enormous amount for their stay. Tired out they took a tram to Terni where they caught a train for Rome. 'The train had only two carriages, full to overflowing. But it had several cattle trucks, and that is how we finally came home in a last lap of four hours. I didn't mind much. I was so tired after last night that I simply put my head on to the rucksack and slept all the way.' They reached the college in time for a bath and a shave before supper. 'We gathered a huge circle in the Common Room afterwards to sing them our songs and recount all the goings on. Only one gita had any yarns to compare with ours – Prod Williams – whose group had stayed a night with monks who (they were convinced) had gone utterly mad. In their huge refectory each man had his own table, and they sat shouting at each other throughout the meal. Our men got quite scared.'

Bert had one last story to tell as he completed his long letter home. He described how the madness lasted one more day, when he was asked to be the assistant priest at a Confirmation,

> where nobody had the foggiest idea of what was supposed to be happening, least of all myself. I dropped the bishop's crozier once and bent it, and when I didn't know what to do next I got hold of a mitre and stuck it on the bishop's head. If he already had one on I took it off. But it went off alright. You have to come to Rome to get a laugh out of your ceremonies.
>
> *Love Hubert*

Just six days later, back to his studies, he had completed for the Venerabile magazine a serious review of Ronald Knox's *Epistles and Gospels for Sundays*. Bert greatly appreciated Knox, with both priests having the benefit of Greek, giving them insights into understanding texts that raised difficulties. Bert describes Knox's 'excellent work' with 'The Epistles of St Paul which we once found almost without meaning, suddenly become in this book surprisingly intelligible, not only because we can read them in English we can understand, but because we have at the same time a clear and simple commentary.' Mgr Knox was doing exactly what Pius XII had encouraged in the 1943 encyclical, by studying the New Testament texts with a knowledge of ancient languages, to gain insights into exact meanings of particular words. Bert gave the example of Knox giving a more accurate 'learned to believe' in place of 'have believed' (in earlier translations), which implied that they had stopped believing.

It is surprising that, in only his first year at the Biblicum, Bert had the confidence to point out that the famous Monsignor 'does not seem to take sufficient account of the peculiarities of hellenistic Greek, which is the language of the New Testament.' But he approves Knox for bearing in mind the influence of the Semitic idiom in the New Testament. The long scholarly article gave examples that compare the Latin Vulgate and Greek texts where two alternative meanings were possible. Bert admired Knox's 'dexterity in the use of the English language. Where the Greek or the Latin will bear of two alternative meanings, he has with great ingenuity often managed by his rendering to convey both.' He also praised the author for the explanatory notes after each Sunday epistle and gospel. 'Here the mind of the sacred author is unravelled, so that we do not merely get the general drift of what he is saying, but perceive his argument through and through, for here the background is fitted in, the implications are filled out, and the connections of thought explained. It is for this reason that the book will be found so useful on Saturday evening ... Among the faithful too the book should find readers; Mgr Knox himself explains that his dream reader is the hostess who will salvage the ruined Sunday luncheon conversation with the consecrated formula: "We'll see what Knox has to say about it afterwards".' Bert points out that she must not be disappointed when she realises that some explanations require a knowledge of Greek.

The diary entries for the rest of the year are brief, but well illustrated with photographs. There are glimpses of the fun loving Bert still contributing his skills and sharing his enthusiasm for Rome with the college students and staff. He described how some enthusiastic students had thrown an iron bench into the Tank. Spud was bet £1 that he wouldn't go and sit on it fully clothed. Of course he did. On the Canonisation of Saint Nicolas de Flue, Bert forged a ticket to get in. He wasn't the only one to get in illegally. 'Sutherland was in borrowed monsignorials attending a bishop. Carson managed by getting a pile of books to hand out. Lowery had used a letter Peters got from Cardinal Pizzardo (whom he legitimately attended) to get in. Gallagher found his way in among the canons of St Peter's.' Bert and the others appear on the official canonisation photograph. He was still drawing the cartoons for *Chi Lo Sa?* and contributing for the concerts, making sets and doing the make up. He enjoyed a quieter gita at Whitsun, on Capri, and returned to swat for his exams gaining the BA in scripture.

Bert travelled home for the summer with Peters, walking through the St Bernard Pass into Switzerland, during which he caught sunstroke. He met up with his parents in Lucerne for the rest of the journey home, where he enjoyed weeks amongst his family. He met his English College friends in London, and supplied for a month in the Ruislip church, to give Fr Sutton a holiday. In August he spent six days joining an experimental Cross

Pilgrimage to Walsingham, organised by Charles Osborne. A month later he went with a few of the 'Roman' priests on the annual mini pilgrimage to the shrine of Our Lady. Bert had recommended this to the college early on in his studies only to have the idea rejected; but his friends joined him every year. With the holiday nearly over, Bert and Farrow returned to Rome, stopping off in Florence for a few days on the way.

Bert's studies continued, with hours of lectures and days spent in the Biblicum library. He presided at Masses across the city, and took part in college evenings. Early in the term there was a lengthy public meeting for the students. On the last day Bert decided to 'chip in again with a speech about Walsingham – my two visits there in the summer, and the motion passed in the early 40s that the college would make a public pilgrimage there upon news of returning to Rome, a motion shamefully withdrawn on the grounds that we could not legislate for the future generations! I proposed a new motion 'that we add the prayer 'Our Lady of Walsingham pray for us' into our night prayers'; another motion 'that we raise a subscription to buy a statue of OLW to be placed somewhere in the college'; and finally a suggestion that during the England holiday 'we have a tendency to go to Walsingham'.' Both motions were defeated.

On 20 November they celebrated the wedding of Princess Elizabeth and Philip with wonderful coffee and liqus added to the good meal, and 'The best CR ever, the boys going absolutely mad. Mgr Heard intervened.' In December there was a General Strike, not taken very seriously, with Bert finding the only inconvenience being the lack of mail from home. He asked Tito, the servant for his corridor, who was as busy as usual: 'Aren't you and the servants striking?' 'Yes, fra poco, when we've finished our work.' Christmas was enjoyed with concerts, exhibitions, football matches, visits to the theatre, much CR singing, fireworks, good food, drink, and plenty of tabs or pipes. Bert attended Christmas liturgies in many of the basilicas and churches. He welcomed in the New Year in Alan Clark's room with a bottle of Lacrima Xti.

CHAPTER SIX

Two more years at the Biblicum
1948-1949

1948 was a decisive year for the young Father Richards. In every way it pointed to the path his life was to follow in the future. He had clearly settled in at the Biblical Institute and was able to devote more time to keeping his diary. He had passed his first major exams with great success and was less anxious about his studies. Again he reports events in detail, giving more insights into the ongoing life in the English College, and to the political situation in Italy. He comments frequently now on his scripture studies and on the lecturers, especially on his relationship with his tutor, Fr Bob Dyson SJ. It is clear that this Jesuit priest thought very highly of his English student priest.

Bert started the year with full participation in the English College concert, performing a highly original mime of *Sound the Trumpet*, with Spud, Lowery and Derbyshire as '2 Tenors and 2 Basses'. The mime sketch included dance, using props of a wheelbarrow, hats, handkerchiefs, telephone, gunshots and motorhorn, cigarettes and beer, and finally singing in harmony. It sounds as creative as a Monty Python sketch of later years, rather than a student effort of the 1940s. Some claimed it as 'the most marvellous ever'. Throughout the year Bert commented on all the plays and performances, in some of which he became involved. There was appreciation of the Beda students for polished performances, and very strong criticism for the college *Mikado*. There was a wonderful skit on three Christmas plays by Spud, who could always raise laughs, especially when he included impromptu asides, which left Bert 'weak with laughter'. A great success was Bert's own contribution at Christmas with his version of Gilbert and Sullivan's Heavy Dragoon in *Patience*.

If you want a receipt for that nebulous entity
Commonly called Venerabilita ...
Take lots of ingredients of varied identity
Rattle them off two or three to the bar....

1. A characteristic assortment of Englishmen
   Middlesex, Birmingham, Cheshire and York,
   A rather large quota of all kinds of Irishmen,
   Dublin, Kildare, Johnny Balfe, County Cork;
   A very small sprinkling of Welsh, just a touch of it,
   One every five or six years is enough;
   A little of Malta, but not very much of it –
   Can't have a smooth without taking the rough.
   Split them all up in a manner methodical,
   Half philosophic and half theological;
   Several OND just to make it all uniform,
   Four or five canonists, one mad on cuneiform;
   Ripetitore, and, to be precise,
   One bishops' agent, a Boss and a Vice ...
   Take of these elements all that is fusible,
   Melt them all down in a pipkin or crucible,
   Set them to simmer, and take off the scum ...
   Venerabilita is the residuum.

2. If you want a prescription for Venerability
   Get at the essence of every Sem:
   A typical southern irresponsibility
   Mixed with a typical northerly phlegm;
   The spirit of Ushaw in all its barbarity,
   Predisposition to Romanised Pot,
   Fun of St Edmund's without its vulgarity,
   Constant and faithful aversion to swot;
   A Bedian largeness unhampered by piety,
   Primness of Cross with its classic propriety,
   Dash of the Service types, sparkling verbosity,
   Cackle of Oscott and Birminghamosity,
   Rubrical taste of Upholland and all
   Sense of tradition from St Mary's Hall ...
   Take of these elements all that is fusible,
   Melt them all down in a pipkin or crucible,
   Set them to simmer, and take off the scum...
   Venerabilita is the residuum.

A highlight this year for Bert was the Beethoven concert,

with the 6th and the 9th symphonies, at the Argentina, conducted by Victor De Sabata, with 'masterly control, his gestures to the drums, as if bursting a bubble.' He attended a show at the Holy Office for priests – a *Pinnochio in English*, strange, but extremely well done. Never wasting a moment, Hubert visited and re-visited museums and galleries, sometimes just to view a single object that threw light on his studies.

There were good evening debates and visiting speakers to enjoy. The year began with a debate 'That England is now at the height of her glory' with 'fiery and fine speeches, especially from Alan Clark. I had drawn up some debating points about honour today paid us only to ingratiate, USA in the ascendancy, England having had her day and should be willing to acknowledge it – but in the light of the brilliance around, I forbore. Prod Williams suggested that all this talk of victories and literature and art were a waste of time, since the Debate was on her glory, which is cricket, England's mission to the world.' Later in the year the Italian Society Debate was on whether it was the college or Rome that 'makes a Venerabilino'. Not surprisingly, Bert was the main speaker for Rome. 'Grech, defending the motion (for the college), was a fine fellow, but really a heretic, and quite, quite mad.'

Of the visiting speakers to the Literary Society, Bert wrote most appreciatively of the Chinese Ambassador to the Holy See, who mainly answered questions put to him. 'A remarkable man, whose respect for the clergy made you feel about so big.' His thesis was about analysing Christianity in the East and the West. Christianity was born in the East, but developed in the West, in western form, dress, outlook, philosophy. '(Aristotle's philosophy, Aquinas's theology, Teresa's mysticism, Alfonsus's devotions), and can be stripped without losing the central kernel, which the East must clothe in its own form. A lovely evening)'.

Bert still lead gitas with energy and enthusiasm. He organised a skiing day at Terminillo, the fourteen of them setting out with a bundle of hired skiis. They started on the nursery slopes and 'we slowly graduated from there to a steeper slope with a turn, and bagged it for the rest of the day, even incorporating a small jump into it. My previous experience helped, but the lads picked it up very quickly, especially Derbs, Slim, Spud and Nobby Clark. I had some colossal spills, including landing on my head after the jump, but wasn't hurt. Doc Rickards took the jump so high he dislodged a post. Three on a toboggan went straight into a tree. Tosh sang for two hours on the way back. A magnificent day in the sun, with all the clouds below us.' The gita of the year was 'A hilarious fortnight with Doc Rickards, Spud Murphy O'Connor, Jim lowry, and Meat Howarth' to Mont Blanc and the Matterhorn. The diary account is only four full pages, but Hubert wrote a 30-page account, illustrated with dozens of photographs, bound together in his usual way as a separate file.

They travelled via Turin, and Pre S. Didier, ready to have a first climb on Mont Blanc. When the long delays on trains became frustrating Doc would say in his delightful way: 'It's just a different tempo, dear boy.' Their first sight of the huge mountain covered in snow in the sunlight, 'was indescribable, it was just wonderful.' They climbed up the valley to Courmayeur, where some girls tried to persuade them not to follow out their gita, as three Oxford students had lost their lives in the summer 'and did apparently exactly the same things we were doing, and that we were planning to do!' But the five went on, up and up in a funicular: 'the ground rushing away and getting smaller and smaller. Suddenly you realised that you were in a small box high in the air. Every minute the view got better and better, and always the box was pulled up higher and higher, and now and again giving a sickening bump as it went over one of the pylons holding up the wires.' At the top the view was absolutely impossible to describe: 'You could see *the whole* of the *Alps*, in France, through Italy, through Switzerland, and out again into Italy. We could distinguish clearly the shape of the Matterhorn miles away. And right next to us lay Mont Blanc, smiling in the evening sunshine at the thought of five unprepared, inexperienced, unequipped twerps who were going to try to get to the top of her, the Queen of the Alps, next morning.' Later in the evening, back at the Refuge, they watched the sun set over the mountain, with the whole country bathed in red light. Doc called it 'Frozen music'.

They set out at 6.00am the next day surrounded in a thick

mist, and could only reach the French Refuge in safety, so made
their way down the French side in danger of slipping for miles
when the slope was too steep. 'Then we hit the glacier. Yes
Mamma, a real, fullsized *gletscher*. This was probably the worst
bit of country we crossed on the whole gita. There was a
crevasse every two yards, smiling at us in a toothless grin. They
were easy enough to get over, you just gave a jump.' But you
certainly did not look down. Jim Lowry kept handing out advice to them, very seriously. He leapt over one crevasse, and
walking back slowly he played the rope back to Hubert for him
to jump, and then fell into a crevasse himself. Luckily they were
on even ground; if it had been on a steep slope they would have
pulled each other into the crevasse. The hard 3-hour treck along
the glacier was the only way to return. On reaching a village the
rain began, and did not stop for 48 hours. They half dried their
clothes at the hotel overnight, and set off again, first by train to
the Swiss border, and then what turned out to be a soaking wet,
25 kilometre walk eastwards along a mountain path. It was deserted, 'not even a blooming bike', except for a postman coming
the other way. They told him they were making for Martigny;
he raised his eyes and said 'Mon Dieu.' They saw 'a most glorious avalanche en route, which just suddenly started through a
cleft in the mountain. We heard a roar, and looked up above us
to see a huge spout of water and rocks rushing out from the top.
Half an hour later it was still going.'

They kept on by singing stupid songs, and finally took a
train to Visp, through flooded fields, with the overflowing river
reaching the line itself. They had to settle for a hotel with a grim
manageress, and cursed the Swiss use of electricity because
there were no fires to dry their sodden clothes. Every thing in
their rucksacks was wet too. 'I walked down to supper in a pair
of underpants, khaki jersey and my boots. Nothing else. And
the others looked just as comic. We decided to walk into the dining room with real English sangfroid, as if nothing had happened, and light our damp cigarettes very slowly and stare out
anybody who looked as if he thought we looked strange. But the
Dragon had forestalled us. She nearly fainted when she saw us,
and just managed to stop us scaring all the other guests, by ush-
ering us into the breakfast room.'

Bert celebrated Mass the next day with an enormous congregation spilling out onto the street, before transferring to the Jugenherberge, where the kind Gertrude let them use her iron all morning to try and steam their clothes dry. 'I even ironed the chamois leather case in which I kept my fob watch, and it simply made a rude noise and shrivelled up to nothing.' They had a merry evening with other guests, concluding with a harmonised *Lead Kindly Light* on the stairs. 'Got no office said today, and in the circumstances I dispensed myself.' There was now no chance of the Matterhorn climb, with the weather making it too dangerous. After Mass the next morning they set out for a 40 kilometre walk back into Italy, as the railway lines had been washed away in places. It took 9 hours. Three Swiss climbers had gone up the mountain the day before without a guide, were overtaken by the dark, and had sat still so as not to miss their footing. When searchers found them they were still sitting there, frozen dead. Hubert's party needed a guide to lead the climb over into Italy. It was a difficult one, not the stroll they had expected, as the fresh snow was soft. They sometimes sunk up to their knees. 'All the time the guide was swearing his head of, "Come on you down there, *Gott in Himmel* what are you doing with that rope? ... And you want to climb the Matterhorn! ... *Mein Gott*, use your hands ... And you want to climb the Matterhorn!' Meat finally swore back at the guide: 'I *don't* want to climb the B ... y Matterhorn.' When the guide saw it was safe to leave us he admitted that all guides shout at the climbers, just to keep them alert. 'In fact he thanked us for doing it so well', taking only 3½ hours instead of the usual 5. They sat down and celebrated with sugar, raisins and chocolate sandwiches made the night before. They learnt that three Italian climbers and a guide had died in the avalanche.

They made for Milan by foot, bus and lorry. At one roadhouse they met Charly. 'He had been so delighted by his POW treatment in England that he insisted on fetching three bottles of champagne from his cellar to drink a toast to England, with an overflowing bowl of grapes. We ate some spaghetti, and almost immediately caught two more lifts to Milan. A rather back street lodging, and form filling at the 'hotel', being rather merry we entered some atrocious nonsense for names and addresses. Bed.

Tried to say Mass at the Duomo, but impossible, since it only allows the Ambrosian rite. S. Filippe instead, with all Milan staring at us.' They took a train at Modena at 10.00 pm. 'Crowded, we stood in the corridor of the First Class. Thrown out at Bologna, and put into the Mail Van. Expelled at Florence into the Cattle Van, already crammed tight with a Catholic Action Youth Rally summoned to Rome to support the Pope, who stamped on the fingers of others finally trying to clamber aboard. O Giovinezza! A sleepless night; Rome at 6.30 am. Miraculous rescue of case; dinner at Olga's; tram out to the Villa where I was allowed to sit at the Beaks Table for supper. Said my Office and went to bed flaked, leaving it to the Gioventu to pray for the Pope.'

Bert won the case with Macmillon for ordained priests (OND) to stay at Palazzola. He had 'Three glorious weeks, of golf, of toast and hot wine on the meadow, much swimming in the lake, rock climbing on what has been called Jock's Tooth, Crete de Vong, West Face and South Ridge. Much rum punch drunk. Early walks to Rocca for Mass; cricket match with British Embassy; two gitas; visit from the German college with much singing; return visit to German college on bikes. We ate *spaetzle* with a bishop, and sang *Ad Multos* to each other, listened to their Zickerzacker and replied with a song written by Spud and myself to the tune of *Am Brunnen vor dem Tore*. Hans Küng among the students applauded loudly. At the final Common Room, with much rum punch drunk, the two Murphy O'Connors (Brian had joined Spud, Cormac was to come later) sang Irish songs with such conviction that every one else was scared to interfere.'

Throughout 1948 the students were frequently reminded of the struggle the church was having with communism. It was a big issue during the run up to the elections in April, and unfortunate that a Vatican scandal came to light at that time. In March the communist paper *Unita* headlined a Monsignor Cippico accused of 'pocketing' thousands of Vatican cash. He was caught, but the money was gone. The Christian Democrats hit back at the Cippico scandal, by resurrecting 'a communist banker in jail who won't be voting'. Dyson says the heat is diminishing following the lifting of the ban on Italian travel. 'You'll be able to see when there's real trouble – I will be the first to get out.' Bert also reported that the USA, England and France had voted for Trieste being returned to Italy, with the Communist Party protesting.

The Cippico scandal would not go away, with children greeting the priests and seminarians with 'Cippico', and with posters across the city showing 'a crucifix between Guidetti and Cipicco, with the caption *Il povere Christe fra due ladroni*, 'The poor Christ between two thieves.'

By April the election campaign was becoming 'A madhouse. Every available wall is plastered with posters, layer on layer. Leaflets are even appearing from the sky, dropped on little parachutes, including fake banknotes signed by Togliatti, for the 'Banca dell'Inflazione'.' Bert reported that the Christian Democrats put up a good fight against the communist propoganda poster, that had used the 14 February *Times* article predicting a communist victory. 'We gave our corridor servant, Tito, today's *Times* saying the opposite, and he rushed off to get it printed. He also asked me to do a drawing of Togliatti naked in a barrel running out of Italy into Russia – which he will stick up somewhere. Meanwhile the Fascist MSI headquarters is heavily guarded, spoiling for a fight. And the monarchists have held a huge rally at the Doge, playing *La Campane di Trieste*.' The actual election passed very quietly, with the communist paper *Unita* disputing the results when the Christian Democrats received 48½% of the votes, which sounded conclusive. *Unita* accused the Christian Democrats of adding to their total all the uncertain votes of smaller parties. 'De Gasperri held a meeting in the Corso, and spoke in heroic terms of Liberty and Order. Ovation after every sentence.' Bert noted that: 'English papers have headlined tanks in Rome, and rumours of revolutionary take-overs of churches – but here everything has been as quiet as a mouse.'

All this took place in Holy Week and Easter. The diary shows that Bert was far more interested in the church's liturgy than the country's politics. As in earlier years he reported his participation in the Station Churches, and was pleased to be chosen again to sing *Christus* for the *Matthew Passion* on Palm Sunday. In the afternoon he went 'with Prod Williams to do the seven altars at

St Peter's, and to drink to the winner of the Grand National which he won in the College sweepstake.' In Holy Week he attended Tenebrae in S. Girolamo, and on Good Friday he did the seven churches' that took him five hours. On the same day he visited the Greek church, 'and finally the Russians, who enthralled me with their brilliant singing and ceremony'. On Holy Saturday he volunteered again to do House Blessings, first in the S. Damaso Parish – 'A posher quarter than last year, including some very generous shops, and the Massimo Palace. Finishing early, we were given another stint. 5½ hours. On Easter Sunday he went to St Peter's 'to wish the Pope a happy Easter'.

Bert was curious about Italian feasts and processions which were celebrated in colourful fashion, far more theatrical than any in England. He joined Dad Hulme and Marmy Coonan for the Corpus Christi Procession of the Miraculous Corporal at Orvieto. 'Up at 4.30 ...We arrived at 9.15 and hived off to say Mass, not bothering about permission. Then Marm went off to find breakfast, but Dad and I stayed vested to join the procession, and found ourselves among the Greeks. Miles of participants, some with angel wings, some looking like Hamlet, many in medieval doublet and hose. A fanfare was sounded at each corner we turned. We got our turn at carrying the reliquary – astonishingly heavy. That done we nipped into the next church, unvested, took a short cut back to the Cathedral, vested again, and joined the procession as it returned. During Benediction I wandered around to admire Signorelli's marvellous frescoes. What a cathedral! And what a site! Eventually got some brunch, and while Marmy finally caught up with the celebrations, Dad and I found a field where we slept till 5.15, and caught the 5.30 bus. Back by 9.45. Very tired.'

Bert doesn't disclose what he felt about these 'miraculous' devotions. It seems he wanted to experience local customs, and enter into the spirit of Italian Catholicism. Spiritually he was more drawn to contemplation, quiet prayer, and liturgies that allowed for reflection, which he found in monasteries and particularly in the Russian Church. 'Visited the Russian Church to hear again the thrilling *Gospodi pomilu*.' On the Feast of St Gregory he said Mass at the S. Gregory altar in St Peter's

Basilica. He always celebrated family birthdays in appropriate
churches, always choosing S. Lucia for his mother. 'Monday 13
December Mass for Mamma in the church of S. Lucia, in a
crowded church, but no one followed my Mass at the high altar,
all lining up to kiss her relic at a side altar.' On Christmas day,
after the college Midnight Mass and bed at 3.15 am, he was up at
5.30 , 'dead, to say three Masses, first for my server Tosh Abbot,
second for myself, and the third (in St Peter's) for the family. The
canons singing matins in their chapel made a fine background.
Back for breakfast and High Mass at 10.00, then quickly to catch
Christmas at the Anima, the Russian Church.'

This 1948 diary gives an insight into Bert's time at the
Biblicum. He found Fr Rossiter's seminars 'Solid hours of fast
talking, and even so he doesn't get finished.' At the end of the
month Bert is giving a seminar himself, on The Disposition of the
Jerusalem Walls. 'Gave my seminar today. Dyson was shaken by
my views, and came up to the board to draw his own version.
Yet he congratulated me after with "Keep it up, Father", and
saying it was the best presentation yet. I finished dead on time,
and dead.' Bert continued to work on this thesis, producing it in
March, fully illustrated and bound. Meanwhile exams were taking place in February, for which he had been swotting really
hard. 'The man before me was clearly having a hard time from
Dyson, whom I heard shouting at him. An Italian assured me:
"Inglese? You will be alright!" When it came to my turn, Dyson
did nearly all the talking, with me just saying yes and no, which
he never pressed. Felt very dissatisfied, though no doubt he will
give me a good mark.' The archaeology exam followed two days
later, and the next morning it was one on Egyptian. 'My exam
went perfectly. Dyson, fraud as ever, asked me the English
equivalent of a difficult phrase. "He pulled himself together"
(his own translation). "*Optime, Pater*".'

Clearly Fr Dyson favoured his English student. 'Back to lectures today. Dyson pulled me aside to show me the Sinuhe
Inscription in hieroglyphs which he had written out on a board
to illustrate his lecture on Joshue, and then unveiled it in the
middle of the lecture, with the casual remark, *'Nescio num aliquis
potuerit hunc textum nobis legere? Pater Richards?'* (Who would
like to try and translate this? Father Richards?) So I did, to loud

applause,' Perhaps Bert delighted his professor by the enthusiasm he showed in everything he was taught, especially in his interest in the Egyptian obelisks. Bert was already passing this on
to the younger students at the English College. 'I took 12 of the
lads to the Lateran obelisk, where Bob Dyson explained its history, and read the whole of it to us. Good fun.'

Two new courses were introduced, Lyonnet's biblical theology
and Bea's *Methodus Docenti*. The students were now attending
twenty lectures a week. Bert, often tired, was not helped by the
frequent visitors from England who expected (or perhaps Bert
offered) to be taken around the city. His sisters, Bertha and
Celia, booked a ten day holiday in May which was 'highly successful, though highly tiring, with a marathon of sightseeing'.
He arranged a Papal Audience, concerts at the Argentina, and
La Traviata at the Opera. 'I managed to fit in a few lectures too!'
Within days Peters and Sowerby arrived by motorbike from
England, expecting Bert to spend time with them. He wrote:
'Hard to get back to fulltime swot when I am so tired. Today,
overslept for Meditation and for Rosary after siesta. He had also
been asked to write an article for the Biblical Institute journal,
summarising: 'The Biblical Commission on the sources of the
Pentateuch, and on the historical nature of the early chapters of
Genesis.' At the end of May, Bert received a letter from Papa
telling him of a rumour circulating that he was to be recalled in
the summer to replace Fr Reggie Fuller, who was sick, at the
diocesan seminary.

In June more visitors arrived to be met and entertained, and
only days later, Bert wrote: 'Took my written exams on NT and
OT this week.' Exams in History and the Synoptic Gospels fol-
lowed, which went well. On Saturday 19 June: 'Final exam for
my Licentiate oral. Lyonnet commented on my good written
paper, and told me I had done *optime* in this oral. But Vaccari on
OT was more dodgy, and I felt I hadn't done myself justice.
Surprised therefore to get my final mark, a *summa*! Went out to
celebrate with Fr Jacquemart, an ice cream and Cinzano.' On 21
June he reports a 'Final visit to St Peter's. Final photos of
Farnese. Final haggling for brooches. Final visit to American
Club for ice cream pie for my server. Final visit to Biblicum for
farewell to Bob Dyson: "You're the only man from England to

get a *summa*. Apart from myself. I got three." Rush to the station to get tickets for Venice.' A memorable three-day visit with Terry Walsh, before returning home for a well deserved rest.

The rest only lasted a week, because Bert was a chaplain on the Cross Pilgrimage to Walsingham, which began on 2 July. Groups of pilgrims set out from fourteen different locations round England, each group carrying a large wooden cross. They walked about 200 miles over thirteen days to meet up at the Shrine of Our Lady, where the crosses were erected in the grounds as a Stations of the Cross. They are still there today. Bert was leading the Station IX group from Newcastle-under-Lyme, with Fr Simon Blake OP. The two priests preached on alternate days. Each night the pilgrims slept in church halls, convents, or manor houses, the priests sometimes in the presbytery – in more comfort.

Some days enormous crowds followed the group, or watched along the roadsides. People joined in for part of the walk, some even pushing prams. 'At Hednesford, 700 men came out to meet us in the rain, and 2,500 more met us in the church. Fr Simon preached and was inspired. People wept, and so did I. The veneration of the Cross went on and on for ages.' There were casualties, with many pilgrims having sore feet, or tummy upsets. The two priests were helped by local parishioners walking with them, and taking turns with the heavy cross. Bert became 'strangely oppressed'when at Hinckley people came out with a wreath of roses to welcome them. 'It was as if we were some sort of spectacle. A dark night of the soul descended on me. I wondered if the whole thing was hypocritical. I recovered later when I preached at Lutterworth.' The groups began to converge on entering Norfolk, where Bert's group met up with Wrexham, 'A team of ruffians if ever you saw one, unshaven, half crippled, hobbling on sticks.' Bert reflected later on a strange sense of rivalry amongst the groups. 'What's it got to do with what we're supposed to be doing?'

There were interesting episodes along the way, and the group bonded well. On the shortest leg they spent the whole afternoon in the pub, talking for six hours. They met a strange parish priest, who 'does all the housework himself, partly because he can't afford one. And partly because he can't stand women.' They were supposed to have stayed at Oxborough Hall, in Norfolk, but the Squire's non-Catholic wife objected. Local parishioners took them in, and fed them.

Doc Rickards, a Roman friend, joined the group along the way, and remarked that the 'Holy Ghost had taken over' when Bert preached. Later P. J. Moore, also from Rome, wrote to Bert: 'I have heard from all sorts of unexpected sources – visitors to the college – of the tremendous impression you have made on England.' But Bert arrived home tired and pensive. 'Worried most about what the pilgrims thought we had achieved – for ourselves, for the congregations who hosted us, for the Catholic Church in England. It seems to me that our group has benefitted from the experience. For myself, I worry about spiritual pride.' He found it difficult to get back to 'living normally' on return home, 'as if the real, worthwhile world was back there'. The feeling passed when he 'spent the morning with Cardinal Griffin, assuring me I could stay on in Rome as long as I thought necessary.' He took on supply work in Ruislip throughout August, and then had the joy of that extraordinary gita, 'Mont Blanc and the Matterhorn already described. No sooner had he relaxed in the Villa holiday that followed, and was back in college, than visitors arrived again.

First it was Charles Osborne, the Cross Pilgrimage organiser, who stayed for 'several weary days, wanting long walks to thrash out ideas for a 1950 Pilgimage'. Then it was one of his pilgrim group who, so enthralled by the experience, had walked over 1000 miles to Rome in 50 days, living on bread and milk. He stayed for 10 days and expected Bert to be his daily guide, even though lectures had begun and Bert was preparing to give a lecture to the Biblicum students. 'Thu 4 Nov. Back to work with a vengeance, much of it in the library on my practical exercise, which Dyson wants me to give as the first of several in December, "to set a standard, Father".' Bert gave his lecture on 15 December. 'Dyson interrupted me three times, so it took much longer than I had planned. But he ended by commending my exposition as the clearest and most orderly. How well we English support each other!'

With Christmas approaching Bert was back amongst the students, preparing concerts, and organising and drawing for *Chi*

So La? He broke off to say a Mass in the Mamertine Prison for one of the students he had know for a long time, whose orders had been suspended by the Boss indefinitely. 'A phone call home at Christmas speaking to seven people in three minutes!' The highlight at the end of the year was the English College beating the Scots at football, 2-1, for the third time. 'The Boss awarded smoking after tea.' The diary concludes with a new year resolution: 'To change the subject when the talk gets dirty, as it does more and more. *Sic transit* 1948.' 1949 was to be a difficult year for Bert. He was to leave Rome, and the English College, to face the daunting task of teaching young Westminster seminarians at St Edmund's College, Ware. He determined to pack in all he could before his final exams in June, and the final carefree holiday gita in July. The diary is evidence of enthusiastic revisits to the places he loved or found curious. As one former college friend remarked: 'You live, as Dad Hulme once said people ought to live, 150%.'

1 January started with a typical crazy joke that Bert and Spud played on the college. At breakfast Spud sounded bored at the prospect of entertaining the Scots College and the Beda at the evening concert, so Bert suggested his friend should dress up as his private guest from the Biblicum. Spud decided to go as an American Franciscan, and they set about the transformation, Bert responsible for the hair and beard. Only three others knew of the deception. 'At 5.00 we took a turn up and down the corridor. Spud had developed an amazing American accent, and a limp which changed with every other step. Several people passed, but they just stared at him and sniggered as we passed ... From a distance he looked very credible and I was reassured, especially when the Boss and Vice passed by and made no comment. At table, with much wine, Spud developed a "ghastly" high-pitched laugh.' During the interval, three Scots asked if they had met him before, and Spud played up so well that Bert had to 'stuff my handkerchief into my mouth'. One student was sitting by a genuine visitor from the Biblicum and asked him about the American with Fr Richards. He said that he had never seen him before, 'but then there's some odd types at the Biblicum.'

Bert, unable to bear the strain as the evening went on, left

Spud talking to the students during the second interval. The guise was not spotted until the end of the production when Spud went round the back to congratulate the cast. 'P. J. Moore spotted the joke immediately, and pulled the beard off. We could hardly get back to my room for laughter.' 'At supper I asked Monaghan when he had guessed. Guessed what? I told him. He looked astonished, as did every one else. We kicked ourselves later for not doing something outrageous, like introducing him to Jock Tickle, the Vice.' The jape, as Bert called it, was so successful that Spud decided to take it to the Gregorian University the next day. 'We all skipped our own lectures to see the fun.' Spud arrived, 15 minutes late, balancing a pile of books, inkbottle on top, and an umbrella. 'Tiptoeing past the rostrum, he dropped the lot. Everyone agog. He apologised sweetly to Boyer, and solemnly walked up the steps of the auditorium to the very top, sitting next to Spillane, who nearly had a rupture keeping a straight face.' Just before the bell, Spud rushed down the steps with his books, inkpot and umbrella, said '*Mal di stomacco*' and disappeared. A Franciscan friar who was besieged by the crowd and quite bewildered, said he had never seen him before but his beard suggested he was a missionary. The French suggested he was a friar ordered to come in late for a penance. The next day Italian students took in their friends to 'show them this outlandish monk'. The tale was talked about for a long time afterwards.

This diary is especially illustrated with pages of photographs, letters, programmes and tickets to all the museums, galleries, concerts, catacombs, churches and basilicas visited. Bert reports the Masses and other liturgies, including in the Armenian, Greek, German and Russian churches that he attended. Many of these were on feast days: 'Rome on a *Festa* is amazing, with extraordinary variations in piety, good and bad. Some weird sermons being given.' He joined a packed audience to hear children singing their Christmas songs in all languages; 'The best thing over the whole of this Christmas.' His involvement in the English College events began when he dashed back from his lectures to host a delegation of British MPs in the Library.

In January the College Archives were brought back from their wartime safekeeping. Bert spent hours over them, especially reading 'Bishop Burton's diary, with its brilliant pen sketches, the best of that style I have ever seen. How different that generation was from ours, in learning, knowledge and culture, even in first year students. He composes his own Latin and Greek verse, and has powers of description simply unheard of today. Fascinated by his attitude to the Jesuits, and to the controversial Rosmini.' George Burton was a student at the College in the 1880s, and being older than other students never felt comfortable there. This was even more to do with his scholarship, and sympathy with Rosmini, who was condemned for his opinions, which were in conflict with the strict, unquestioning Roman theology of the day. Burton, who later became Bishop of Clifton, blamed the Jesuits for their part in condemning Rosmini. Bert felt he understood Burton, perhaps sensing, even as a student, that a questioning acceptance of the church's teaching was not necessarily heretical. As a Roman student Bert was unlike George Burton, however, not questioning the teaching, simply admitting at times, that he found some of the theological theses puzzling. He had a great affection for the Pope, and took every opportunity to be present in papal services in St Peter's. On 2 February, he went with Schoenberg, to present candles to the Pope, a tradition on that feast. He was pleased that Pope Pius spoke to his group, 'and was with us at 12.00, when he stopped to say the Angelus with us.'

Later in the month he attended High Mass in the Piazza, with a good view from the roof of the Salvatorians. 'The Pope spoke after, about Mindzcenty and the Papacy and what it stood for. I was more moved than I have ever been before, but found it hard to defend Italian Catholicism at dinner against the cynical carping of Walsh and Shaun Monaghan.' (Cardinal Mindzcenty of Hungary spoke out against communism and the Stalinist persecution of Catholics. He was tortured and given a life sentence in 1949). The Pope's 50th anniversary was approaching, and the Gregorian University had organised a choir, which Bert joined, to sing a piece of Palestrina. He wrote, 'They also wanted to offer a spiritual bouquet, and have asked all colleges to send in "returns" for the number of Masses each will say for him. We promised three each – but what a soul-destroying idea.' The University celebrated with twelve cardinals and many dignitaries. 'The Rector Dezza made one of the most stirring speeches I've ever heard, appealing for loyalty to the Pope, and quoting examples of Stepinac, and other ex-Gregorian students imprisoned. He was almost in tears, as were many others.' On the Jubilee Day itself, Sunday 3 April, Bert was out at 7.30am to get a good place for Pius XII's two Masses, 'the place black with priests, alternating their singing with the Sistine choir, the Acclamations *Christus Vincit* being particularly impressive.' The Basilica echoed with spontaneous cheering that broke out as the Pope left at the end; and Bert and friends went to the American Club 'for a much needed Beer'.

It is very clear from these early diaries that the young Father Richards was eagerly loyal to the church and its hierarchy. One entry this year expressed his intention of responding to a request from England. 'Got myself in a right mess over a circular from the English hierarchy asking for a weekly fast for the success of this year's mission. I decided to join in, and wondered about promoting it in our public meeting. As a motion? As a suggestion? There was so much bitter opposition that I decided to drop it, lest I cause a rift in the house. I shall simply do it myself.' This serious side was, as I've noted, more than balanced by his love of the ridiculous and his sense of community. He includes many brief references to humorous incidents shared by the students. 'Shopping for an E string for his violin, Burtoft was told they didn't have one. "In that case", he said in English, "I'll have a packet of shredded wheat".' One gita this year was unsuccessful. The plan was a day skiing. The Boss would not let them leave before 7.00. The bus was late and it rained. They eventually managed only two hours on the slopes. 'The snow was floury and clogged the skis. Buckley set off alone in deep snow, and when he reached the bottom he had only one ski left. Lowery set off on his own with ice axe and rope. Chaos. We had to leave at 3.00 (more ski sticks and straps lost) to walk through the blizzard for an hour down to the bus. Later, the bus broke down.'

Easter was a happier occasion. Bert wrote 'The post-Lent joy of Easter came home to me more powerfully than ever before, mainly through the breviary.' The next day he set off for Florence on the Easter gita, with Terry Walsh. They met up with 'eleven more of the lads in the hotel, so the refectory was a noisy place, and even more so the balcony later where we sat till 11.00 drinking to Ireland's independence.' They spent four glorious days there before moving on to Siena for one night. 'We should not have tried to "do" this lovely unspoilt city in one day.' Then on to Assisi for the last three days of the holiday, enjoying the company of Canadian priests at supper, 'especially their wise-cracks: "A curate is a mouse training to be a rat".' Bert was most impressed with S. Damiano – 'which keeps the spirit of Francis and Clare. Finally to the Porziuncula, where a vast pilgrimage from Umbria prayed for rain after months of drought. I liked the rose chapel and the statue of Francis with live doves. It rained tonight.'

Although Bert was a postgraduate, he still continued his scripture studies at the Biblicam, taking exams along the way, in preparation for his post in England. He completed a course 'Studia Semitica', and took the exam straight away to 'get some of these subsidiary subjects off my plate'. He found the Egyptian exam very straight forward. This was followed by an oral exam on comparative Semitic, 'with just me and O'Callaghan in his room. He finally asked me what mark I would give myself!' During May and the beginning of June Bert attended lectures, trying hard to find time to 'swat' for the final exams, but was again asked to take unexpected visitors around the city. He arranged papal audiences, and queued for their theatre tickets and sat his exam on 'Biblical Theology'.

Alongside the study Bert researched and wrote a critique of Ronald Knox's 'Old Testament', and prepared an article for the Venerabile publication on the Roman Obelisks, which he sub-mitted in May. It was published in the Venerabile XIV 3 edition, in November 1949. 'These obelisks are truly amazing. And what is still more amazing is that the Roman emperors should have gone to the trouble of dragging these granite colossi thousands of miles to set them up in their capital; for there are thirteen of them poking their noses out of the ground in Rome.' It is a fascin-ating read, inspired by Fr Dyson's enthusiasm, and appreciated by the college. Bert pasted the long article into his diary, and il-lustrated it with sketches of the obelisks in their settings. There is also a card, from the Boss, John Macmillan. 'My dear Bert,

This is not in order to add to the list of Christmas cards you yourself may send out; but after sending my best wishes for a happy Christmas, to let you know that you are missed in your first absence after ten long years, and furthermore – to congratulate you on your article on "Roman Obelisks", which continues the standard you first set up in "Quality Gitas!" Bob Dyson was along the other day; and all the obelisks are still here. Perhaps you may one day have saved enough to come out and dig another up. *Cari Salute*, John Macmillan.'

On 8 June Bert had a hectic day, trying to buy a doll for a niece; going back and forth to the Biblicum to find Dyson about the map he had requested; packing for his departure; searching for travel maps; finding the times of buses, and trying to fit in time to research the Kenites in the Biblicum library. 'In between, unsuccessfully trying to do some study. Woe is me.' That was his last entry written in Rome. He later added the following to his Rome entry, along with dozens of 'Final *nostalgic* photos of Rome'.

> In précis, on Thu June 9 I had a papal audience (bacciamano) in the morning, took my final exams in the afternoon (a 10 and a 9.5), and in the evening went to the garden party at the Br. Embassy. I then took a week off in Capri with Schoenberg, came back to Rome to collect my things, and finally left on the night train on Sat Jun 18, to spend a hilarious month walking through the Dolomites, Austria and Switzerland, and visiting hundreds of relatives in south Germany and north, my parents having met me with the car at Schaffhausen. We got back to England on Wed Jul 20. Will I ever spend more ten such glorious years?

CHAPTER SEVEN

To England and St Edmund's College
1949 onwards

The gita back to England took six weeks, and is recorded in the largest of all Bert's diaries. He addresses it to his friend:

Dear Spud,
Well, me boy, here it is. I say 'is', where I ought to say 'will be', because I have only just started on this *magnum opus*, and it's going to take quite a bit of bashing at the old *macchina* to get it finished. But if you think I'm going to go slow in order not to make any mistakes, you've had it … Well hold tight, we're off.'

Bert describes that last day in Rome with his final exams and the papal audience which 'The Boss had wangled for us … Pius XII looked grand; it was good to see him in such good health after the last time when he looked as if he was going to collapse at any moment. And it was good to have a chat with him as one of the last things to do in Rome. Most people I met on the way home asked me if I had seen him, and were colossally impressed by the fact I had spoken to him personally.' Bert left Rome with his American College friend Schoenberg for a few days in Capri. He returned to Rome to send all his belongings on home, bad farewell to the nuns, and 'a very tearful adieu to the Boss – he gave me such an affectionate handshake that I almost forgave him for being such a blighter for the last ten years'. Then he left in a taxi, with two companions, La and Copper, for the first stage of the gita, seen off in the usual English College way – students leaning out of the windows throwing a bucket of water or two down on the crowd of students on the pavement, passers by wondering what on earth was going on, and the final cheers as the taxi left with 'the roll of bumf trailing behind us and getting longer and longer as we went to the station'.

Bert left his companions in Innsbruck to begin a long stage of his journey alone, to Oberammergau, back into Austria, through Switzerland to meet up with his parents and Margaret, on the

German border at Schaffhausen on 4 July. They crossed the border to Geilingen, where Bert recognised the Gasthaus Zum Schwert, the home of his childhood. All the memories came back, and there was much weeping from the older villagers to see 'their priest'. 'Old Mrs Ruh, shrieked when she saw us, and rushed out to greet us. I just about remembered her – after all I was more in her house than at home as a kid. It was amazing to hear that her two sons with whom we used to play all day long as kids had both been killed on the Russian front. If we hadn't come to England in '28, Frank and I might be pushing up Russian daisies now.' On visiting the church, Bert reflected: 'Who knows, perhaps the beauty of this church first set my mind as a kid to take the path which has landed me where I am now.' The next stop was Weilderstadt, 'and I saw for the first time in 25 years the little town where I was born. What amazed me more than anything else was that I should remember anything about it, since I was only two when we left. But I did.' The beauty of the little town amazed him, with its memorial to Kepler, and its fine church. Bert, with Papa, called on the priest to arrange to say Mass there in the morning, only to find that it had been announced that 'Wednesday evening Mass would be sung by Herr Professor Doktor Richards, the first Weilderstadter to be ordained for 80 years.' It surprised Bert to have an evening Mass, and to find the tabernacle on the left side wall of the sanctuary. It would take years before changes like this came to England. After visiting all the relatives in South Germany and the Rheinland they arrived, weary travellers, back in England on 20 July.

'It was good to be back in England again ... I began to appreciate the beauty there is in our own England, a thing which you can't do until you come home from abroad. It has got beauty, and it is much more delicate than perhaps the glaring beauty of the scenery in Switzerland or Austria. More than ever I was glad to see English people again.' Bert didn't have a long rest, as he had imagined, because he did supply work again in Ruislip for weeks, 'with much confessioning and baptising and holy houring', before taking over the scripture chair from Dr Fuller at St Edmond's College Ware, the Westminster diocesan seminary.

It was a rude awakening. He only had a vague idea of what his work would be. While in Rome he had to write to Fr Fuller to ask what his job entailed. Who was he teaching? What subjects? What years? Was there a study programme he could see? It was daunting to arrive at the college to be introduced to everyone as Dr Richards, and was grateful to the Rector Bagshawe telling him he would be free to teach scripture as he wanted. Papa, Mamma, Margaret, Bertha and Herbert escorted Bert to his new job. 'The room I have inherited from Brian Campbell, a dismal sight, with broken pictures and filthy walls. Herbert was so shocked he gave me £10 and told me to get it painted. But when they left me to it, I got it reasonably shipshape, and with the radio going, it is home. I think I shall enjoy it.' He described his surroundings in more detail the next day, when he realised, 'I have two rooms, en suite. Both need much work doing on them, from the wiring, to loose bookcases, to droopy curtains, to broken chairs.' Not unlike early days at Stonyhurst.

Bert continued: 'But the body is remarkably well provided for, with excellent meals (the Blue nuns look after us), mid-morning tea, and a glass of milk brought to the room after night prayers. The students arrived slowly today – they look a lively lot. Dick Sutherland, relegated from Rome, a little sad among them. Rosary after supper, walking around the corridors in pairs, a sigh of prayer from 100 separate mouths, most impressive.' Bert felt for Dick Sutherland, a student he knew so well from Rome; he was to look out for him over the years. They remained life-long friends until Fr Sutherland's too early death in 1974. Lectures began two days later with the new scripture professor very nervous, shaking life a leaf as he began his first lecture. 'But by half-way I had worked my way in, and felt more at home. What impression did I make?'

Those first weeks were difficult for Bert. He reports that, as in Rome, he was the butt of attacks on scripture at table. 'Will no one take the scriptures seriously?' This insistence that scripture was a minor subject in the Catholic Church dogged Bert all his life, with jibes even from his friends. It was not long before Fr Brian Campbell, a canon lawyer, 'amused his class yesterday by reading out the latest Roman document on the need for scripture professors to set a good example by being more than normally pious. I retaliated today: "For the benefit of those taking canon law, I would simply remark that if the Pope issues a document about scripture professors, it is only because the idea of a scripture professor giving good example does not strike him as absolutely ridiculous. He has issued no such document on canon law professors".'

Bert was teaching two distinct courses, one for the younger seminarians, the philosophers, and a different one for the theologians (divines). He had to provide notes for them continually. In addition he had to teach Latin twice a week and, by request, Hebrew twice. He had the students' sermons to check and criticise. He was responsible for the college tobacconist accounts, a job he disliked intensely. Three weeks after his arrival he is writing: 'Spent the whole evening browsing through the earlier pages of this diary, and marvelling at the pace of life we enjoyed in Rome. In comparison life here is dull. Busy enough, but always on one plane, not on a hundred as in Rome.' He was invited to be chaplain to the Legion of Mary. 'The place seems to be overrun with pious societies: CSG, YCW, Legion, Weekly Holy Hour, etc … Yet no one keeps the rules! I have declined on the grounds of too much work.' He was also asked to become leader of a scout group someone wanted to start. 'What nonsense!' But he did respond to Charles Davis when asked to share his chapel of ease at Walkern.

If Bert found the life busy in 1949 he was going to get a shock as the years went by, when many more tasks were added to his responsibilities. But he found that the evenings at St Edmund's did improve, with some concerts and common rooms, and the possibility to introduce Gilbert and Sullivan. Already in November he could write:

Tue 8 Nov SEC
The whole evening went on writing notes for my talk on Gilbert and Sullivan, illustrated with excerpts from my records. It went down extraordinarily well, and I can see us producing some G & S here. They liked best the joke about 'Bloodigores'. Back to my room at 10.15 with all the office still to say.

What is evident in all the diaries is that Bert looked for positives, and saw community as most important, and fundamental to Christianity. He was disturbed at this time by remarks made by Bishop Heenan, on the occasion of the Remembrance Sunday service from the Cenotaph. 'I felt proud of England's Christian tradition, and disagree with Bishop Heenan that England is mostly pagan. Why not make capital of the Christianity we have, instead of saying it doesn't exist?' Bert always recognised that Christ was present outside the Catholic Church.

As the term progressed, Bert was able to relax and enjoy the company of students and staff, especially those who were 'Romans'. He described his first St Edmund's Day, with Bishops Myers, Beck, Craven and Petit joining them the evening before, with enthusiasm. 'Today we woke up to a blanket of frost, and the absence of Cardinal Griffin, fog-bound in London. So Myers sang the High Mass, and Beck preached beautifully, oozing with Pauline ideas. The binge in the Douai Hall was, with plenty of wine, easily got rid of by our circle of Romans (Me, Ekbery, McCreavy, Campbell, Pooh Pritchard, Pat Kelly, Mick Groarke, Digger Brown). Bagshawe gave a dreadful speech. Kip, tea with Petit, Vespers, Veneration of the Relic, Procession to 30 verses of Wiseman (I was hoarse) and Benediction. More wine at supper, and a concert. A tiring day.' A week later Bert is writing a review of an excellent performance of *The Unguarded Hour* given by the 'lads'. Soon after, on the feast of St Andrew, they put on a scratch concert, which delighted him. 'It was quite like old times. The lads have something of a Venerabile spirit.'

Of course he missed Rome, but he had other compensations. His family were near, and he was able to see a great deal of them. He occasionally got over to Ruislip, and Papa or Frank would drive out to take him for a meal. He began the tradition of meeting up with friends from Rome, starting with Tyler, where they had a rather serious discussion over lunch at Les Gourmets about ascetics. He joined his first Venerabile Reunion at the Knights Cub, where 30 attended, 'and it was good to be with them. Joe Pledger, thrown out of Wonersh for his ideas, discussed lecturing with me.' (Bert was still worried about it.) Uncle Bill Godfrey gave a good speech, more or less taking responsibility for all English Episcopal appointments. Then to Leicester Square with Tyler, Kelly and Plunk O'Leary to see a News Film.'

Over the sixteen years he was at SEC Bert continued to meet up with his VEC priest friends, especially Spud Murphy O'Connor. He always enjoyed their reunions in London, and in 1951 started the annual summer 'pilgrimage' to Walsingham, with fifteen other 'Romans'. They enjoyed the pub lunch 'binge' as much as the prayerful reflections at the shrine. It was this ease with which Bert could move from the mundane to the spiritual, from simplicity to depth, that endeared him to so many. He wrote: 'I lunched at the Crown & Falcon, Puckeridge, and had tea at King's Lynn. Prod Williams and Amy Johnson were waiting for me at Fakenham, and we got to Walsingham in time to sing *T'Adoriam* at benediction. By 10pm all 15 had collected, and we did the Holy Mile barefoot on a newly flinted road, very unprayerfully. Booted again, we sang panto songs all the way back, and drank beer until 1.00 am ... I was celebrant the next day at Mass, and we sang (as ever) *O Roma Felix*.' For years the visits to Walsingham continued, often with Dick Sutherland organising them as Bert became more involved in his responsibilities. Years later Bert and I resumed the annual pilgrimage to the shrine, to sing *Salve Regina*, reflect by his cross and have a good meal, with beer, at the pub.

A year after his arrival in St Edmund's work began to accumulate. He was appointed to the Westminster Board of Censors. 'I suppose it is an honour', he wrote. He was soon to find it a burden. On average he had to read and report on about 34 manuscripts/books each year. Some were Latin texts and the German of Karl Rahner. His most important work was as a reader for Ronald Knox's *Old Testament*. Bert's knowledge of Greek and Hebrew was important because Knox made his translation of the Latin Vulgate Bible checking with the Greek. Bert had already written a critical review of Knox's *Epistles & Gospels for Sundays*, while at the Biblicum, where he criticised the Monsignor for not always using Hellenistic Greek in his translations. Knox's commissions by the hierarchy to translate the Bible were more on account of his classical training and his fine English prose than on any scripture expertise. He had no qualifications as a biblical scholar. Bert felt privileged that a warm friendship developed between them, and was delighted to discover that the rooms he inherited in SEC were those used by Knox when he was teaching there from 1918 to 1926. The publication of the definitive edition of the Monsignor's Bible was marked by a dinner in London, on 14 November 1955. Bert was one of the 200 or so eminent guests. He wrote: 'A most ceremonious occasion at the Hyde Park Hotel for the launching of Knox's completing his translation of the Bible. Reggie Butcher (SEC president) and I arrived at the same time as Knox himself, lionised all the way up to the entrance by his worshippers, whom I expected to follow us in, but they were not even invited! What an embarrassment for the poor man. The meal (hors d'oeuvre, sole and lamb) was exquisite, with the most brilliant wines. Woodruff made a great speech in honour of Knox, but Knox's own preceding – that was a wow. And, he mentioned only two names of the various 'correctors' appointed to oversee his translation, Patsy Redmond and Hubert Richards, "who persuaded me to make a change on page 1 which I would never have dared make myself: he insisted that "Spirit of God" must read "breath of God". What a nerve I've got.

'Less than a year later, Ronald Knox died at the age of 69. Bert wrote an obituary for the Allan Hall magazine. He began: 'One Sunday in the early 1920s, a rather retiring young priest, then occupying 16 St Edmund's, was taking his turn at the country Mass-centre supplied from SEC, and was approached, over his breakfast, by an eminent lady who had heard that the famous R. A. Knox was now teaching at the College. Would the priest convey her kindest regards to dear Ronnie? Fr Ronnie Knox assured her that he would.

'In the early 1950s, a rather awestruck new scripture professor, then occupying the same room, was asked to make a catalogue of the changes he felt should be introduced into the recently published Knox version of Genesis, and tentatively submitted a long list of suggestions, drawing particular attention to the unfamiliar appearance of the divine name Yahweh as "Jave", a word which he was always tempted to (and still is) rhyme with "shave". He was surprised to receive a graceful letter thanking him for the suggestions, 90% of which were immediately adopted ... I shall not turn in my "grahwey" the letter concluded, "except over Yahweh".' After describing Knox's brilliant career at Oxford and in the Anglican Church, Bert described why he was

mourned at SEC 'with a sense of personal loss. His conversion
and acceptance of a teaching post at St Edmund's must have appeared to the outside world as a sort of suicide. Yet the seven
years he spent here were clearly some of the happiest in his life.
There is scarcely a page in the *Edmundian* for those years which
has not some reference to the versatile activities of R. A. K., and
whether he was composing one of his elegant latin memorials,
or dashing off a lighthearted review of the Westminster *Ordo*,
writing another detective novel or doing "farmyard imitations"
for a Shrove concert, he was obviously very much at home here.'
It is easy to see why the two priests got on well together.

It was the first two years at SEC that really set up the future
programme for the young priest as he became ever more involved in life within and without the seminary. Papa bought a
second hand car for him, and immediately he was the staff's
chauffeur in and out of London, in what seems like constant fog
and recurrent car trouble. Those were the days of chokes, crank-
ing up the engine and battery failure. There was, however, little
traffic and Bert was known to speed up when necessary, occasionally with the police in tow.

1950 saw Bert leading his first of many pilgrimages. It was
the Holy Year, and the Grail (a secular institute of women)
asked him to lead a pilgrimage to Rome.

2 Mar SEC
The Grail, having phoned for advice on a Rome itinerary for
Holy Year, today sent the Baroness to ask me to be chaplain
to the 80 going! All expenses paid, and no duties except daily
Mass. I am enormously attracted by the prospect of seeing
Rome and the lads again, but hesitate about the advisability
of returning so soon and of getting no Easter break. But it is
an attractive offer.

He accepted the offer, shocked at first to see its size; a group
of 80 young women. Even more shocked on discovering that the
leader, a Mrs Fox, had no idea what that entailed, Bert took over
much of the organising after a chaotic journey with carriages not
booked and two sleepless nights. The five days in Rome gave
Bert wonderful reunions with his friends. He would take the
group to their destination and dash back to the college. 'Back to

VEC to see the final rush of publishing the new *Chi Lo Sa?*, (some wonderful cartoons), and at midday off with Tosh Abbott to catch the Pope's blessing in St Peter's Square. Came back to VEC with Mick English for a reasonable binge, and a wonderful Common Room circle after, with great roars over the Latin howlers of my students. Stayed for tea and Solemn Benediction. Then out with Spud to the Gianicolo, where we sat on a wall while he told me all the recent concerts, and I nearly fell off the wall. Later a taxi back to the girls after a demand to come and do Benediction. Talked about the Four Basilicas after, and then heard 24 confessions. And still all my office to say!'

The last five days of the pilgrimage were spent in Assisi, which was a great success, especially as seven college friends joined them all. It meant much story telling, wine drinking and singing, including an *Ad Multos Annos* for the Baroness on her birthday. It was probably this pilgrimage that gave Bert the confidence to organise so many successful pilgrimages to the Holy Land later on. The Grail girls were thrilled with their days in Rome and Assisi, many writing that they intended to return the next year. The Baroness wrote her thanks 'for all your help and quiet unobtrusive kindness throughout the entire pilgrimage'. It is that 'quiet unobtrusive kindness' that so many people recall when speaking of Bert. The pilgrimage forged a great friendship between Bert and the Grail community in Pinner. The pilgrimage left him 'feeling very Romesick, not only for the VEC but for the sense of companionship in the group, which I miss. Wrote many letters today, all nostalging over Rome and Assisi, and describing my inability to get down to the loads of work waiting for me. When will this mood pass?' A few days later it was his turn to lead the Rogation procession and Community Mass. He writes: 'Great relief at having a congregation with me again. How crazy that in a houseful of priests we all hive off to our own little corners to do our own thing, instead of concelebrating to emphasise the unity of the Corpus Christi.' He was very much ahead of his time.

In 1951 Bert was given additional tasks. First, tutorial responsibility for the Westminster Diploma Course, involving tutoring, reading and correcting scripture essays. He was drawing maps for the Catholic Commentary, and taking on extra classes for students struggling with Latin. He was invited to give lectures at the Grail and to the Assumption nuns. Already helping out at the Walken Mass centre, he was asked to take care of local Irish workmen.

> *Sun Sep 23 SEC*
> My first visit to Aston, where I have been given the 'cure' of the Irish workmen building the new town of Stevenage. Of the hundred there (and 400 more are due soon) about 70 attended in a very ramshackle Nissen hut, rather sullenly. No confessions and nobody went to communion (this must be remedied quickly). I said that I would give no sermon and take no collections, and grinned, but there was no response at all. How to approach these people? I feel a terrible responsibility.'

A week later he reports:

> 80 men came to the second Mass at Aston, and three came to confession and communion. I brought the altar down to floor level, and must ask them to come up closer. I shall ask them all to answer (or do I need permission for that?)

Over time everything improved at Aston, with numbers increasing in attendance and the sacraments, with communicants even willing to miss their breakfasts. Bert's ability to create community was in evidence. He became good friends to Mr Hayes, the works manager, and to many of the workers. But he was soon to find opposition from the parish priest at Stevenage. 'Today (19 Feb 1952) tried to see Fr Ormiston at Stevenage about his continued opposition to the Mass that Mr Hayes has asked me to say for his Irish labourers at Aston. He had even phoned Hayes to protest about the missioner Fr Sheil SJ preaching heresy and in an unauthorised place! I was told he was out, but through the curtains I thought I saw he was actually there.' A month later Bert noted that his Irish congregation liked his preaching on St Patrick. On Easter Sunday they renewed their baptismal vows in a flower filled 'church', and presented Bert with a Ronson lighter and a money gift.

By June, when the Irish workers were to move from Aston to Monkswood, Bert did get to speak with Fr Ormiston. The

Stevenage priest was determined that the Irish should join his church. Bert comments: 'The men will certainly not go to O., and my presence has at least kept them on lines. Perhaps we just have to wait for Bp Cravens's visitation. Sadly the decision was to make the new town development part of Fr Ormiston's parish, and I must guarantee a Mass each Sunday up there, and all proceeds (stipends) to go to Ormiston. Can I bear to be his "curate", and tie SEC to such an arrangement? Yet I loathe letting the Irishmen down, who continue to greet me with effusion.' For Bert the new arrangement was difficult, 'a silent Mass with no permission to communicate with the people.' I wonder if many of the Irish turned up.

In September 1953 Bert offered to take over the Mass at Hadham chapel of ease, which was held in a stable loft at the manor house. 'I am clearly going to enjoy this pastoral experience.' Westminster had bought a derelict army hostel that was going to take some serious work to make it into a small church. It took over two years to complete the building, but from the start Bert built up a fine community by hard work and calm patience. He made home visits that included Sunday breakfast at one house and Sunday lunch with another family. In between he called in on others. He wrote a great deal about his Hadham parishioners, with amusement, anxiety and affection. Some remained in touch with him until he died. 'After the Hadham Mass, to breakfast with one parishioner, most frightfully frightful, and namedropping by the hour: "Dear Fr Vincent – he spoke of me as his elder sister", "You see I know my Aquinas", "Did you know Jung? Of course he's getting old now, but he's so right", "Do you know Harding?" "Dear Kathleen (Kenyon) wanted me to come on a dig", etc.' Another interesting inhabitant was a Mrs G. 'Mrs G in Hadham invited me to tea to meet Maria T, "an adultress who knows she is doing wrong but has not the strength to do otherwise." She promises to write to see if I can sort her out. Mrs G is a vegetarian cat lover and mystic with a great reputation for sanctity. I found her narrow, vinegary and basically unhappy.'

Over the years he had charming letters from the children. 'Dear Fr Richards, I hope you had a very nice holiday and enjoyed seeing your 280 relations ... Bridget.' He offered to collect elderly Mass-goers in his car, which they could hardly believe. Within a few months he was celebrating Mass at Hadham on some weekdays, and even taking parishioners with him to concerts.

Fri 18 Dec SEC
In the fog, took some of the Hadhamites over to St Alban's for *The Messiah*. Under the new interchurch laws, we were allowed to say the 'Our Father' with everyone else. Mrs W. proved what a good Catholic she was by clamming up at the 'For thine is the Kingdom'. What have we done to poor people like this?'

It was not until May 1954, after endless meetings with the diocese and architects, that work actually started on the new church. Bert was full of ideas himself, especially with employing artists for original works. He had already befriended a local struggling artist, Reg Lloyd. 'Met architect Blake today, an interesting man. Am quite sanguine about the prospects. Why not get Lloyd to do something? And even Henry Moore might be persuaded to do a small statue.' The famous sculptor lived close by and Bert got to know him quite well. Sadly it was often the local clergy who caused difficulties. 'A near row with the chaplain at St Elizabeth's, who is always talking about the new church at Hadham, but has done nothing about it over the 14 months since we bought the property.' So Bert took everything into his own hands. A week later he took seven divines to the land army hut where they all set to, taking down the 20 partitioning walls. 'Warner telling us that his boss would pay 3/- an hour for workmen so keen.'

Over the coming months Bert took his 'work party volunteers' to the Hadham building site. They scraped old tar-paper off the floor, 'sweated our guts out digging 24 holes 2ft deep for fence posts around the ground' and scrubbed the walls in preparation for painting sessions. Behind the scenes he was in endless sensitive negotiations to commission Reg Lloyd to paint the 'Stations of the Cross', and to insist upon Blake that the paints he ordered were far too expensive and had to be sent back. He managed to persuade Fr Bently in Marylebone to give him the church bell lying in the garden since his church was bombed. He left with the bell and £50 to buy the tabernacle. The work was 'slow but highly satisfying, with lads like Heekin slogging away unassumingly'. At times he had 18 students laying the hard core and shovelling soil for the site, and as the summer term ended he wrote: 'The last day of work at Hadham produced 24 volunteers. The ladies provided a magnificent tea for them in the hall.' In November there was a mad scramble to finish all the work, as the Cardinal was to bless the new church at the end of that month. The publicity meant that visitors 'came in droves to be shown around. I have also quite a job going around to appease all the little jealousies of people whom the press did not mention!' The chapel of ease in the loft was emptied, the 'Stations' erected, choir practices held, and floodlights collected and set up.

On Sunday 27 November the Church of The Holy Cross was blessed and Bert celebrated the first Mass. In the late afternoon his whole family arrived with Spud Murphy O'Connor, to join about 200 parishioners and visitors. The new church bell rang for 15 minutes as 'Cardinal Griffin arrived by floodlight to the packed church. The singing increased in volume, the best being the *Old Hundredth*, where all sang their heads off, including the three Protestants helping in the kitchen. The Cardinal graciously mentioned my qualities of leadership.' He also mentioned that the cost to the diocese would have been much more 'had it not been for the students, led by Fr Richards'. Sherry, tea and cakes followed in the packed hall with Frank (Hubert's brother) declaring that it was better than the opening of a new pub. Later in the evening at SEC there was a Common Room to celebrate the occasion. 'I drank mightily, got Spud to accompany me on a series of mountain songs, and finally persuaded Fred Miles to do all his hilarious imitations. We finished by all singing carols. Bed at 1.00, with a lecture on Habbakkuk to deliver tomorrow!' Much Hadham parish grew from strength to strength, not least because from the very beginning Bert was instructing new converts. Some months he would be holding two or three classes a week, recognising that individuals needed to be guided individually. The hall now needed the same treatment as the church – scrubbing, sanding, and painting. He was never short of help, but some of the older inhabitants needed gentle handling.

Sun 29 Jan '56 SEC

Today took breakfast at the Warners, to show there's no hard feelings over them finally refusing the caretaker job at the church. Charlie W. refused to come in from the kitchen, and shouted out a few remarks behind closed doors. Obviously jealous over the fact that I have effectively taken charge, where it was he who used to run the show. He is also strongly opposed to a dialogue Mass in which everyone chimes in, and (most vehemently) to standing for the Preface. But I admire the fact that he still comes!

In June, after weeks of hectic preparation, the new parish held its first bazaar: 'And it rained all day. We had asked Mrs Hughes Hallet to open it, having hosted us for years down the road when we used her stable attic for a chapel ... In the event, we had gathered so much stuff that we made a clear profit of £170 – the village had never seen anything like it!'

It was in these early years that Bert noted in his diary the tension between prayer and his busy activities. He spent a retreat week with the Cistercians on Caldey Island, later calling in on occasions to the monks at Mt Saint Bernard's Abbey. On the first occasion he wrote: 'The beauty and simplicity of the church is overwhelming, and the silence hits you like a battering ram. I continued to look out of the car window for 10m after we left, till the strong tower was lost to sight. Could I belong here?' For a few years this was a recurring reflection. It is no surprise that he was attracted by the Russian liturgy that allows for quiet contemplation. Bert was a quiet man of prayer, in the midst of activity.

The Hadham years meant a great deal to Bert; he had fond memories of the community, his only taste of parish life. He was much loved, learnt a great deal about families' struggles and about the church's need to listen to the laity rather than lord it over them. In spite of all his commitments at the seminary he found time to visit everyone and respond to their needs. After one holiday he reports: I caught up with my Hadham parishioners, and visited the Hunts, Warners, Saviolis, Edel (hospital), Mrs Ross, Jennings, Mrs Kearsey, and Giuseppe & Libera.' The same week he visited: 'the Grisewoods, Pawles, Morrisseys,

Parkers and Mynotts,' a few days later: 'more pastoral visits to Hunter Johnstons, O'Connors, Shipps, Ward Thomas, Powells, Fishers and Vanstones. Afternoon took the divines to Hadham for catechism, and did a baptism.'

All his devoted work at Hadham went alongside other new commitments, yet he found time to make up a complete photo record of his little parish, just as he lovingly kept a photo record of his family throughout his life.

The diaries record every marriage, birth, celebration, and family holiday in photographs and letters. He also noted how much he enjoyed giving treats to the nieces and nephews. 'A visit to town to take Brian and John to the Schoolboys Own Exhibition: a vast mass of kids twiddling knobs. 12 Jan 56.' On his few days off or on holidays he spent time helping his parents with jobs at home. One way he helped his butcher father was with chickens for Christmas. Chickens were reared on the land at St Edmund's, under the care of Fr Eckbury. The diaries suggests that Papa bought his chickens from the college, as annually Hubert would make several van trips with a load of the birds to the butcher shop in Portobello Road.

Bert's work kept on increasing. He was in demand for talks, from his Finchley Grammar School, from the Grail for their chaplains, from bishops inviting him to give their clergy retreats or diocesan clergy days. As early as 1954 Bishop Dwyer invited him to 'be one on which I can call from time to time. I am thinking of building up a list from all the seminaries and indeed from all over the country ... to have the opportunity of learning from the experience of non-Catholics in various gatherings.' He was invited by Val Elwes to lecture at Oxford to 400 students. He found it a 'most charming weekend. What extraordinarily rounded (and privileged) people all these are. I spoke on the *Credibility of the Gospel Record*, and it seemed to go well. Elwes giving me a dozen assurances that it did ... This has set me up for the rest of the term.' He looked forward to this annual invitation. But it was the Religious Orders who were the first to recognise the importance of scripture, asking for courses and conferences that were to influence thousands over the years.

Tue 7 Feb 1956 SEC

At the instigation of Mth Mary Catherine of the Oxford HCJ's, I have volunteered to teach a weekly scripture course in London, to replace the rather inadequate Diploma Course currently in operation. Mgr Barton (who rather treats me as his protégé) has given it his blessing, and I began tonight at the Bayswater Sion from 7 to 8pm. About twenty attended.)

Monsignor Barton, an elderly, scholarly priest in the Diocese, had the same enthusiasm for scripture as Bert. He was highly knowledgeable, reading every new scripture publication which he would recommend (or not) to Bert. His hand written notes appear often in the diaries.

Dec 14 1956

Dear Fr Richards

I am glad you are discussing the matter in the CR apropos of *Origines*. (I used the same author's *Adieux du Seigneur* when I was preparing my Lent addresses at the Cathedral at the beginning of the year, and wasn't much impressed. Père Huby's little book, though far shorter, is also, I think, a better treatment). You may have Fr Sucliffe on your trail, but he is most depressingly conservative. I remember very well the 1954 CCES at Ampleforth, when a mildly pro-evolutionary paper was read, and Fr S. was up in arms with all sorts of literature from retired colonels and the like who, like the famous Soapy Sam (and Dizzy) were 'on the side of the angels'.

Monsignor Barton must have given Bert some comfort, as he had little support from the older seminary professors. The saddest note in the diaries the next year was Bert's disappointment in his teacher at the Biblicum, Fr Bob Dyson. He had such good memories of him, but now realised that the lectures in Rome were without the research into biblical exegesis encouraged by Pius XII, and that Dyson had never thought for himself. Fourteen years had gone by since the encyclical *Divino Afflante Spiritu*, and Dyson had contributed little to the new thinking. When Bert was asked to read the proofs of The 1958 Luxury Edition of the Douay Bible he was aghast at the whole production, which showed some parts taken from the Westminster Version, spellings not consistent, in spite of Bert checking them earlier himself; and Dyson's contribution on the Psalms a pitiful attempt with text markings in 'arbitrary divisions and headings, and written notes without further reference to these divisions. Was nobody given this to read before it was sent to the printer?'

Encouragement came from those who attended Bert's rapidly increasing lectures. In 1958, following talks at a study weekend at Harborne Hall, Birmingham, he wrote in the diary:

> The first evening went very well, though the discussion worried me somewhat, given that my views on the historical character of the gospels are rather near the knuckle. But (as I find out again and again) I am only putting into words what the majority have been thinking for years.

The year was a busy one. Besides the weekly Newman lectures Bert was preparing a course of 24 lectures on 'The writings of St John' for a London University extension course. Requests for talks from convents poured in, from Ursulines, Sacred Heart sisters, Missionaries of Mary and Notre Dame sisters. The year had already started with his appointment as editor of the forthcoming *Catholic Commentary*; more map work for the Rainbow Bible; and he was 'sweating over an article on Genesis for the *Clergy Review*'. Bert wrote several contributions for Coulson's book, *Saints*. A few months later he was made secretary for the Catholic Biblical Association, wrote articles for the *Catholic Herald* and more for the *Clergy Review*. He wrote a CTS pamphlet on *Divorce*, struggled with reading German books for Herders, and still worried that his reading 'showed how superficial my own scripture knowledge is.'

Meanwhile, Bert had many converts to instruct this year, but found that he was upsetting the local priest. 'Contretemps with the Ware PP Boddy. Yesterday evening, while I was instructing Mrs Ross, he walked in. Surprise all round. He asked me to leave the room, and for 20 minutes scolded her, insisting that her instruction in the faith would be finished by him. When he had gone, she burst into tears, and asked to call the whole thing off. I went to see him today, and realised my lack of diplomacy in acting in his territory without his leave. Including several baptisms of children actually in his parish boundaries. With my apologies, he agreed to let me continue the instructions.' He also had difficulties with the Vicar General about 'the need for translators of foreign scholarly works to be allowed to make their own translation of scripture in order to make the point being made in the original. Glad to say that I have won.' This was in reference to his translation of Charlier's *Christian Approach to the Bible*. In December he heard from Sands that they had already sold 3,000 copies, which meant £300 to share with Brendan Peters. The good news was even better as their translation had an excellent review in *Theology*.

The year ended with 'a shrewd note from Papa asking me whether there is any difference between Archbishop Godfrey's unwilling obedience to Pius XII on scripture (of which I complained), and my unwilling obedience to Godfrey. A nice point, but the fact remains that obedience to something that is wrong is itself wrong ...'

CHAPTER EIGHT

Hard Work and Enjoyable Breaks
1959 onwards

1959 saw even more books to censor and review, monthly articles for journals and Catholic papers, Bible Schemes for the CTS,
work on translations for the *Jerusalem Bible,* and more invitations
for lectures around the country. 'Four days to conduct the Easter
Study week at Spode for 50 Catholic students on the Old
Testament. Not easy, given their innocence about the OT, my
own fairly radical views, and the presence of Archbishop
Grimshaw of Birmingham for part of it. Both in speaking there
and writing to me after, he seems torn between the unimagin-
able dangers of modern scripture studies and a desire to support me and recommend me as a safe and reliable guide. The
lectures went well, and provoked some good discussion. But
perhaps the most enjoyable part were the social occasions where
four girls, dressed as J, E, D and P won the prize, and we had a
singalong with the guitar.'

Later, Bert sitting next to Bishop Craven, was pleased to hear
that the bishop 'professed himself smitten by my interpretation
of Original Sin'. The bishop may not have been so happy to hear
that Bert had recently composed his own 'non-denominational'
service for the burial of a parishioner, Ellen Warner, in the Old
Hall Green Cemetery.

His work in Hadham never stopped, with growing numbers,
baptisms, First Communions, deaths, problems over school ad-
missions, instructions now in German as well as many in
English, children's parties, entertaining groups from the parish
attending celebrations at the college, and hours listening to trou-
bled parishioners.

College work went on as usual, but Bert gave an unusual
opening lecture to his divines in October. Written on the back of
old notes he wrote out what he was going to say – as he did for
any lecture. (He always seemed to remember what he had written because he never referred to the notes when he spoke.) He
pasted the scribbled notes in the diary:

I read during the summer of death of Fr Robert Dyson SJ.

Want to say few words becos was my prof. I sat at feet both in seminary and after the war, when taking degree at PBl Rome.

Perhaps yourselves come across his name: co-author Fr Jones Kdm of Promise (1946 – outstanding for the time) Co-author … etc.

Old Bob (as known) was a v. loveable character. I think true to say was loved by all students of many generations. All the scripture men you've ever heard of passed thro his hands (Jones of UpHolland, Johnston, McHugh of Wonersh, … all recent Americans, McKenzie etc …)

All sat at his feet – & have great affection.

This affection, oddly enough, not for his brilliance – but for the opposite.

Because Old Bob was absolute scoundrel, unscrupulous, shameless plagianiser. But we did all know it – & I think he knew we knew it, & so everybody was happy. Used to issue notes & you'd read & say 'gosh, good stuff' – and then found lifted bodily from book by Lagrange (and of course we all do it but not so blatantly), etc.

When I first came here to teach, presented me w book, in which each page neatly sliced out w. razor blade 'Keep dark from students – can put individual pages in lecture notes – find very useful.'! (But then always tearing up books. When brought to me to lecture, say 'V. fine illustr. Here, perh. like pass around' – rip!)

I remember once collared me before lecture in Rome & asked me to look over blackboard facing wall. I had been doing course on Egyptian hierogl. (all had to do one eastern language on top of Hebrew, Aramaic, Greek). He had written out famous descr. of Palestinian (Simabe). Asked me to make sure I would get it straight. In middle of lecture (Joshue) – he turned: 'I don't know if one of my students … Fr R?' I rattled it off. Cheers! People hardly dared speak to me.

I think it was that element of showmanship w. endeared him to us. We all saw thro it, but it didn't matter. By fair means or foul, he made a colossal impression, and that impression lasted. Old Bob, the first class showman, and in spite of it all (or becos of it all), inspired us w. trem. love of scripture. Certainly without him I wd never have arrived at this desk. Used to love to read out a ch. of Nahum to us – & did it so superbly, wd think it the prophet himself on rostrum. He was, for all his faults and acting, a tremendous teacher: what he taught stuck, and for that alone one prays that he will receive his reward.

Hope you will remember him in your prayers.

Lecturing was always more enjoyable than the marking of exam papers.

Fri 17 Jul SEC
A depressing job marking 80 exam papers, some of which give the impression that no lectures had ever been given on these subjects. But some amusing answers to the question, 'What is the Johannine Comma?'
•   Given St John's style, his Comma is conspicuous by its absence.
•   The Comma was St John's contribution to the grammar of his day.
•   John's Comma was the trance in which he wrote the Apocalypse.
•   John's Comma is much the same as St Paul's Comma.

The year ended with three deaths.

Tragic news today that John Deeble Rogers aged 1, hospitalised yesterday after (it seems) bungling by the doctor, died this morning. I went over to find Laurie and Madeleine inconsolable, and I held their hands and read some scripture.

Today the funeral of Vicenzo's 2-day-old baby, who died on the farm next to the Deeble Rogers only days after their tragedy. Vicenzo and I decided to do it on our own, without undertakers, so I was in vestments and a prayerbook, and he carried the little box in the passenger seat in my car. After, I took him home, where we both had a very stiff aniseed.

Charlie Warner (in hospital) was too weak for Communion. No one has yet told him he is on the edge of death, so I did. He was so grateful that he called all the family in one by one to speak to them and then he asked me to bring him Communion. Most edifying.

Charlie Warner died on Monday. I dashed over to Hadham to pray with Elsie. A good turnout on Tuesday evening when we processed the coffin to our little church. Today a solemn high Requiem with 8 divines singing, and several clergy attending. Terrible todo at the Old Hall Green graveyard when the 82 year-old undertaker stumbled at the deep grave edge and fell in: he had to have a ladder sent down to get him out!

January 1960 began with serious work at the Grail on the translation of the Gelineau psalms. Bert devoted much time to this work until the final publication in 1963. In late January he conducted Morning Service from St Edmund's on the BBC Home Service, 'A Meditation based on the Psalms in the Gelineau Version.' The choirmaster was Fr Alec Wells, who was so enthusiastic about the Psalms that the college choir had recorded some of them with Philips' Records. Bert spent hours on his sermon only to have it cause problems for him with the producer of the programme, Fr Songhurst. 'He took everyone for a practice, mostly for balance. My session with him came after night prayers. He had already expressed qualms about my piece on the Coming of Christ on the grounds of obscurity. He timed me as I read through all my pieces. Added to the choir it came to exactly the 46 minutes, allowing the final psalm to be faded out. But he refused to allow this, and finally insisted I cut three minutes of my part. I groaned as we deleted prayers, and the page on the Coming of Christ. Went to bed a worried man, and slept abominably.'

By morning Songhurst had relented a little, and just before going on air told Bert that if, near the end he saw there was time in hand he could put back the prayers. There was time in hand so Bert decided not to add the prayers, but to insert the excised part of his sermon. '… I mentioned the older carols. In fact, this thinking about the child born in a manger, is something quite recent. The original idea of Christmas was to celebrate the Coming of Christ in glory at the end of the world. Does that strike us as odd? And yet, just think of it. What was it that we looked forward to in that period before Christmas – "Advent", the time of Christ's Coming? You thought it referred to his Coming at

Bethlehem? But that happened nearly 2000 years ago. How can you look forward to that? How can you pray for something that has been given to you in the past? No, it's his future Coming that the church is longing for. And Christmas when it comes is a foretaste of it, God's annual guarantee that just as certainly as he came in Jesus Christ 2000 years ago, so will he come again in the end to judge the living and the dead. Christ is here present among us. He has already come back, to those who have the eyes to see it.'

Fr Songhurst was livid. He paced up and down as Bert delivered his words, and later told him that he had ruined the whole broadcast. 'He stomped off, refusing to speak to me further. But I was glad to get my bit in.' In fact, praise came from all quarters about Bert's preaching. Everyone crowded round to congratulate him, including Fr Dan Higgins, the organist, who told Bert how 'good the sermon was, not just in meaning but in delivery and "authority". Very different from the parsonic delivery so frequently heard.' Within minutes a phone call came through from the Grail, who were delighted and thrilled with his presentation 'of our psalms'. The Baroness later wrote: 'You gave us meat and wholemeal bread. This is the stuff we want; it was enthralling, satisfying, prayerful in the truest sense. We (the laity) are hungry for this food … Incidentally you are a born broadcaster, a natural. It sounded so effortless and clear and utterly convinced from within, no pious platitudes, no clichés, just God and scripture'. Another Grail member wrote: 'Everybody here was thrilled, and your part in the broadcast ranked highest of all.' Pop Parsons, his old headmaster, wrote: 'If today's service in the College Chapel can be a matter for congratulations, I send them cordially and warmly – a real Counter-Reformation feat!' The most interesting and unexpected praise came from a Buddhist listener: 'My intellectual knowledge is substantiated by my intuitive sense, when listening to your graceful and thoughtful service, that of all churches here in the west the Roman Catholic alone truly understands the message it has been given.'

Somehow Bert's calm presentation of his thoughts, both in lectures and in church, suggest that he found sharing his insights easy, without anxiety. This was far from the truth. Throughout his life, before every event – lecture, seminar, or sermon – he spent hours of preparation and was always surprised when he received praise. His worries vanished as soon as he had time with his friends, especially his gita companions. The great holidays were greeted with relief. Back in 1951 Bert was able to enjoy a real family holiday with Ma, Pa and his youngest sister, Margaret, on a five week European journey, taking them through France and Italy, where they visited Rome and Assisi, before visiting Germany. In the south, with the family in Nagelsberg, Bert realised 'that a good deal of the strange local dialect (spoken by his relatives) is clearly related to Yiddish and Hebrew. For instance: To steal is 'gaufe' (= *ganav*), Bad is 'schoufel' (= *shaphal*). To eat well is 'achile, achle' (=*achal*). People sometimes remarked that Bert had a 'Jewish nose'. Did he have a Yiddish ancestor? The relatives cried when the family left Nagelsberg, and Bert wrote: 'What have we done to deserve such loving relatives? Here and in Bruhl and Broich, in the Rhineland.'

Climbing and skiing were the gitas the friends most enjoyed. In 1952 Spud, anticipating an Easter climb, expressed his feelings in poetic form, as he often did:

> Think of it, just a few days of that old feeling again, a gita during gita time. The rugged rocks, the open sky, the songs, the jokes, the eats, the smokes. Not to mention the climbing itself. How can you possibly refuse? As I perform my daily and weekly duties, the necessities, the humdrumity, the awful totalitarianism that is beginning to pervade every nook and cranny of this life, tugs and drags and weighs down my soul. One hears of God and mammon knowing in whose powers the moderns are. One sees and peers at periodicals filled with the devilment of our time, and one smells the stink of foulness in one's nostrils until the body revolts and the soul cries out for refuge if only for a while – to breathe – to breathe – to breathe. I know no finer place this side of heaven than those mighty carved forms, pyramids of gaunt rock, which stark and clear shine forth in summertime, and barely clad; but when the winds and cruelty in their due time come, then full of beauty, their forms covered by the

purest mantle for our gaze, they reflect to our poor spirits the aweful Presence which made us both.

Later, in reply to Bert's response, Spud sent another note:

Your pen is like a golden alpenstock, the paper you write on a stretch of virgin snow untrod by man. Your thoughts pour themselves forth, sweeping on like a veritable avalanche, stopping only to leave a silence lovelier still. Your eyes like twin icicles allowing no mist before you, no clouds to mar the distance of your gaze. Strength is your body, the strength of rock. Who shall stand in your path? A puny ridge? A timid overhang? A deep crevasse? Come forth ye winds and snows, come forth ye storms and blizzards! Silence, ever silence. You have seen with your mind's eye that light, that everlasting dawn, the eternity of God which is the spirit of the Mountains. Can I say more?

The Easter gita was in Wales, with walks, climbs and mountain songs. At Trefiw, asking for Cinzanos before supper, the proprietress remarking on their accurate pronunciation of the word, was told: 'We are priests.' 'What a waste!' she replied. 'Can I come and discuss theology with you later?' Over the next few years there were other climbs, with Spud, Lowry and Byron; on the Isle of Skye, where 'We didn't dare put on our climbing gear on Sunday: the Curries were even scandalised that we had music in our room ('Fancy, foor meenisters playing the floot on the Sabbath'). Just as well they didn't interrupt the game of Thirty-Ones I taught the others, with shillings changing hands all day.' There were the climbs in the Dolomites and the Alps. There were skiing holidays with Peters, joining Bert's sister, Margaret, in Austrian resorts where she was working. There were more summer holidays with the family, with Spud joining the 1953 visit to Germany for a family wedding. It was a car journey with Papa, Mama, Anita and Spud through the Rhineland, with a stop off by the climbing duo in Austria and Italy, reuniting with the others in Stuttgart before going to Nagelsberg for Elsbeth's wedding to Eugen. It was a family party talked about, even in later years, because of the humour and fun that Spud brought to the occasion.

The summer of 1959 saw Bert join his parents and Margaret for a long holiday in Canada, again visiting relatives. His brother Frank, and sister Teresa, had both emigrated there some years previously. He had hoped to give a few lectures in Canada – to pay for the holiday, but all the centres were themselves on holiday. He went over to New York for five days to attend, with Reggie Fuller and Bernard Orchard, the 'American Catholic Biblical Association' AGM. He found the hospitality 'Overwhelming. Private rooms. Own showers. A lounge with free beer and ice cream all the time. Cafeteria meals of **** hotel standard. Fullsized swimming pool, and outings into New York.' There were dozens of 20-minute papers, some extremely good. Bert also managed to arrange four lectures for nuns at the College of New Rochelle, which were very well received, and earned him $80 which helped pay some of his expenses.

There were two quite different holidays with Spud. The first was in 1956, giving Spud's friends, Jack and Cynthia, help on their farm in Devon. It was memorable for Bert because while hedging with a hook he damaged his right hand. The swelling needed penicillin, followed by an emergency hospital visit with an operation under gas. 'It gave me an absolutely wild dream, where I was a penguin finding it difficult to articulate words with such a large beak. They had to cut my hand to the bone to root out the infection . Back to hedging the next day, and a glorious chase across twelve fields in the dark looking for some of our sheep that had strayed.' The most enjoyable gita he had with Spud was when he most needed it, in the summer of 1964, after a dreadful year. They explored, mostly on foot, the Holy Land. He could not have had a better companion.

He had already visited Palestine in 1960 in very different company; but it was never a gita. Fr Bernard Orchard, the Ealing Benedictine, organised a three-month journey 'From the Nile to the Tiber' by land rover. The press reported 'Three Benedictines and a diocesan priest have set out to follow the flight from Egypt of the Hebrews with Moses, and to retrace the missionary journeys of Paul.' The other two Benedictines were Piers Grant-Ferris and an American, Blaise Turch. Fr Orchard had pressed Bert to go with him, and had asked the Rector, Mgr Butcher, to allow him an extension to the summer holiday and to obtain cash from the diocese. Bert reported that 'Cardinal Godfrey has suddenly had cold feet over the size of the expedition and the fact it is hoped a film will be made which could be used to raise funds for Ealing Abbey. He writes: "I had understood that this journey was to be in the nature of a pilgrimage which would be of great help to you in your scripture studies and, because of the delicate situation in the Middle East, I was most anxious that publicity be avoided and that interviews should not be given to the Press." He asked me to come and see him. It turned out that he's only worried that 'The Jews' do not capitalise on our trip!'

For Bert it certainly was a pilgrimage, and he recorded every moment in his diary, later making a bound copy of all the long letters he sent home. The photographing became a nuisance to him as it caused so many delays. He also wrote: 'With a party of four, we always seem to start ½ hour later than arranged. I fret a good deal about the wasted time when there is so much to see.' The diary does show how much he gained from the experience: he could associate well with every biblical location, as a few examples will show.

> Of Tyre we could only see the modern city, the biblical one (Ezekiel 27) being covered by the sea. I discovered that tomorrow's gospel, 11th after Pentecost, begins 'Jesus came into the area of Tyre and Sidon.' One felt one had just missed him.
>
> In Damascus, August 22. We were up by 5.30, and put anoraks on. Sunrise over Mt Herman was like the Transfiguration, and the shepherds wandering into our tent Mass was like Bethlehem. From Damascus into Jordan (where by fluke they saw King Hussein 'going out for a flip in his helicopter, where he waved to us') south to Nebo to see Moses' view of the Promised Land. We read the last chapters of Deuteronomy. Light hazy, but the view was still impressive.

They rode through Petra on horseback (18 shillings each).

> Fantastic beauty. Met some archeologists from the Ashmolean. A bit sore from the horse ride, especially when my horse took it into his evil mind to canter and gallop.

On our return up north, I suggested we leave the road to photograph some black beduin tents. Invited in with courtesy, carpets spread, coffee poured, the womenfolk, some with babies at the breast, gathered round in wonderment. Toffees to the kids, eyes large and solemn. Tobacco exchanged, all conversation in sign language. Hens pecking around. A fire is lit, obviously to roast a lamb: we protested, because we want to race on to Nebo. Abraham receiving the heavenly guests?

Through Jericho (where the land rover suffered on rocky ground) across the floor of the valley, 1,000 feet below sea; up and up, past the sign post saying sea level, 28 miles – a day's journey at least on foot for Christ and the disciples; past Bethany, and there, suddenly, the Holy City lay before us, with only the Kidron gash between us and the temple area. I was thrilled. Through St Stephen's Gate at 2.55 and just caught the Friday Stations of the Cross. Very moving to traverse the streets that Christ walked on the Via Dolorosa. Lithostrotos and Mother Ita's scholarly explanation. Stories compellingly genuine. Christ walked here. Also St Paul.

Jerusalem like Assisi. Charm and peace. Holy Sepulchre. Mess, clutter and clobber. Constantine's basilica a perfect plan, now just a shambles. Squabbles. Dirt. A fireplace in the Greek choir. Hideous dust covers over the chandeliers.

Bethesda. Alec Jones had spoken of archaeology as a fourth dimension, and how he had put his foot into the pool without knowing. Wondering how he could be so stupid, I did exactly the same. White Fathers digging out a Byzantine basilica. Archeology in the making.

Later the four had an audience with His Beatitude Archbishop Athenagoras who was known for his ecumenical hopes. It was the highlight for Bert. 'A is a charming old man of 70, full of life, with a grey flowing beard and warm sympathetic eyes. The utter simplicity of his house and garb – why cannot our bishops live like this? His bookshelf contained the RSV, the RB and the *Annuario Pontificio*. He was touched by our desire to see him. When we told him where we had been, he asked "What did you find in Jerusalem?" I said, "Disunity." He was not satisfied with this. "Surely" he said, 'you found Jesus Christ. Are you a Christian? So am I. We worship the same Lord, we are baptised with the same baptism, we have the same sacraments, we have shed the same blood for Christ (he referred to the moving inscriptions in the Roman catacombs, with Latin names next to Greek). What then divides us? Surely only superficial things, which we can leave to the theologians to discuss to keep them occupied, while we get on with the real unity." Whenever he spoke of the journeys of St Paul his eyes filled with tears. As we left, he gathered all four of us into his arms and asked, "What is the most important thing? What was Christ's last will? Peace, Unity, Love" and with tears gathering in his eyes he smiled broadly at us as if to say "What are we waiting for?" We were too moved for words. As we kissed his hands to leave, he bent down to kiss each of us on the cheek.'

They finished their journey in Rome. But it was a Benedictine trip and they did not stay at the English College. They called for tea but found everyone in retreat and unable to entertain them. They did get a place in the Sala Ducale to 'watch Pope John process by on his way to a capella for Pius XI. We had hoped that our strange garb might attract his attention sufficiently to make him stop and say "Who the hell are you?" but he just passed through in utter recollection, with an obvious desire to avoid publicity, unlike Pius XII.' The short stay was disappointing for Bert. He noted in the diary that he had 'Seen hardly anything of Rome, but I still have all tomorrow morning.' The next day he wrote: 'Vain hope. My last hours with the party proved to be the most frustrating in the whole three months. Mrs Dory (a friend of Fr Orchard who had flown into Rome to meet up with him) arrived for Mass, dressed to kill. Bernard insisted we breakfast with her, in the centre of town, which took till 9.30.' Intense traffic delayed the return to the Benedictines at St Paul's to pack, 'with Bernard needing to unload three cases before he was ready. Then to an early lunch date with Mrs Dory, which was great, but I had to wolf the second course in order to dash out and catch my train, which I only just made.' Bert was relieved to be on his own.

He had a great welcome back at St Edmund's, with catcalls over his crew-cut; all reading at table off in his honour; drinks with the Rector, and cheers for his first appearance at lectures. His congregation at Hadham were delighted to have him back, not least Mrs Kearsey, who had written to him on the eve of the journey: 'I am unaccountably sad at your going, and given to morbid reflection that I may not see you again, which is utter nonsense and sits ill upon me ... You have a little corner in the parish, and in the hearts of many of us.'

Bert's favourite gita of all was his 1964 'hilarious visit to the holy Land with Spud' after his 'dreadful term'. Carefree and 'carrying only two rucksacks for luggage, one of them almost exclusively occupied by a guitar,' it was just what he needed. His long account in the diary are excerpts from letters he sent back to his parents. They reveal that deep love for the Holy Land that led him to lead more than twenty future pilgrim groups to share his enthusiasm, and sense that closeness to the gospel Jesus not found anywhere else. In his usual desire to share his findings he later invited his divines to a diary reading of the trip. He put a colourful, hand written notice on the notice board:

THE HOLY LAND BY BUS AND ON FOOT

FR RICHARDS WILL READ THE DIARY OF HIS
1964 TOUR, INCLUDING

The Miracle on Mount Carmel
The Italian Nun with the Saucy Songs
Franciscan Objections to Love-Making
Pere Gauthier on Pope Paul
Soap Made from Dead Jews
Oily Breakfast in the Sacristy
The girl with the Bikini & the Shotgun
The Nun looking for a hermit's cave
The Bus Station at the Foot of Calvary

TUESDAY 4.30 pm
LECTURE HALL
Anyone interested is welcome

Many turned up for the 90 minute reading, and there was 'resounding applause'. The accounts are full of good stories, meetings with strange, amusing and unusual characters, happy evenings with the guitar, and the many deep experiences felt at the 'Holy Places'. What was the Miracle on Mt Carmel and who was that Italian Nun? Bert and Spud arrived in Palestine at Haifa, on a Turkish Tramp Steamer. They walked the steep hill to the Carmelite Monastery, arriving for the 10.30 Mass at the 'shrine (memories of the fierce prophet Elijah and later Christian hermits who dedicated themselves to Our Lady here).' A pious American Lady rushed up to them, having missed the Mass. She had been praying for a miracle, that a pilgrim priest would turn up so that she could 'assist at it'. Bert obliged, and she insisted he took a $1 from her.

Later, staying at the Franciscan Convent on the Mount of Beatitudes, Spud and Bert entertained the community, sitting on the front steps overlooking the Sea of Galilee. They did their cork and match tricks and 'ran through our repertoire of Italian mountain songs with the guitar. One of the more lively nuns helped us with the words, but every now and again stopped to ask permission from the Reverend Mother (a dear old soul) when the words became a little saucy.'

The diary account is full of references to the gospel Jesus, bringing to life the biblical scenes that Bert would have read out to his congregations at Mass. Writing of their stay with these nuns, Bert reflected: 'The most lasting impression was of the countryside and scenery and landscape which Christ and his apostles knew, heat and all. Mass each morning reminded us of the Sermon on the Mount which this house commemorates, and our way to the lake between vineyards and cornfields called forth constant echoes of it: grain growing on good and bad soil, thorns and thistles, stony ground, the birds of the air, the lilies of the field, the vine and it's branches.' Bert was to share these reflections with so many of us who, later, went on his Easter pilgrimages. On the morning before they left 'this high spot in the gita, not easily forgotten', in the middle of his 7.15 Mass, Bert was tapped on the shoulder and addressed in English '"Oi, I booked Mass at 7.30." It was my erstwhile classmate and quondam Vice Rector in Rome, Mgr (Nobby) Clark, and he was dead serious. We put matters straight when we accepted a lift in his coach to Tiberias and regaled him with our adventure. He was impressed by our walking, and sympathetic over our infinite capacity for drinking iced grapefruit. "Have you tried concentrated salt tablets? They take away your thirst." "We don't want our thirst taken away. We like it!"'

On another evening they ran into Nobby Clark again. They joined his group for the evening entertainments and Bert wrote: 'Through the smoke haze and wine fumes I vaguely remember my amazement at a retired Indian army type urging me to stick needles & pins into my thigh, up to the heads as he was doing. I didn't try. An Ampleforth monk in full pontificals, who had been sitting impassively sipping an orange juice all evening, surprised me by catching me as we were leaving, warmly wringing my hands, and thanking me for the "*Ab*solutely *splen*ded enter*tain*ment." I introduced him to the pins and needles merchant and left them at it.'

Spud and Bert loved walking by the Lake and on a visit to Capharnaum chose a bathing spot near the chapel on the shore, 'commemorating Christ's command to Peter to feed his lambs and his sheep – how accurately it is hard to say, but the words were spoken somewhere on this lakeside. With these thoughts it was a little embarrassing to find a German Franciscan giving a rather different idea of Christianity to the dozens of Jews who were using their Sabbath holiday to picnic and swim on the lakeside. The Frats owned the most apt bit of beach, where rocks gave good diving, trees good shelter, and above all a strong waterfall from a spring gave fresh water for camping. The Jews arrived by car load to enter by the only gateway. Obviously they wanted the beach, but he objected to "all this kissing and love making" going on under the trees, and stood there with a hoe threatening anyone who tried to enter. It was not very effective as many families found their way in and were delightfully innocent, eating melons and sandwiches and drinking beer in the sun. I was horrified at the scandal our religion can give to non believers.'

By way of contrast Bert wrote with deep admiration of a French worker-priest in Nazareth. He had been determined to seek out Père Gauthier who had been reported as 'doing wonders among the Nazareth poor. Everyone we questioned had no time for him – it made us more determined to see him.' They found him on the hillside addressing a crowd. 'Slim, graceful, ascetic face with the look of one who had suffered much, kind but compelling eyes.' He showed utmost patience with heckling questioners. They waited three hours for his Mass, 'for he was always putting himself at the disposal of the new groups arriving on the hillside. I was reminded of true poverty – consisting in service; and the poorest being he who puts himself entirely at the mercy of others.' His church was a cave, probably a dwelling place in Christ's time. 'A plain wooden altar on four tree trunks, an oil lamp and two old icons. A stone bench had been carved out on the sides, and a rush mat on the floor for others to sit. The Blessed Sacrament was in a tiny inner cave – probably once a manger. A few simple flowers before it. Sublime simplicity. We said our office while waiting.'

He was asked about the Pope's visit, and he recalled the letter he had written imploring the Pope not to miss the perfect opportunity of showing the world what the church was – 'A community in the service of people. If in Bethlehem he went to see a refugee camp (because Christ was one); if in Nazareth he came to see the poor and labourers among whom Gauthier works (because Christ was one); and if in Jerusalem he went to visit the prison (because Christ was there) then his journey would show all men what the church today stood for.' Bert half expected 'some terribly avant-garde Mass in French, in the lay clothes he wore. But he told the people, as he vested, that he belonged to the Eastern rite, which demanded Mass in the language of the people, in this case French. Priests present in lay clothes, like Bert and Spud, were invited to stand close to the altar after the consecration to receive in both kinds from their own hands. 'It was one of the most devout Masses I have ever been at.'

Later, our two priests stayed in a youth hostel at Engeddi, on the Dead Sea, and discovered a local buffet opened twice a day, where they could stock up with bread, fruit and tinned food. 'The girl who served the buffet wore a bikini and a shotgun, reputedly because of border troubles, but she may have had her own personal problems too.' It was there that they encountered the 'French-speaking Argentinian nun, who has a vocation (so

she maintains) to be a hermit, and who is wandering Israel looking for a cave to live in.'

Their next stop was Jerusalem, so crowded that it was difficult to find lodgings. They spent one night of their stay in a convent of Arabic nuns, where 'We were established in the sacristy
and with typical Arab hospitality, mountains of food began to
arrive, all rather lukewarm and greasy, but in monumental pro-
portions, soup, salads, meat, chips, aubergines, beans, tomatoes,
cheeses, fruit and coffee. We managed about 1/8 of what was
set out, and repaid the generosity by offering to play the guitar
for the nuns during their recreation ... Spud was in good form
and more and more guests and neighbours were brought in.
Perhaps the most amazing thing in the evening was the nuns
singing in Arabic to Italian hymn tunes, me accompanying.' Of
course the highlight of the stay in Jerusalem was their visit to the
Holy Sepulchre Church. 'When Spud said Mass in the church on
Calvary, what with the perambulating pilgrims and the noise of
workmen, he referred to it as the Holy Shambles. Myself I found
the noise of hammering rather suggestive.' They were fortunate
to have their own guide to every corner of the great church (as to
many other places around Jerusalem) because Spud's cousin,
Jerome Murphy O'Connor OP, was studying at the Dominican
École Biblique in Jerusalem.

There was the same noisy hustle and bustle along the Via
Dolorosa when the two priests joined a Stations of the Cross.
'All the while Muslim Jerusalem continued unaffected, with
Turkish coffee, hubbly bubblys, hooting cars, donkeys, and the
voice of Cairo from a dozen different radios. I was stopped in
the middle of it all by a chap trying to sell me slides. Charles
Osborne, near me, was almost livid with exasperation over the
utter chaos and lack of recollection. I assured him there couldn't
have been much recollection during the first Way of the Cross.'
A visit to Bethlehem nearby was especially important to Bert. 'I
had the joy of saying Mass in the crypt where St Jerome had
lived in a cave next to the Nativity to translate the Bible into
Latin (The Vulgate) ... I said the Nativity Mass and it felt like
Christmas all the rest of the day.'

Another serious reflection came at David's Tomb on the Zion
Hill: 'The memorial commemorates the millions of Jews mur-

dered in Nazi Germany. Room upon room of commemorative tablets, walls blackened with votive candles burnt by the thousands of Jews visiting. Showcases of horrors, the most revolting being a piece of soap which wartime Germany made from dead Jews. Two Israelis with us were weeping quietly.' Later they took a bus out of the city to the much larger Yad Vashem Memorial to the murdered Jews. 'The little exhibition on the Zion Hill was a more personal affair, this was more of a documentary, room upon room reconstructing the story of the Jews in Poland, in Czechoslovakia, in Germany etc ... Most overwhelming of all was the bunkerlike building, with little light, a black mosaic floor on which 20 ceramic panels named the concentrations camps – Dachau, Auschwitz, Belsen etc. In the middle a large gas flame. I stared at the place for minutes in silence. One of the most oppressive sights yet.'

In later years Bert was to take his Easter pilgrim groups to visit most of the places he and Spud explored on this gita. They usually stayed in the hotel next door to the noisy bus station. Behind it was the 'Garden Tomb' – 'a low church attempt to discredit the Holy Sepulchre by finding something more *simpatico* in the open ground outside the present walls, with a Calvary rather sadly overlooking the pandemonium of the Bus Station.' Many of his pilgrims liked to visit this site very early on Easter morning for prayerful meditation. On Spud and Bert's last day in the Holy Land they 'payed a last visit to the Holy Sepulchre at a time when work had ceased and pilgrims had eased off, so that there was enough peace to meditate and pray. Then we went home to pack. (Next day left by air to spend over a week in Rome, but that's another story.)'

It was utter joy for them, staying first at the Venerabile and both able to say a Mass in St Peter's. 'Rather overwhelmed by the row upon row of seats fitted out for the 3000 bishops in Council, and finishing by visiting the tomb of John XXIII;' and then joining the students for a week at the Villa Palazzola. The new rector, Leo Alston had made some changes and found the students singing his praises. 'He has gauged very accurately the temper of today's students, and has won their sympathy. The nightly Compline, (asked for and refused by Jock for years) was a joy to attend, the daily dialogue Mass (ditto) a model, and the

Sunday High Mass (the only Mass I was interested to see, because Cardinal Heenan had just about fired me into outer space for trying to introduce the same at St Edmund's) rightly, had a homily every week (I was inveigled into doing it). He has unbuttoned the rather rigid and unrealistic discipline of former times. The lads are happy and as keen as mustard.' During the week Bert read a whole volume of Rahner and reviewed it for the *Venerabile*, poured over the old *Chi Lo Sas*, and college diaries; attended a public audience at Castel Gandolfo, and 'gave the lads two sessions in the common room with the guitar, with such success that the rector postponed night prayers'. They flew back to England with United Arab Airlines. 'But Spud stopped me wearing my keffish'.

Hubert and Clare Richards enjoying the surroundings of their local pub.

Family portrait from 1935. *Top, l to r:* Celia, Frank, Hubert, Bertha. *Front, l to r:* Margaret, Papa, Mama, Terese

Above: A happy Hubert (second from left) in the Forum, Rome.

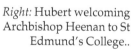

Right: Hubert welcoming Archbishop Heenan to St Edmund's College..

Above: A break between lectures.

Below: Hubert as chaplain to the
Walsingham Cross Pilgrimage, 1948.

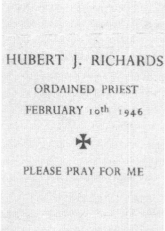

HUBERT J. RICHARDS

ORDAINED PRIEST

FEBRUARY 10th 1946

✠

PLEASE PRAY FOR ME

Above: Front and back of Hubert's prayer booklet which he received upon his ordination in 1946.

Below: Fr Richards' Mass Centre at Hadham.

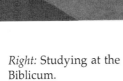

Left: Gospel Songs at Spode House.

Right: Studying at the Biblicum.

Above: Hubert (right) as Major General in *The Pirates of Penzance.*

Above: Family Photo. Clockwise from left: Hubert, Blanca, Pedro and Clare.

Left: Bedtime story with Blanca and Pedro

Right: With Blanca's baby son, 2009. Cian's first Christmas, Grandpa's last.

Students' gift on Bert's Silver Jubilee.

Above: Where most of Bert's books were written.

Below: Cardinal Cormac Murphy O' Connor launches Bert's final publication, *The Four Gospels,* in 2007.

CHAPTER NINE

Vatican Council and All Change
1962-1965

Back a year to 1963. Life for Bert at the seminary began brightly. The Vatican Council was in progress and he had high hopes that changes in liturgical practice would result, and that scripture would, at last, be given its 'proper' place in the Roman Catholic mind. In January Bert was at Southwell House for the AGM of the Catholic Biblical Association, where he contributed a piece on scripture and the liturgy. John McHugh and Pat Fannon gave a lively report of what was going on at the Council, with 'my old Alma Mater, the Pontifical Biblical Institute (PIB) under considerable fire from Ottaviani and the conservatives.' He gives a summary of McHugh's talk in scribbled notes.

Vogt's History of Controversies:

1954	Rumours against PIB
1955	Dyson & North accused
1958	More calumnies against PIB

Osservatore attacts 'Introd. a la Bible'.

1959	Divinitas makes attacks public
1960	USA/Argentina conclude Holy Office supports conservatives
1961	Vogt says attacks are against Pius XII's *Divino Affl. Spiritu*
	Spadafora says DAS was imposed on poor ignorant P.Pius
	Aug. *Osservatore* contradicts DAS
	Congreg. imposes the article as norm for teaching
1962	Rumours everywhere that PIB condemned by Rome
	Ottaviani asks for Lyonnet & Zerwick removed
	General of SJs refuses becos no reasons given
	Calumnies:
	Historicity of Promise to Peter denied
	Rom.5:12 weakens proof for Original Sin
	No acceptance of Tradition

Historicity of Annunciation denied
Holy Office says 2/3 of Bishops at Council are Modernists!
Bps themselves scandalised by the battle, and condemnation
of Rahner.
Ottaviani & Pizzardo plan to abolish University status of
Roman houses.
Meanwhile:
PIB prepared a motion for the Bps at Council –
>There are not two sources of Revelation, Tradition and
>Scripture but only one: God.
>Sacramental efficacy of Scripture should be underlined.
>Historicity of the Gospels.
>DAS should be made norm for Scripture Studies'.

In 1963 Bert had reason to be optimistic for the future. The
Council was such good news. Early in 1959 Pope John had astonished the bishops by calling for the Second Vatican Council.
Commissions were set up immediately to prepare for it. It
opened over three years later, on 11 October 1962. *The
Constitution on Divine Revelation, Dei Verbum,* is regarded as one
of the fundamental documents produced by the Council. A pre-
liminary draft, by the Theological Commission, was presented
to the bishops a month later. Meeting with criticism, it was put
to the vote to decide if it should be completely rewritten. 60%
approved of it, but regulations demanded a 2/3 majority. The
Pope made a 'famous intervention' and overrode the regulation
by supporting the commission, and setting up a joint commission to recast some of the text. It was good news for the
Pontifical Biblical Institute because an original chapter, 'Two
Sources of Revelation' – Scripture and Tradition – was replaced
by two chapters, one on revelation, and one on its transmission.
Scripture and Tradition were not expressed as separate sources.

The text was far less philosophical and emphasis was more
on modern methods of interpretation of scripture, much in accordance with *Divino Afflante Spiritu.* In its final re-writing by
November 1965, it presented scripture as containing 'revelation'
(a manifestation of God), but stated that not all scripture is revelation, with parts being of human reactions to it. Tradition was
said to include much that was of human origin, and therefore

needed continual interpretation, and had to be given new ex-
pressions from time to time as new problems arose. The church
had its important role to play as custodian of the Word of God.

The Constitution on the Liturgy was the first completed work
of the Council. This was not surprising because, as Bert had
been aware for many years, a vigorous movement for liturgical
renewal had been going on in Europe. It became even more international, including America's experience, resulting in 1956
with a Congress in Assisi, about which the Pope (as Cardinal
Roncalli) had been enthusiastic. There were many great liturgical pioneers, such as the Jesuit, Joseph Jungmann, making the
Liturgical Commission's work much easier. They were able to
produce a fine document, with 'its tone altogether biblical', for
the bishops to debate by 22 October 1962. It was accepted on 14
November by a massive majority of 2162 votes to 46.
Amendments were made, and it was promulgated about a year
later by Pope Paul VI. Pope John had died on 3 June 1963, and
when Pope Paul was elected he eliminated the vow of secrecy
that the Council had enforced. This meant that the constitution
was immediately translated into action.

Our English bishops were listening to all this. Reports were
coming back from Rome that they were not contributing very
much and seemed conservative. Not good news for Bert.
Around this time he was accepting invitations to spend time
teaching at the Catechetical College Lumen Vitae in Brussels. He
had already been invited in 1961, giving a series of scripture lectures, alongside Congar 'speaking powerfully on the laity', and
Fisher on liturgy and the psalms. On these visits he was able to
experience the exciting liturgies at 'La Bouverie' where a radical
new way of celebrating with the community was being introduced. 'Rumour was that the parish priest had been excommu-
nicated by his bishop. Reality was that the bishop had asked
him to conform, and he refused, so they agreed not to discuss
further.' Bert was impressed by what he saw, finding it involving the laity in the way he had always hoped for. He saw the
plan for a new church building, 'with its wealth of symbolism.
The baptistery itself has three steps down entitled "Buried with
Christ", and then three steps going up, entitled "Risen with
Christ". The reservation of the Sacrament is to be echoed by the

reservation of the Word of God.' Exactly what Bert envisaged. Before his return to England he had another update on the Council from Fr Fischer just back from Rome, and made good friends with the English Fr Adrian Smith.

Later that January, Bert was staying with the Catholic Missionary Society priests ('a very agreeable bunch') to speak on 'The Prophets and the Gospels'. He decided to concentrate 'because of modern scripture studies – on what they were not.' The talks were received very well. It seemed that the clergy were having no problems with the advance of scripture study coming from the Biblicum (PIB). News came through on the final evening that Cardinal William Godfrey had died. The funeral at Westminster, with about 1,000 priests 'deeply upset' Bert because: 'all the singing, except for "Amen", was done by the choir so that we were silent for 2½ hours; and that the absolution of the poor old man had to be repeated five times, and that so many of the bishops and monsignors were Romans.' He was cheered up by the fact that Hertfordshire was covered in snow and ice for weeks. He could ski with Fred Miles, Pat Hegarty and John Lafferty on all the local slopes.

On Ash Wednesday he received the first copy of 'our new publication *The Paschal Mystery*' and he had his usual crowded day: 'Tried all day to get down to writing more articles for the Virtue book, but failed by reading Sr Gabriel's paper from yesterday, and making some comments; letters; preparing slides for the next talk; arranging servers for the next two months; reading C. S. Lewis on the Psalms; checking an article for the *Clergy Review*; reading the *Worship* magazine which arrived today; giving an opinion on three new booklets from Ireland, first class; leading the Stations at Hadham; preparing a lecture for tomorrow. Not to mention the Office.' Later in the year his next publication came out: *God Speaks To Us*. He was on more committees, including the one for the Canonisation of the English Martyrs, and he records in his diary the death of Pope John, 'He will be missed.'

The entry for Tue 10 Sep SEC is the one that signalled the end of his priestly life as it was:

A very worrying summer, which I had left free to do much

writing for the Virtue encyclopedia as possible. Considerably disrupted by the Devon visit (to help out Peters), four days at a Conference at Spode, much work at Hadham (including McEnroy's death and funeral), and finally (the bombshell) the stroke which disabled the president Reggie Butcher, leaving me (under instructions from Worlock at Westminster) to act as his deputy while he is in 'St John And Elizabeth's' in London. Bp Craven gave me the title of 'acting president', but this was soon changed to 'acting vice-president' (whatever that implies), and the bombshell gave a final burst of flames when it was announced last w/e that Heenan is appointed to Westminster. May the Lord Save us.'

It became obvious later that it was Heenan who made him vice-president. Understandably there are no diary entries for a few days.

He resumed:

This has meant a flurry of things to worry about over the last few days: reading through Butcher's files and trying to make sense of them; arranging the visit of the new Archbishop; worrying about banns and dismissorial letters for the forthcoming ordinations; organising the catering for that day; applying and signing and replying to all the letters dealing with educational grants; seeing to visiting priests; preparing for St Edmund's Day later in the term; wondering whether to hand over the Hadham parish to someone else; writing to bishops about students that are leaving and new students coming; all of them will need to be interviewed; assigning rooms; arranging for retreat priest and the bishop for ordinations; etc.

Went up to London several times to see Butcher, partly to consult him, but mainly to reassure him I was keeping his seat warm.

The divines arrived a week later and Bert gave them a free day before their retreat, given by Bernard Orchard. Bishop Craven came for the three-hour Ordination Mass and the diary reports: 'I finally ushered the bishop out at 2.30, and Orchard

out at 3.00. Archbishop Heenan arrived at 5.15, with everyone
lined up on the drive to welcome him. It was my job to introduce everyone. I mumbled a few words of welcome and distress
that this was not being done by Butcher, and so led him to the
Douay Hall to address us. He is a clever speaker, and ingratiated
himself very well to everyone. He then came to the Common
Room where he was open, easy and free for all. The nuns may
have Dialogue Mass, the divines may have a holiday at Easter,
and Chas Davis is to be invited for the next session of the
Council in Rome as a *peritus*!' There is a fine photograph of Bert,
amongst older seminary priests, greeting the archbishop. No
wonder some friends and family presumed he could have been
chosen as the future president. Only two short diary entries appear for October, and by mid November he is writing of a day
full of depressing thoughts.

> The president has now been ill since end of July.
> Potter is sick with pneumonia since 1 Oct.
> Jim Molloy has been in hospital for a month.
> B. Westbrook has left to do parish work, rather unwillingly.
> Alec Wells has left hurriedly and very mysteriously.
> Chas Davis is absent at the Council for the duration.
> Many students are sick.
> Bp Craven is full of promises, but does nothing to help.
> Nor does the new Archbishop.
> A final blow that Tony Kenny has asked for laicisation –
> why?
> The fact that in Liverpool he was Heenan's subject does not
> help.
> A time for tears.

The next day was another 'mad one', giving his own lectures;
having a priest to lunch; visiting the hospital to speak with the
doctor about Butcher '(very uncommunicative but I wd say
quite bleak)'; quick visit to his parents; a night prayers pep talk
to the divines which he felt gained their approval. He also had a
letter from Chas Davis. 'He writes from Rome about the extraordinary blocking powers of Ottaviani and the Holy Office, and
the poor showing that our English hierarchy is making compared with America and others. Having no specific job, he feels

embarrassed there (though deadly interested).' Davis had made it very clear that it was Ottaviani who was the problem at the Council. He wrote: 'The tussle in the commissions, particularly in the Theological Commission still continues. Ottaviani refuses to be guided by the clear vote on collegiality and acts as if the Council was under the judgement of the Holy Office – represented by himself in the Theological Commission. According to Häring, the progressive bishops who have the majority in the Theological Commission, are showing endless patience and skill, but on the whole they are stymied.' The letter shows quite clearly that Davis was not welcomed by the English bishops to take a full role as a *peritus*. 'I seethed with exasperation the other night when they held the second meeting of the committee of English-speaking nations about liturgical changes. Archbishop Young of Hobart, whom I have got to know well, expressly asked for me to come in on the work. (Deickmann and McManus are brought in as experts by the American bishops.) Grimshaw, who is the representative of the English hierarchy, said no – 'because I was committed'. Even before this I have several times thanked God for delivering Westminster from Grimshaw.' Davis decided in the end to come home early. As much as he enjoyed the experience, he saw no point in his presence there. In retrospect it seemed possible that Heenan had simply found a way to remove Davis from the college.

1964 began with the joyous Golden Wedding anniversary of Mamma and Papa. The preparations, the Mass and the reception 'went extraordinarily well, with the right blend of formality and spontaneity. The Hola (the traditional family song for special occasions) written by Margaret and me was a joy to sing before such an appreciative audience. Everyone went away happy.' By the end of January it became official that Reggie Butcher would not return to the college. Speculation was rife about the new appointment. Two days later the first of many letters came from the archbishop complaining about 'changes' Bert had made without permission.

'The Vicar General has been informed that a number of liturgical changes have been made while you have been in charge at St Edmund's. I shall be grateful if you could let me know the extent of the changes. It would be very difficult if the new

President had to begin by abolishing the innovations. This might cause resentment among the students and ruin his influence.' Archbishop Heenan then told Bert that if any changes had been made, then 'you must without delay re-introduce the liturgy and community exercises as they were before.'

In his reply Bert explained that he had talked over all the minor changes he suggested with Monsignor Butcher, on his hospital visits, and had his full approval. They were:

- Dialogue Mass for the nuns. Approval given already.
- A Dialogue Mass for the Divines after discussing it with them.
- Occasional combining of the two Sunday Masses into the one High Mass when only one priest was available, as the others were committed to the nuns, the parish, and several Mass centres.
- We abolished the kissing of hands & birettas because the President objected to it.
- Because of difficulty for some students in singing, which caused anxiety, we have experimented in speaking the Grace at table instead of chanting it.
- I have asked the subdeacon to face the people instead of the altar when singing the epistle – to make the student aware that he is proclaiming the Word of God to his people.

In his reply Archbishop Heenan told him that Butcher had not been in any condition to agree with changes, and all had to go back to normal. He asked Bert to come and see him. His diary response: 'Hey flippin ho.' Three months later the new President was announced, a Fr Maurice Kelleher. It was not a name very familiar, so 'De Rosa and I looked up his record in the mark-book kept in the president's room.' They found that he regularly got low marks in everything. It was clear that he would do exactly what Heenan wanted. It was to lead to a very unhappy, if not disastrous, time at St Edmund's for staff and students. By 16 January, Bert described 'a sense of deep depression'. He was very worried about Mamma's health, in and out of hospital; worried too for Celia, whose husband Jo was also in hospital, and for Bertha having her own anxieties. At the same time life at St Edmund's was very difficult.

Here the College is in a mess, with progressive deterioration
since Kelleher came:

- Headmaster Britt Compton is livid that he has gone
  ahead with changes in the school without any consultation.
- His total disregard of anything intellectual, esp. in theology. The ideal curate is an obedient and unthinking navvy.
- He has reversed all the burgeoning new ideas in liturgy.
- He is increasingly distrustful of the students, and they are
  increasingly antagonistic to him.
- His lack of leadership has split the staff in two, some
  openly ingratiating themselves and sharing his opposition to the proposed new study syllabus.

Meanwhile the Archbishop continues to delay his visit, ('I'm
taking a long cold look at SEC'), and the air is full of rumours
– that he thinks Peter de Rosa is unsuitable as a prof; that he
disapproves of profs giving lectures outside the college; and
that he wants to censor what Davis is writing for the *Clergy
Review*. Davis and De Rosa are beginning to say they might
out and run. Perhaps I should too.

The new study programme, enthusiastically researched and
proposed earlier by the staff, was 'shot to pieces'; everything the
three had proposed were 'dead meat'. For Bert the saddest result of the staff meeting was in the discussion of Orders, where
Kelleher's men were 'on a witch hunt' for a forward looking student. Bert and Peter de Rosa defended him, but recognised he
stood little chance. He was sent home. A few days later
Archbishop Heenan arrived, 'full of grace and charm as always,
but clearly determined to get Davis out, as the main source of
tension with Kelleher over what a seminary should be.' He was
offered either a sabbatical or pastoral experience in a parish with
a Secondary Modern school attached. He simply refused both.
The next day Bert was in trouble for 'the non-rubrical voice I use
at Mass for the *Orate Fratres*, the Canon and the *Domine Non Sum
Dignus* ... I feel rebellious. At the staff meeting tonight, the word
catechetics was so much part of the discussion that one felt that
would soon go too.'

The final staff meeting of the year was carefully predeter-

mined so that there could be no real discussion. There was
'Severe castigation of criticism of the church, of novelty, and of
opinions as distinct from dogma. New jobs were created for the
safe men on the staff, in preaching, discipline, catechetics, and
Kelleher himself will take all the Mass practices. The students
are not to be forewarned of the changes. Davis wonders whether
he can continue in such a stifling atmosphere.'

A few days later Bert decided to speak with Kelleher, 'out of
a sense of duty, to point out the extent of the discontent in the
college, inviting him to tell me to leave at any point.' Bert was
distressed for the students and felt they needed a voice, which
he would give. He told Kelleher how scared they were of him
because they had never seen him in their Common Room. 'They
only see you as restrictive, untrustful, and uncommunicating.
Butcher they trusted because he treated them as responsible
adults, and under him they had a zeal for study and the rules
and their future pastoral role. They see you as very frequently
absent, imposing new rules (car, telephone, Wednesdays) without explanation. And they are distressed that you have monop-
olised their Community Mass, which you insist on doing in the
old style, in silence.' Bert spoke of the way most of the staff felt,
untrusted, accused of novelty and disloyalty to the church. 'You
seem to imagine we are conniving at revolution, whereas we are
in fact a restraining influence through our patience, and the students trust in us. You never consult us, and you give us the impression you wish to bury the influence of Reggie Butcher, in
whom we all had confidence.' He didn't feel the session did
much good, Kelleher simply explaining the differences away.
'But at least he knows'.

Bert felt that he had nothing to lose, as his departure from the
college was clearly imminent.

Two weeks earlier he had poured his heart out to Len
Johnston at Ushaw in a long letter, apologising that he was not
able to write on Isaiah for the *Commentary*. He had tried for
weeks to get down to it, but 'nothing would come. I think
"breakdown" would be too dramatic a word for it. It's been
something far more intangible, of which the only visible clue is
the long-term result, viz. that I have done nothing creative or
worthwhile since last September' (eight months). He described

the worrying and busy time he had standing in for Butcher, but 'what has happened since makes that previous period look now like a Paradise Lost.' He described Kelleher as 'easy, affable, companiable, kind and oozing with charm as you no doubt saw, but about as forward looking as Ottaviani.' He described how, within a month of his arrival, Butcher's policy of treating students as adults, at last paying off in a sense of community and responsibility, 'had been shot to hell by niggling pettifoggery and an attitude of distrust which had reduced them again to schoolboys. Nor has this distrust been reserved for the divines; Davis, Peter De Rosa and I have had it made pretty clear to us (in the politest manner) that we have been a baneful influence. The only thing Kelleher picked up from his tour of the seminaries is more ideas on how to remain in the sixteenth century.'

Len Johnston's reply was equally depressing. He began, 'If it weren't so tragic it would be amusing: you remember Tom telling you about their experience with Heenan in Liverpool – and now you have it yourself; and you may recall my veiled and not-so-veiled references to our situation here – and this is what you are now experiencing. And the result is exactly what it is for me. What you say about your own state of mind or/and health fits mine exactly – it would be too much to call it a breakdown, but I could spend hours reading and find that nothing at all had gone in … I solved mine – temporally – by just opting out of everything that could possibly be dodged. But isn't it all terribly sad?'

Johnston goes on to describe exactly the same problems at Ushaw, with a complete breakdown of community, with conflicts and factions, with the regime being 'directed to the production of slick automata (made in the image and likeness of Heenan himself, or else Godfrey)'. He discussed all the possible ways of acting: continue to argue and protest (and help the students privately); or to opt out and leave the seminary, 'but in the first place in our diocese – as in yours too now – this means exchanging one lunatic situation for another; we have a Canon Lawyer as bishop who has explicitly said that "I'm just not interested in liturgy or theology" – my God: the successor of the apostles, our father in the faith! – and you can have no idea what this means until you see it in practice; there is quite literally one

criteria for action – the code, *ad mentum* (no, that's rank flattery –
ad nutum) *episcopi*: anything that lives and moves is put under
the dead hand of law.'

Len Johnston gave one last form of opting out as staying put,
doing one's job, disclaiming any interest in the institution as a
whole; just living there, and meeting up with friends. He asked
Bert for any ideas what to do about it, and to share them with
him. He wondered if it would be an idea for him and Davis to
write articles in the *Clergy Review*, and if a meeting of seminary
professors could be arranged. 'Remember I was urging you to
do this when we thought you might become the new president.'
Bert's reply was to give the new SEC definition of their jobs: 'To
prepare the students to be obedient assistants to their PP's.
Therefore to concentrate on their spiritual lives and their character. And then, of course, there are the studies as well.' He
thanked for such sympathy but said that he was, at the moment
'quite honestly in no mood to fight back'. Davis had made efforts to write in the *Clergy Review* (he was editor), but Heenan
was threatening to take it away from him '(I kid you not). Off to
Palestine next week to try to forget it all. But I know perfectly
well that I shall be coming back to hell at the end of it … *Viscera
mea, viscera me.*'

Soon after his return to St Edmund's, Bert gave up his
Hadham Parish. A scroll, signed by everyone, including the
children, says: 'To Father Richards, We wish you Godspeed, remembering with gratitude your devotion to our church.' His
reply, at a presentation, is scribbled down in rough notes. He
said it surprised him that they believed he had done something
extraordinary for them, when 'you taught me so much: how to
be simple in sermons and brief; I learnt from your kindness and
patience with me; you allowed me to share in your sorrows and
bereavements, and in your joys – weddings, births, First
Communions. You always had such consideration for me.' He
commended the new priest to them: 'Be sure to give him the
same love, loyalty, and friendship you have given me over these
10 happy years. I am sure Mrs Kearsy will brew him many cups
of tea as she did for me, treating me like a son.' He gave the reason for his going – that he became so interested in them that he
was 'in danger of neglecting his first work which was at the col-

lege. I assure you that I will remember you always in my prayers as I have done ever since I have known you.'

Ten days later, 8 October, news came that Mamma, already in hospital, had taken a turn for the worse. 'I dashed up to find her unconscious. I anointed her and said all the prayers in the ritual over her. Same again on Saturday and Sunday. What concerned us most in a family discussion was the possibility of her recovering when, as the doctor rather brutally said to Margaret, 'She'll never be anything other than a cabbage.' I drove up again this afternoon, with the nurse relieved to see me, since she had been trying to phone Papa and Celia with the news that Mamma had died at 4 pm. I said the prayers for her at 4.10, glad that I was there so soon after.' Kelleher and six students attended the Requiem, with Spud and Peters, deacon and sub deacon. 'A beautiful ceremony with relatives galore, deeply moved, all commenting on how "brave" I was as celebrant, but all I could think of was of Mamma's happy release from her dreadful illness. When visitors had gone, we had a relaxed family gathering at 54, glad to huddle together.'

As the year approached its end, the three Westminster seminary professors, Davis (Theology), De Rosa (Philosophy) and Richards (Scripture), felt increasing pressure and anxiety. Peter De Rosa was openly challenged to say whether he had written a recent article in the *Catholic Herald*, suggesting that if he did he would have to go. 'Peter simply kept silent.' At the St Edmund's Day celebration on 17 November, Denys Lucas preached 'a very forward looking sermon, which was tangibly resented by the main body of the visiting clergy, who then gave a great ovation (led by Bishop Pat Casey) to Kelleher's after dinner speech, which was in turn tangibly resented by the seminarians. The cleavage is perhaps even greater now than it has been.'

Bert finished the year giving the Leicester Square lectures, signing the contract with the Catholic Biblical Association Committee for the Catholic edition of the RSV Bible, and interviewing a close friend of Edith Stein for the cause of canonisation, 'when I got to know her very well over the 5½ hours interview, and grew fond of her.' He spent as much time as he could with his father, who was very lonely for Mamma. As Christmas approached, with Davis back from Rome to continue lecturing, the diary entry states: 'It seems that Heenan has not yet found a way of sacking him, but sees him as forming a trio with De Rosa and me, and is looking for work that the three of us could do outside SEC.' In January 1965 Bert escaped to Davos for a skiing fortnight with the St Edmund's School party, led by Frs Peter Bourne, Michael Pinot and Tony Potter. He was to make this winter skiing break with the school party his annual holiday for a number of years to come.

Term began with an afternoon at Westminster for a Requiem Mass for Churchill, celebrated by Archbishop Heenan, followed by a conference for the diocesan clergy. Bert reports the agenda: schools, finance including debts, the current discussions at Vatican II on Religious Liberty. 'But the longest section was Heenan's view on the ongoing argument about contraception. Much harm has been done by ventilating so many ideas, with many foolish things said, and Catholics no longer know where to stand. We must await the Pope's decision. If he says that Pius XI and XII were wrong, we will accept that, and tell our people that this does not mean the church erred! If, *e contra*, he agrees with his predecessors, then we accept that just as quickly, with no questions asked. Infallibility does not depend on the latest issue of the *Clergy Review*. (The mind boggles!)'

A month later, on the 19th anniversary of Bert's ordination, (11 February) he received a note from Papa, encouraging him to accept disappointments. His father was clearly aware of the stress his son was feeling. 'In a life that is full of change, we must again and again be ready for disappointments. No one can escape them, and they have an important role to fulfil: they help us to become thoughtful. There is no such thing as a life without disappointments, so we have to expect them, and mentally make allowances for them. Disappointments make us more tranquil, more sensitive, and more patient. They also help us to see how fate governs our lives far more powerfully than we imagine. But they can also give us a clearer vision, and show us the road ahead. Disappointments must teach us never to give in, but with a new maturity and resolve to make a new beginning, and go on our way confident that the sun will shine again.'

Things moved quickly. On 2 March Bert was called to Westminster 'to see Heenan about the possible opening of a

Catechetical College in London. Press statements to be made soon.' Two days later he was in London speaking with the Sion sisters 'who had offered us a site for such a college'. From all that followed immediately, it is evident that Bert was asked to lead the new venture, but he does not have anything to say about the talk with Heenan, (now a Cardinal). It is unclear whether the Sion Sisters had set the ball rolling, or if it was Heenan's idea. Did the idea come from the SEC trio, having given up any hope of staying at St Edmund's, and offering Heenan a reason to introduce the changes he was clearly determined to do at the seminary? Before a week is out the opening of 'A new Catholic College' is headlined in a number of national and Catholic papers, with Bert announced as the principal. He entered into the challenge with that 'Resolve to make a new beginning, with confidence that the sun would shine again', as Papa had predicted.

CHAPTER TEN

Corpus Christi College, London
1965-1972

On 9 March 1965 a press statement from Archbishop's House announced the opening of a Catechetical College, with Reverend Hubert Richards as the Principal. It seems most probable that it was Mother Loreto of Sion who recommended Bert for the principal's post. For years he had been supported by the Sion Sisters. He was a friend of the Jewish community as they were, with his insistence on recognising the Jewish Jesus. (He would never let his students speak of the 'Old Testament', only of the Jewish scriptures). The Sisters gave their premises in Bayswater to the Archdiocese for the new college. The history of the catechetical movement since Pius X's 'Catechism' in 1908 was often in crisis through an almost inevitable clash between forward looking 'prophets' and the cautious 'guardians' of Catholic belief. Why would Cardinal Heenan, a ruthless 'guardian', agree to establish a college knowing that the Council was encouraging new thinking and experimentation which he could never embrace, but the college would? As early as the 1930s catechists were presenting their teaching, in the words of Fr S. J. Gosling, 'as an intense desire to spread the gospel of Christ as life to be lived,' (Fr Richards) 'and not simply as a truth to be apprehended.' (Heenan).

The Cardinal announced that Fr Richards, Fr Davis and Fr De Rosa would be replaced at St Edmund's by Fr Lionel Swain, Fr Michael Ashdowne and Fr Peter Bourne in the autumn. Charles Davis was appointed, alongside Fr Bernard Leeming SJ, to the theology faculty at the Jesuit Heythrop College that had been raised from a seminary to university status, offering degrees to students from diocesan seminaries, religious orders and to the laity. Peter De Rosa's future was less certain. Bert wanted him to assist at the new college, but Heenan couldn't make a decision. Meanwhile, as well as their teaching and other commitments, Bert and Peter made preparations for the opening of the college, with much travelling at home and abroad. Bert was

aware of the great work achieved by Canon Drinkwater in catechetics, and suggested that the college be named after him.
'Today off again to see Heenan to continue discussions. I suggested calling the place Drinkwater Centre in honour of the
great catechist. He said, "You may as well call it Contraception
Centre" (!) I have decided to call it Corpus Christi.'

Bert made visits to the National Catechetical Centre, to the
Major Religious Superiors to ask for their best students, and
went on a round trip (with Peter) of all the European Catechetical Centres for ideas. In April Archbishop Beck asked to see
him, 'not about Corpus Christi College, but about doing a supply at Christ's College Liverpool for Alec Jones, who needs time
off to complete the new English edition of the Jerusalem Bible.
When? This coming May till July! He has already got the agreement of Kelleher to release me now from SEC (what does that
imply?), and promises to fly me back and forth to keep up my
Leicester Square commitments. All this on the top of a million
details for the opening of CCC.' In between all of this Bert was
across the country interviewing prospective students, and arranging for a team of permanent and visiting lecturers.

Wed 14 July SEC
Left Liverpool to return to SEC to say goodbye to the students, who left on the 16th. I stayed on to pack my things in
tea chests.

What a sad farewell, with no celebration, for the 16 years he
gave to the seminary.

Early summer was spent, with Peter 'entertaining 500 teachers at Hopwood Hall with lectures on the sacraments, I developing their scriptural background, and he applying them to the
modern world. Joseph McGhee bishop of Galloway was present
and highly appreciative, as were the teachers, giving us an encouraging send-off for our new venture. We eventually published the lectures as *Christ in our World*, (Chapman 1966).' Then
hard work in Denbigh Road, W 11, turning four former guest
houses into the college with offices, lecture room, seminar room,
and accommodation for 16 men, with a new building put up for
the dining room and library. Most students had to find accommodation in local convents, or parishes. Bert had finally been

able to convince the Cardinal that Peter De Rosa should be his assistant. Heenan wrote: 'you must not read too much into what I said about Father De Rosa. I merely wanted to know what qualifications he has for catechetics. Remember that I still am somewhat of a stranger. I did not know that he had studied Religious Psychology and Anthropology. I am more than satisfied that you will make a great success of Corpus Christi and if you are happy about Father De Rosa that is enough for me.' He asked that Peter should spend two September weeks in Cardinal Griffin School. 'If reports can be believed, this is an eye opener. It is an absolutely up-to-date building and all the pupils are Catholics. I am told, however, that a very large number have lapsed from the faith and some no longer believe in God. If you spend some time studying these boys and girls you will be in a much better position to teach those who are going to deal with them in years to come.'

Peter was clearly glad to be working with Bert and early on had written a very warm appreciation of his colleague in the *Catholic Herald*.

Father Hubert Richards … is a man of many parts. He is about as far from the parsonic type of the 'Punch' cartoon tradition as it is possible to be. Quiet, modest, pipe-puffing, ever relaxed, he likes dangerous things – such as fast (but careful) driving, skiing and mountaineering. His private study contains a huge shelf packed tight with records from Beethoven to the Beatles and on the wall hangs a guitar which he strums in his leisure moments with more than an amateur touch. The wall is also adorned with modern paintings commissioned by himself, pieces of pottery and other bric-a-brac culled in his travels, an Arab water bottle for the desert, and a sturdy grappling rope for rock climbing.

Peter described his family and study background, commenting that, 'at the Biblicum in Rome where he gained his teaching degree in scripture, 'Leather-pants' was what one of the teachers, a pungent little Jesuit, Fr Dyson, used to call him, an allusion to his unflagging devotion to studies … Although he has a fine grasp of German, French and Italian and though he has taught Greek and Hebrew to the students in the seminary, Fr

Richards is modest about his academic attainments. He looks upon himself as more of a propagandist of the Word of God than as an original researcher.'

Peter then described his writings, his collaboration on the Grail Psalter, his contributions to journals, and, 'As his numerous publications show, he was ahead of most of his contemporaries in his understanding of liturgy and in his efforts to develop the relationship between scripture and liturgy.' He described Bert's lecture series that had grown to 500 people (doubled later) regularly making for the hall of the French Church in Leicester Square. 'This is why, apart from priests and lay teachers, there are to be seen on Tuesday evenings clusters of nuns looking like well trained platoons of penguins striding purposefully through the brightly-lit streets of London. He has ruthlessly eliminated from his vocabulary all scholastic and bureaucratic jargon and shows a marked preference for plain Anglo-Saxon words and image-thinking which he claims is truly Semitic. When Christ was asked "Who is my neighbour?", he likes to say, he did not give a definition but told a story. Such is his own method. He has looked upon his whole academic career simply as a priestly task, as a means and an opportunity to communicating the truth about God.' He concluded: 'His audiences all over the country, but especially at St Edmund's, will testify to Fr Richards' sympathy and charm. Always an essentially practical and pastoral priest, he possesses what David Hume called a "gross earthly mixture".'

The desire by enlightened priests for a development of catechetics was not something new. It was discussed in the 1920s in *The Sower*, founded by Drinkwater in 1919, for this purpose. The European influence was introduced in the 1930s, when work from Louvain was reported and adopted by the Birmingham Archdiocese. Lumen Vitae Institute in Brussels was founded in 1946, with one founded the same year in Lyons, France. In 1958 Cardinal Godfrey set up the National Catechetical Centre (NCC) at Cavendish Square, London, with Bishop Beck its director. At this time a Belgian nun Sister Romain, living in London, was a great influence in her enthusiastic work for the catechetical movement. In 1960, writing in *The Sower*, Drinkwater was expressing the need for England to show less depen-

dence on the European models. It led to Summer Schools in
Britain, with the well-known names from abroad, Hofinger
being the first, giving the lectures. 'He stressed that catechetics
was concerned not with the transmission of a system of ideas
but with the proclamation of a message.' Interest grew in most
dioceses.

In 1963 Fr Nigel Larne was appointed national director of the
NCC. Father Somerville edited *The Sower* and helped prepare a
new, national catechism. An important aspect of the more dy-
namic methods of teaching came with the establishment of an
audio/visual department developed and set up by Desmond
Brennan, who was also teaching part time at Strawberry Hill,
following study at Lumen Vitae. Another graduate from the
Brussels' college was Sister Margaret of Jesus (Ruth). She had a
unique role in catechesis, travelling around diocesan centres
lecturing hundreds of teachers, guiding them into the new
thinking about teaching adolescents. In a chapter on Corpus
Christi College in his thesis, Brother Damian Lundy comments
that Cardinal Heenan seemed completely unaware of all these
developments, by Drinkwater and others, which were reported
in *The Sower*. Heenan went to Liverpool in 1956, and with a good
pastoral manner, and awareness of teachers needing guidance,
he changed his diocesan religious inspectors into religious ad-
visers. It seemed a very good change. But it was not carried
through, as he continued to talk of 'instructions', and his revised
catechism and school textbooks 'read like a lighter, more attractive version of a traditional apologetic presentation and defence
of Catholicism'. Heenan was never going to change, and this
would lead to the subsequent sad rift between Bert and the
Cardinal, the 'prophet and the guardian'.

In the 1960s before Vatican II, and during the Council, the
catechetical movement was focused on the liturgy and the Bible.
Bert had seen their natural relationship many years previously.
His diary reflections, even from Stonyhurst days, worried over
the muddled liturgies he witnessed, where preaching would ignore the scripture readings; where the Word of God would be
mumbled; where seminary students sang the epistle with their
backs to the congregation. For the Cardinal the age old rubrics
seemed always more important than the proclamation of the

Word, as Bert had discovered when Acting Vice President at St Edmund's. The Cardinal's anxiety over liturgy continued throughout the Corpus Christi years, even before the first students arrived.

> *24 September 1965 Letter from Cardinal Heeenan*
> I asked Archbishop Beck what he thinks of daily concelebration and he feels that it would soon lose its attraction if it became too commonplace. I shall write again when I have asked advice from the concilium and have had the views of the other bishops …

In his reply Bert pointed out that there could be as great a danger in privately celebrated Masses where there is no sense of community. There were 27 priests in the first year, and some might tend to give up their personal celebration to attend the community Mass. It is clear from the early correspondence that Heenan had a warm relationship with Bert, who in turn showed deep respect for his superior. In November the Cardinal writes:

> You will be glad to know that on the pilgrimage of bishops it was quite impossible to find altars and we thoroughly enjoyed the experience of concelebration. Yesterday twenty-four of us concelebrated on Mount Carmel – *sub umbra Carmeli* with a vengeance.

The hectic summer term in Liverpool at Christ's College; the summer schools; the employment of staff; negotiations with visiting lecturers from home and abroad; the setting up the First Year Programme; the continual interviewing of students; the financial arrangements; accommodation issues – all of this must have made Bert wonder what he had taken on. He continued to serve on Committees and Boards as before, and in addition he took over as Director of the National Catechetical Centre. He embraced it with his outwardly calm presence and the college opened on 3 October. His diary entry sets the tone for all the subsequent entries over the coming Corpus Christi years. They are factual and brief, with only the occasional reflection. The long thoughtful, analytical entries only appear when there is real conflict and personal sadness.

3-9 Oct CCC

First Week of all days, the plumbing went wrong on Sunday, meaning that residents could not use their washbowls. Redfaced apology on the notice board.

A Sunday evening Mass concelebrated by me and 4 others. Then a get-together, speeches of welcome, and Night Prayers.

Monday to Friday, Bouyer gave both morning lectures, solid liturgy and scripture.

Tues. the usual Leic. Sq. stint for me.

Wed. a meeting of Catechetical Inspectors at the Knights Club, finishing with a tour of the new CCC.

Sat. the Catechism Committee met here instead of Cromwell Road.

The lecture team were Fr Richards, Fr De Rosa, Sr Romain, and Sr Aloysius, with Des Brennan running the audio visual department. Fr Bouyer from Paris was the first of many visiting, distinguished lecturers. Bert had described the type of course that the college would offer when it was announced in March. The aim was to make teachers aware 'of what they're going to teach, of whom they're going to teach, and how they are going to teach'. The content, based on scripture, would be 'A study of how the good news is revealed to us in scripture, is systematised in theology, is made actual in the liturgy, and is lived in the life of the church.' Educational psychology would be explored to help teachers understand the thought processes of the different age-groups. The most recent developments in teaching methods, using audio-visual aids and more open discussion, rather than 'instruction', would be introduced. The college students themselves would have only two lectures a day, to allow time for seminar group discussion, and personal study.

In retrospect it is obvious that the seeds of discord between Heenan and the staff were already there in the very concept of this catechetical venture. The staff were enthusiastic and optimistic, keen to bring the forward-looking church of Vatican II into life, with its return to the scriptures, with its recognition of the role of the laity, with its approach to ecumenism, and with its understanding of the needs of the modern world. It was the

Pastoral Constitution on the Church in the Modern World (Gaudium et Spes) that was the key text for the Corpus Christ staff.

Cardinal Heenan was not so enthusiastic; he was patronising towards the laity, focusing his attention on the 'dignity' of the priesthood. The Council challenged his views. He saw the Council *Decree on the Ministry and Life of the Priesthood, Presbyterorum Ordinis,* as the key to everything that the Council stood for. In 1951 he had written that 'The priest has no right to consider himself as an ordinary man.' He never changed his view. He quickly lost confidence in his decision to establish a college for priests, nuns, laity – male and female, as he later suggested it should change to become a male establishment only – a kind of seminary. Yet it is recorded in the Westminster Diocesan Archives that the Cardinal, on the complaints of Mgr Kelleher, removed the three professors from St Edmund's because they did not fit in with his idea of a seminary training. De Rosa wrote later of Kelleher's regime: 'Students were never trained for their role as educators of the Christian people. Students they were and students they remained until they were ordained.' Damian Lundy writes of the Cardinal's 'ingrained sense of the distinction between clergy and the rank-and-file. He used the distinctively Vatican II phrase 'the People of God', but wrote of 'them' – as if unconsciously setting himself apart from (or above) the people of God. He distinguished between priests attending Corpus Christi and other 'pupils'!' Heenan was not happy that the Council placed more emphasis on priestly ministry than on priestly life. 'A priest must live apart from the citizens of this world', he wrote.

The Cardinal was not alone in his anxiety about this new venture. It did not take shape as he had envisaged. The bishops were reluctant to respond to the idea, and later on, very quick to criticise. In this first year there were 90 students, 29 of whom were priests, but only 7 were from English dioceses; 7 were from Ireland, the remainder from religious orders, (4 from abroad). Over the next few years Heenan expressed his concern over an increasing number of issues: the relaxed atmosphere between staff and students; the use of Christian names; the relaxation in dress; the international mix of students; an ecumenical dimension that the staff welcomed; the seminar experience where the

'faith' was discussed, allowing questioning and personal response; and the usual concern about 'experiments in liturgy',
which Heenan often described as 'antics'; and the 'jargon' language of the catechist. 'There is no need to talk about Christ-cen-
tred theology. If it is good theology it is bound to be Christ-cen-
tured. Nor should we cease to talk about faith. It is something
more than the Christian message. Surely the Christian message
is given to Protestants of all kinds – including Salvationists who
reject the sacraments. The jargon can easily kill the lovely new
learning. A foolish secretary who is now in the Newman London
Circle no longer says Mass but the Eucharistic Celebration.'

One problem never went away, Bert's treatment of students
who should never have been sent by their superiors to study.
They came carrying personal problems. The Cardinal was sympathetic, but wanted them sent back to their religious order, or
diocese. Bert felt that the college community could help them
come to terms with their difficulties. He was successful in many
cases. In a letter to Heenan he wrote: 'A desperate case I have on
my hands at the moment could have been "solved" by reporting
the man to his superiors. I know this would have ruined him.
Instead I have, after long and painful sessions with him, been
able to persuade him to go to his superiors of his own accord
and ask for the psychiatric help he needs. I am convinced that
any other action would have been wrong.'

Many of the complaints coming from the bishops were also
about the Leicester Square lectures. It was hardly surprising that
a handful of the (now) 1,200 teachers would complain about the
'new ideas and language'. Even the Cardinal understood that
this would be so, but his reasons were patronising. He wrote to
Fr Richards in March 1967: 'I have no doubt at all that the lectures have been orthodox. It is a question, I think, of methods of
expression. Some of the audience have a fairly low educational
background and, for all I know, do not have a very high I.Q.
These are probably the people who have picked up the wrong
ideas. Some have certainly been scandalised but I think they are
probably the middle-aged.' At this time Rome was asking for a
report about the college and the Leicester Square lectures, so
Heenan was asking for all the lecturers' qualifications, and for
lists of visiting lecturers at the college and Leicester Square.

It was, however, a number of major external events that caused the greatest problems for Bert and Corpus Christi College. The first was when the theologian, Charles Davis, left the priesthood and the church in a blaze of publicity. It shook Bert, who had known and worked with Davis for 17 years. He wrote of his immediate reaction:

Wed 21 Dec CCC (1966)
Bombshell! Yesterday a quick phone call from Charlie Davis to warn me about today's press release; he is leaving the priesthood, the church, his job, the lot. Gobsmacked. Why not a private exit on the quiet? No – he is a central figure in the church in England, and needs a very public exit! The fact that he lectured here (and offers to do the same next year if I let him!) makes the issue red hot. The pages that follow give some idea of the issues, but there is a 2 inch thick file along-side as well.

The press, National and Catholic, were quick to analyse the situation, with much sympathy for Davis, and criticism of the church. The headlines varied from 'Professor to leave Church. Roman system attacked' (*Times*), 'Catholic professor quits: I'm going to marry' (*Daily Mail*); 'The Defection of Dr Davis' (*Irish Independent*); 'The Path from Rome' (*Spectator*); 'Priest quits Church: To marry' (*Telegraph*). Davis held a press conference in London where he insisted that he was not leaving the church in order to marry. 'I am marrying to rebuild my life upon a personal love I recognise as true after a life surrounded in the church by so much that is at best irrelevant and at worst an obstacle.' He also stated that 'I do not think that the claim the church makes as an institution rests upon any adequate biblical and historical basis. I am still a Christian but I reject the institution of the church.' Opinions and press articles appeared over a number of weeks, from Norman St John-Stevas who recognised it as 'a seri-ous blow to Catholic intellectual life in Britain'; from Fr Peter Hebblethwaite SJ who gave reasons 'why I need the church', stating that 'One does not have to defend the indefensible. The recognition of sinfulness in the church is not a matter for shocked alarm but for repentance and renewal.' He favoured re-maining in the institution to influence from inside, and wrote of the example of Henri de Lubac and Yves Congar, who both suffered 'at the hands of bureaucrats' and were, after patient waiting, recognised finally at the Council. The Dominican, Fr Herbert McCabe, editor of *New Blackfriars*, in support of Davis, wrote that: 'The church is very plainly corrupt.' He was removed as editor by his superiors.

Bert was deeply affected by the situation, not recognising the Davis he knew. He agonised over it, as is evident in the diary where there are four A4 pages of notes in very small writing, scribblings of his analysis of the situation after watching his friend on the *David Frost Show*. He made notes to share with the students. He made more notes after visiting Davis himself, on 14 January. 'Surprised that the situation was so different from what I expected. CD was in no way nervous, hesitant, or even belligerent – treated the whole thing as the most normal thing in the world, (apparently) calm and happy. Willing to tell all how he felt. He had to leave the church while still sharing their views, but the onus laid on them! He had not left the church as they all saw it, but they! It was a logical conclusion of all he had ever said and done. "I remain perfectly willing to lecture for you at CCC. It is you who will have to positively refuse me." He admitted that he had had no positive persecution.' Bert had expected that he would find Florence, his future wife, the dominating force in this, as she had already 'left' the church, and claimed that they had been engaged for a year. But he wrote: 'I doubt now very much whether it was her crisis of faith or hurt which swung CD. She really did seem to be secondary to the whole issue.' He found Davis too easily 'swiping' at difficult doctrines, and too readily 'repeated set pieces about historical disintegration'.

Bert concluded that there were three positions:

Some say: 'This was expected. Should have been dealt with before.'
Others say: 'This is simply rationalisation to go off with a girl.'
If from honesty & knowledge I cannot accept either, I am forced into a third. Much of what he holds I stand for myself. Where does that leave me?

Bert visited Desmond Fisher, former editor of the *Catholic*

Herald and the friend of Davis with whom he had gone to stay. He summarised this visit. 'Jan 14 was a big act. CD always had capacity for calm and confidence. Here it was a cover for deepest fears and doubts. (He was anxious about the meeting.) Florence did leave the church two months ago. This must have been an element in decision. His intellectual pride wd not allow him to leave Ch quietly. Too humiliating.' A week later Bert had a conversation with Davis' brother, Frank, who was able to give him a most sensitive analysis of the situation. It was understandable and made more sense. Frank gave three reasons for what had happened:

1. From childhood CD has been a recluse, buried in books. Even today, holidays at home mean a suitcase full of books. On family visits he wd take book along & read. Himself admits 'As if immense wall between me & other people.' This over cerebral existence long been cause for concern. He will crack up.

2. We don't suffic. realise pain of: (a) The way Walkern (built up 15 years) taken from him without consultation (incl. stoppage of catechetics etc.).

(b) Not being invited back for first St Edmund's Day.

(c) The isolation in Heythrop. He felt he didn't belong. Could not see any future pattern emerging. A wounded man like many today.

3. It is in this situation that Fl.H appeared. Apparently first person to break through his wall. In the crisis of her faith what was he to do – the one person who was real in his life? An emotional crisis. The intellectual case is largely a rationalisation.

Is he charging the church with the *very* thing he found most difficult, personal relationships?

Less than two weeks later Charles and Florence married in an Anglican Church. They were sad that his two friends, Peter and Bert, felt they had to refuse an invitation to be present. They sent their best wishes and visited the couple later. They had earlier written a kind letter to the Cardinal expressing their concern for him over the situation. Heenan was gracious in his short statement to the press, not judging Davis. 'His conscience and

his personal relationships are his own concern. We now best
show our friendship by praying that God will guide him in all
his undertakings.' Bert always appreciated this sensitivity of the
Cardinal.

It is clear from the diary that the upheaval, so widely debated
in the press, caused difficulties for the college. It confirmed the
bishops' anxiety about the teaching. Bert had started this second
year with his quiet enthusiasm. He had brought three of the first
year's outstanding students onto the staff, Fathers John Perry,
Peter Wetz, and Brother Drostan. Sr Margaret (Ruth) was to join
them when her contract in Wales finished towards the end of
the year. The third year, 1967-68 was more settled, with impressive visiting lecturers: John Robinson, Denis Nineham,
Barnabus Aherne, Archbishop Bloom, Van Caster from Lumen
Vitae, Bissonier, Owen Hardwicke and Donald Nichol.
However, the stress on Bert took its toll. In the second week of
October he was 'whipped into St John and Elizabeth's hospital'
following severe chest pains. He noted: 'A beautiful card from
all the students. Also a hand-made one from the students and
nuns at St Edmund's (but not the staff!) Cardinal Heenan wrote
a sympathetic note from Rome.' He was ordered rest for six
weeks, with Len Johnston taking over his lectures.

The year ended with Cardinal Heenan officiating at a concelebrated Mass. Bert spoke to the students; he wrote his notes in
the diary:

> He is our founder and supporter, when all the rest have
> given up on us, so welcome him: this is not a visitation! I
> would be grateful if all priests cd wear a collar, out of cour-
> tesy. I wd like the Mass to be solemn, festive and characteris-
> tic as possible. So I will warn him about spontaneous bidding
> prayers, singing the doxology, pax and communion under
> both kinds, silent thanksgiving. On some minor points he
> disagrees with me, so we will modify: the consecration (his
> prayer *par excellence*) to be said, not sung, communion out of
> the ciborium, not basket, we might surprise him, silent dur-
> ing the Confiteor (our joining in would throw him).
>
> Are we being dishonest in adopting these changes? My
> answer is that they are minor points not worth arguing

about, and we give in to him as our guest. Then how will he ever learn? I answer, not in half an hour. The Mass is too sacred to be made a battleground. But if you feel strongly, don't hesitate to come and discuss with me.

In the event, all went smoothly.

This is typical of Bert's manner of acting; he was the peacemaker, always trying to understand both sides of any argument, and always listening to other points of view, with a willingness to make changes. The summer of 1968 was a busy one for the staff. From 26 July to 9 August half the staff ran a Summer School at Keswick Hall College, Norwich, while the rest, including Bert, ran another at Bangor University. Then came the second bombshell, which was to cause more problems for Corpus Christi.

The long awaited encyclical *Humanae Vitae* came out during the first week, and raised such a rumpus in the press that I hired a car to drive to Norfolk to console the staff. In fact, they were so busy that the news had only slightly percolated, and the matter was not even referred to. Whereas at Bangor, it was the only topic of conversation, and Peter Harris did a magnificent job of keeping a balance under questioning of his 'dogma' lectures.

There was widespread dismay at the Pope's decision to continue the ban for Catholics on any form of 'artificial' birth control, after three years of deliberation. There was great hope that Paul VI would take the advice of the many theologians, clergy and lay advisors who had expressed the opinion that a change was needed. The Catholic Church was, once again, headlines in the press, and almost unanimously condemned for a decision that would have far reaching effects across the world, and in relationship with other churches. The decision was described in headlines, 'Bewildering', 'A stunning blow', 'Pope's veto brings storm', 'Putting the clocks back'. The *Daily Telegraph* commented on the effect in Latin America: 'A Jesuit priest prominent in education here said; "This is a step backwards. It will be very disconcerting to priests who have close contact with the poor in this Continent, and who have, to a certain extent, been teaching along lines which would have been favoured by a contrary verdict from Rome. The problem for the church will be to maintain obedience to Rome while adopting an attitude consistent with individual opinion and conscience".' The Paris newspaper, *Le Monde*, reported that 'Since the recommendation of Vatican II on "responsible fatherhood", many thousands of French Catholics have practised contraception with the approval or acquiescence of priests. *Le Monde* considers it 'remarkable' that the Pope chose to adopt the views of a minority of the Vatican Commission. The majority had rejected the evidence for the "natural law" on which the encyclical was based.'

As was expected, the Cardinal pointed out that the decision could never have been on a majority vote. In his pastoral letter he wrote: 'It was always understood (in the Commission) that the decision must be by him alone as Christ's Vicar. The law of God cannot be decided by majority vote. The Pope has given his decision. While accepting it, we look forward to further pastoral guidance on the whole question of family life. Meanwhile the church has compassion on the many for whom the ruling will bring hardship. Those who have been accustomed to using methods which are unlawful may not be able at once to resist temptation. They must not despair. Above all they must not abstain from the sacraments. However often they fail they must ask God's grace to find strength to obey his law.' These words infuriated and upset many people, priests and laity. It was saying, use contraception, but then go to confession to acknowledge your sin. The result, in fact, meant many simply left the church. Some bishops did speak out against the encyclical, especially in Holland. Bert has pages of press cuttings in the diary with his underlinings of important statements, including the statement of 117 Dutch theologians who wrote in support of their bishops, who had expressed concern. He underlined these words: 'We are grateful that you, as pastors in Christ's church have not restrained us, by any argument on authority, but instead have drawn attention to the essential human values at stake.' In England it was only the Jesuit Archbishop Roberts who spoke out, saying that he had never understood the argument that natural law forbids contraception. 'It has always been my conviction that intelligence must give consent. The question now is: "Is all contraception forbidden by God – or only by the Pope?"'

Charles Davis took this opportunity to comment on the Cardinal's pastoral letter in a Catholic paper. He noted that Heenan had pastoral concerns for the laity, and that 'his zeal to serve ordinary Catholics is outstanding'. Davis used the occasion to back up his opposition to the papacy, a reason he 'left the church'. He writes of the 'bankruptcy of the papal teaching', and that 'it should now be clear that any genuine reform will have to oppose and break that structure.' This fuelled again the irritation of the English hierarchy. It caused less harm to the college, however, than the publicity signed by Peter De Rosa, the cause of Bert's next tussle with Cardinal Heenan. The situation was settling down when De Rosa and two other priests sent the text of a letter they were going to send to *The Times* to the bishops of England and Wales. They also collected 55 signatures of other priests. They wrote that while respecting the Pope's decision: '… We deeply regret, however, that according to our consciences we cannot give loyal internal and external obedience to the view that all such means of contraception are in all circumstances wrong.' Fr De Rosa made the mistake of using the name of Corpus Christi as his address. He should have realised that it was implying the consent of the college.

The Cardinal saw the letter before it was published and immediately wrote to Bert. He was sending a diocesan priest to the college for the following year, but the priest asked to withdraw, not being sure that he would be happy there. 'He does not say so but I imagine that the antics of Peter De Rosa has something to do with his decision … I deplore more than I can say that Corpus Christi is being used once more as a centre for collecting signatures of protesting priests.' Bert replied that the college had never had anything to do with collecting signatures. 'You suggest almost that the letter in question has been officially organised from here. The fact is that the encyclical has not been lectured upon or discussed either by the staff or the students. The letter was an entirely private venture of Peter. If the Press has referred to him as a member of the staff it is because this is his position. If he has given this college as his address, it is because he has no other.' Peter offered his resignation from Corpus Christi, but the Cardinal refused it. It may have been better for the college had he accepted it, as its reputation was

permanently damaged. In future years there was a great reluc-
tance of bishops to send diocesan priests to the college.

Bert's own comment on the *Humanae Vitae* debate was written on a small piece of paper and stuck in the diary.

> *August '68*
> To an intolerable situation there are two reactions.
> 1. To speak out loudly and clearly, so that no one should be
> in any doubt that it is intolerable. Prophet's task.
> 2. To suffer it in order to remain with those who can't escape
> it. Pastor's task. To ensure something is done from within the
> situation to better it.
> Both reactions possible and honest. Must chose.
> We admire fearlessness of Pope for doing something unpop-
> ular according to conscience.
> Should we not at least refrain from judging the fearlessness
> with which some do something equally unpopular for sake
> of own conscience?

Bert then escaped from the stress by going on a gita with
Spud to spend two weeks on Mount Athos, writing up his detailed account of the whole experience. College opened for its
fourth year, on 6 October 1968. Of the 82 students, 36 were
priests, but only 5 were from English dioceses, with no priest sent
from Westminster. It was a peaceful college year, with Bert invited to lecture in Canada, where he could also meet up with his
brother Frank, and sister Therese. Papa had died in November.
'… A merciful release after weeks of painful, undignified and
fruitless attempts to restore him. Poor old fellow. I did the funeral
service, and we buried him next to Mamma in Ruislip.' Two
days later Bert flew to Paris for a weekend meeting with the
'Équipe Europeenne', the annual conference for directors of
European catechetical centres; there were other visits to catechetical establishments at home and abroad. As usual he was
also giving lectures across the country, to training colleges,
Jewish groups, convents, to ecumenical societies, and to schools
and universities. He found time during these first years of
Corpus Christi to give some attention to his writings. He managed to persuade 'Virtues' to allow him to put the articles he
had contributed to their encyclopedia into a publication: *ABC of*

the Bible. Published in 1967, he later regarded it as the most help-ful book he ever wrote. The same year his popular book on the Apocalypse, *What the Spirit says to the Churches*, was published, translated into French the following year. His last 1968 entry in his personal diary states: 'My desk diary contains the last words for 1968: "I bet Peters £5 that we will have a married clergy in England 1973".' Ever the optimist!

Only 56 students attended the fifth year of Corpus Christi, 1969-70, with only three English diocesan priests out of the 22; a sure sign of the damage done to the college by the *Humanae Vitae* Affair. The year passed without any drama, and with no detailed entries in the diary, except that the end of term December staff meeting 'ended with smoked salmon sandwiches and wine.' Only 57 students applied for the next year, 1970-71, with just one diocesan priest (Westminster) out of the 20 priests attending. It was understandable that the Cardinal informed Bert: 'that the College will in the future be a Westminster re-sponsibility exclusively. It was agreed "that while continuing to offer places to students from elsewhere, Corpus Christi College shall be subject to the jurisdiction of the Archbishop of Westminster". It is absurd to regard the college as national if the rest of the country was not willing to support it.' Des Brennan had suggested that a DES Report might help to improve their image for the hierarchy. The HMI inspection was completed on 27 November, and Bert wrote that they 'eventually published a glowing report.' Copies were sent to the bishops and Catholic Training Colleges.

There was praise from Bishop Worlock of Portsmouth. Archbishop Dwyer of Birmingham wrote: 'It certainly is a great tribute to the college.' The principal of Fenham College replied: 'I am delighted that you have such a firm and wholly appreci-ative vindication of the excellent courses you are giving … I felt that the Inspectors thoroughly caught the spirit of the college, and their report read more like an advertising prospectus than a cool government report. In these days of uninformed criticism of colleges and their courses including your own, it is good to have such firm support at the level of the DES.' Fr Cronin, of the Westminster Catholic Parents Centre, wrote: 'I have seen many such reports in my time, and was involved in two of them; but I

don't think I have ever read one that was so outstandingly
favourable to the college concerned as yours was. Congratulations!' Cardinal Heenan only made a comment six months
later: 'The only thing I did not like about the report was the insistence upon group dynamics.' This was interesting because
Bishop Alan Clark had written: 'I am wondering whether really
all this praise redounds to your good name. Is it necessarily a
good thing "when theological or philosophical topics are introduced by the staff, there is no attempt to impose a specific point
of view"? Is it necessarily a great achievement for a Catholic college for it to be said that "one of the most impressive features of
the course is the liberality and breadth of view of both staff and
students?".'

Bert replied: 'Thank you for your letter. It is odd that all the
letters of unqualified congratulations we received on the HMI
Report were from those who have been up to their necks in
education for a long time. The two which expressed reservations
were from bishops. Which suggests that what we disagree on is
not religion but how you set about educating people in religion.
"Imposing specific points of view" is something you do not
even to infants today. You want to try and do it with mature students! But it is very odd that you should complain about us not
imposing a specific point of view. I thought the charges against
Corpus Christi were that we did and that it was unacceptable!
You cannot have it both ways.'

The spring term 1971 was a happy one for Bert. He celebrated
his silver jubilee of ordination on 11 February. 'About 90 people
came, some as early as lunchtime! We had an evening Mass,
where I preached on forgiveness. A magnificent party after in
the lecture room, with an artificial tree brought in by Be, growing £10 notes!' Later his 9 friends from the English College arrived for their special celebration with him. 'Our VEC Ordination
Year gathered at CCC for an evening concelebration in our orat-
ory, and then a slap up meal at the Knights. Four of them stayed
overnight.' The Easter holiday, as usual, was spent leading his
Pilgrimage to the Holy Land. Returning to Bayswater he was
'greeted' by post from Heenan; his diary heading 'Trouble
Ahead'. The summer term started badly. At the Bishop's Low
Week Meeting it had become clear that they were not support-

ing David Konstant's appointment as director of the Catechetical Conference, as Bert had hoped. 'Feeling about cate-chetics is running very high at the moment and if David is iden-tified with Corpus Christi I think that he will be turned down. We shall have to have another long discussion … I want to talk to you about people who give the courses. I feel that Perry is not a really safe guide to priests and nuns. He was in a collar and tie when I made my last visit to Corpus Christi.'

Another letter from the Cardinal followed to inform Bert that the bishops were not prepared to appoint a national director of catechetics. It was not a problem with catechetics, but a question of theology. They did agree with Heenan's proposal for a 2-day catechetical conference in December at which they would be present with the diocesan directors. It would be held at Corpus Christi, where they could attend the sessions, to judge lectures for themselves. 'I would like you to arrange to come along early one day for lunch so that we can have another talk. One or two of the bishops were sceptical of the possibility of hearing exactly the same lectures as are given to the students.'

Maybe it was this lack of trust in the staff that finally broke Peter De Rosa's spirit. He decided to leave CCC and the priest-hood. Bert wrote in the diary that he was 'worn out by the ongo-ing saga of *Humanae Vitae* ever since 1968, the continued suspi-cion over his orthodoxy, and the miserable prospect of having to go on and on fighting the authorities to stay true to one's con-science.' Bert made notes to point out to his friend. 'To leave would give all the cards to the critics, who would only throw more mud. Bishops and superiors would lose all their confid-ence in CCC which till now has depended strongly on his pres-ence and views. Any past students feeling shaky will lose heart totally. Yet there is a need to speak out and play the part of a prophet, to be true to one's conscience.' He listed, in the diary, all the other possible reactions to the news, ending with 'But there is gloom all round. Neither "side" is winning.' Peter stayed on until the end of the term. John Perry joined him in leaving both the college and the priesthood. Bert felt a great sense of loss and bewilderment.

CHAPTER ELEVEN

The Beginning of the End
1971-1972

As the college year drew to a close (July 1971), the Cardinal asked to have a long talk with Bert. A bishop had comlained that 'you were giving Holy Communion to a Methodist. I am afraid that if I passed this on to the bishops they would be disturbed.' He was also concerned hearing of the 'antics' of a missionary college where the Mass is occasionally said sitting around a table, no vestments worn. Somebody has said that the same kind of thing goes on at Corpus Christi.' Heenan went to the college in July and had a session with Bert in his room, before the staff meeting. The short diary notes record the outcome. Bert was asked: 'Would I remain as Director of the Catechetical Centre, and allow David Konstant to come as Principal to Corpus Christi?'

At the staff meeting there was no surprise to hear again of the Cardinal's concern about 'the priest students having no more reverence, respect and docility'. But Bert was clearly shocked to be remonstrated again about: 'my attendance at N.Sym's wedding reception: a priest, principal, celebrating with a renegade priest about to live in sin. My Reply: "Would not Christ have done the same?" Reply: "As well say Christ would have had premarital intercourse!" Indication of my unfittedness for this position. *More* shocking than any signed letter to *The Times*. Heenan continued: If CD went 4 years ago, and PDeR now, what if I went in two years time! That would be the end of CCC? Bert reflected: All this to test my perseverance? Or to offer me an option out if I would, as more acceptable? Or to play part of *advocatus diaboli*?'

When the Cardinal left, the staff assured Bert that any move of him, even within the building, and they would lose all public confidence. For the forseable future they could only try to continue coping. The discussion in their last staff meeting had been about extending the course to a two-year study. Now they were just hanging on. Bert shared his anxiety with Peter De Rosa. 'Is it possible he looks on me as a bad risk, as ringleader of trio, as imprudent & possibly permissive? In spite of his kindness & assurance of confidence, has he really lost confidence in me (as bps have) & wd dearly like me out (else why jump the gun with D Konstant?), but refuses to fire me?' He was most upset by the Cardinal's question about his priesthood. 'First reaction. "Hell, – pressure from a brother priest?" Second reaction: "Hell, Do you have more right than me to determine what the future of the Ch. shd be?" Third reaction: "You win. The pressure is too great. I wd happily have stayed, but with this determination to oust me, why sh'd I resist?"' In characteristic manner Bert then wrote to the Cardinal to share these thoughts with him. His reply was not very encouraging:

> ... the bishops were gratified to hear that Peter is leaving. They obviously hope that there will be a really new regime at Corpus Christi ... I have been searching for staff. Next year we are not going to have those visiting lecturers – the doctors, the Maynooth men – the students have complained about the lack of teaching. On the recommendation of Arch. Dwyer I have approached Leeds for Michael Keegan. He has a degree in theology, a teacher's certificate and a diploma from Lumen vitae. His Lordship would not release him if you are staying on. I imagine that I am going to run into this difficulty with all the bishops and religious superiors. I have heard from Bp Guazzelli that Peter intends to announce his defection at a press conference. Have you no influence over him? Or do you feel like Charles Davis & Peter, that ex-priests should make a very public exit? I shall do what I can to offset the scandal by issuing a statement promising substantial changes at Corpus Christi.
>
> With an affectionate blessing, + John Card. Heenan

Bert left for a summer lecture tour in Saskatoon and Edmonton, Canada, staying on for a family visit in Toronto and Peterborough. On his return to England his sister Therese wrote:

> Hubert, that was a lovely holiday you spent with us. Don't ever think of leaving the priesthood, no matter what troubles you may have to face on your return to England. You should see your relaxed & happy expression on your face when you are asleep – it is a face of a happy man knowing he is doing

his best (& doing it very well). After 25 years you still say Mass as though for the first time. You are convinced, you are not bored nor exasperated. We all felt your strength and benefited from it. We pray that God may keep it alive as well as your true humbleness.

God bless you. Love Therese

Her brother returned home to find that 'the papers had a field day' following Peter's Press Statement. The Cardinal's Press Release, titled: 'The New Corpus Christi College', was written with great care, and though blaming the decline of the college on the Peter De Rosa's *Humanae Vitae* letter, he wrote: 'At no time, however, has Fr De Rosa or any of the staff spoken against the Encyclical in lectures. The undertaking to this effect given to the Cardinal has at all times been honourably observed. Past students are responsible for much of the excellent work being done in the catechetical field in this country and abroad.' The statement also pointed out that the Cardinal had defended catechists following criticism of the new catechetics by parents, teachers and priests. 'He pointed out that new methods are as necessary in RE as in every other branch of teaching.'

The next correspondence between the Cardinal, Bert and the staff of the college is critical in trying to understand the events of the final year of the 'Old Corpus Christi College'. A complete copy of the letter Bert sent to the Cardinal on 21 August 1971 is placed in his diary. It was also signed by Srs Ruth and Rena, and Frs Wetz and Sommerville.

My dear Cardinal,
I had intended after a staff meeting to write to you, to put on record our conversation, and to tell you of the Staff's response to it.

The further conversation I had last Thursday with Fred Miles was a considerable surprise to me because it resumed matters which I had brought up with you, and on which (although I knew you were unhappy) you did not seem to me to wish to push me beyond what I presumed the rest of the CCC staff could take.

The most important of these was the question of visiting lecturers ...

Bert names the four 'eminent' lecturers who had been at the college before and were invited for the next year. 'Fred now tells me that you wish me to cancel these invitations, because they might nullify the steps you are taking to restore confidence in CCC. I understand your difficulty but the staff agree with me that such a cancellation would at this stage be impossible ... Your action in this respect suggests that you feel CCC should put forward one point of view only, as if it were possible to express the "official teaching of the church" as simply as that. This is so close to the line taken by the *Pro Fide* group that the staff could not associate themselves with such a policy.' *Pro Fide*, a group of very 'traditional' Catholics, were vigorously campaigning against the new catechetics, and much else in the post Vatican II church. Bert concludes with the suggestion that because of 'such a divergence of understanding on the nature of religious education it would be inappropriate for us to remain as a staff in charge of your college.' They realised that it would not be appropriate to go immediately and so 'we are willing to serve you here for the coming year on the understanding that we continue to enjoy for that period the academic freedom we have enjoyed so far. This means our resignation would become effective from July 1972.'

Bert's entry for 18 September is an important one, as would become evident three months later.

18 Sep. To the Cardinal to discuss the future, and again on the 22. He speaks of Michael Keegan possibly replacing me, but has agreed that the present staff may stay on for the coming year 1971/72, and even beyond that if things settle down. We have agreed on holding a December meeting with as many bishops as care to come – and have high hopes of sorting out our differences.'

Bert sent a summary of their discussions to the Cardinal, 'To serve as a record of what we discussed.'

1. We are happy that you have accepted our offer to serve you for another year and that you have left open the possibility of our continuing to enjoy your trust and confidence even beyond that. Neither we nor yourself are proposing any further

changes in the permanent staff nor in the lecturers we have
invited for this coming year's work ...

   2. We look forward to meeting you again in order to discuss arrangements for the meeting of bishops at Corpus
Christi in December and to talk with you about the future
programme of studies ...'

It seems that Cardinal Heenan, perhaps under pressure from
his bishops, would later choose to ignore this memorandum.

Meanwhile, five months earlier, I had received a letter from
Fr Richards 'To inform you officially that you have been accepted
as a student in Corpus Christi College for the year 1971-72. The
scholastic year will open with an evening Mass on Sunday 3
October.' The letter included a list of 15 books I was expected to
have read before arriving. Having attended the Leicester Square
lectures, I was anticipating a wonderful year as a resident student. It surpassed all my expectations. We knew nothing of the
strain the staff were under. The diary for this year is different
from all the others. The weekly summaries of college lectures,
events, and Bert's other engagements are brief, leaving room for
the letters to and from the Cardinal, newspaper cuttings and
press statements, especially beginning in December following
the 'Bishops Meeting'. There are scribbled pages (difficult to
read) of soul-searching reflections on the developing situation –
sometimes optimistic, sometimes showing anxious frustrations
at the Cardinal's seeming misunderstanding of what had been
discussed previously, and his constant references to minor issues, always fed to him by a bishop.

We were intrigued to hear that 28 bishops and the Cardinal
were coming for three days, to sit in on our lectures and seminars.
Bishop Alan Clark took over my room. From our point of view
we understood that the bishops were interested, not hostile. They
certainly seemed so from our talks with them, especially over
drinks before supper. I recall Bishop Guazzelli telling me that he
wished he could enrol as a student, it seemed so refreshing and
exciting, explaining, 'I have not had time to read one book since
I became a bishop.' Maybe few of the bishops had, and it may
explain everything! The mood of their visit took a new turn on
the last day of lectures when the students asked the bishops to

name the 'heresies' that worried them. Bert, lecturing on the 'Resurrection of Christ', was heckled by Bishop Holland, interrupting to accuse him of not believing in the physical, bodily resurrection. As Bert patiently explained what he was saying, Bishop Butler left his seat, went to the front and defended the language that Bert had used, telling the bishop that he was not correct. I glanced at the Cardinal – he was purple with anger as the student body applauded Bishop Butler.

Later at dinner (we sat amongst the bishops), the conversation on our table was enlightening. We four students sat back and listened to the two bishops not agreeing about their understanding of the 'historical' event. Fr John Dacey spoke up, asking the bishops to listen to themselves. Could they now appreciate the difficulties teachers have in their task, 'We need your understanding and support!' We students did not know that the Cardinal had already told the staff, as the meeting was about to begin, that he had accepted their resignation, and a new principal was already found. They were stunned. What was the point of the bishops being there in that case? It did not tie in with the dialogue Bert had with Heenan in preparation for the event. In early December the Cardinal had written: 'Thank you for the agenda. Any framework can serve for the discussions, which are the main purpose of the meeting. Its success will depend on the frankness of these discussions. I hope that the bishops will disclose whatever misgivings they have. I know that the staff will be equally frank in reply … We can arrange another meeting with the staff in the New Year.'

The letter had clearly given Bert and the staff some hope for the future. After the event itself he scribbled a few notes:

Purpose of visit? Opportunity for long dialogue, enter into problems, see for selves what lines must be followed. Optimistic. Fear of the unknown (us as well as bps) High hopes of outcome, to restore confidence in staff. Or to confront, inspect.

Or to provide background for announcement of changes wd make sense – to let them see the dangerous theology (which we wd not hide) to discredit CCC. Also the dangerous famil-

iarity. If so, it certainly succeeded for sure. But for others, inspired. Some certainly discovered the issues.

He noted that some bishops wrote to thank him, appreciating the problems. Yet, 'Cardinal says all knew of our offer to resign, and none had suggested refusal. But some may have
thought (as we) that it was still negotiable, compromisable.' The
staff asked the Cardinal to announce that he had accepted the
resignation to the assembled bishops. But he refused. Why?
'Was he afraid of a reaction?' Certainly the several bishops I
spoke to were not aware of what was going on.

There was one clear misunderstanding between Bert and the
Cardinal, which may have led to his sudden decision. New staff
were needed to replace Peter De Rosa and John Perry, and it was
agreed that Heenan and Bert should look for possible replacements. Bert made the mistake of actually finding two willing
priests to take over, and on 10 December, informing the Cardinal
who was still looking for replacements himself. Heenan was
angry, saying that it was up to the new principal to look for staff.
It was clear that he had already asked Fr Michael Keegan to take
over before the bishops meeting later in the week. Bert's comment in the diary for the evening of the bishop's departure was:
'The staff had as it were a Last Supper at the Knights Club, before the final crucifixion.'

The Cardinal wrote immediately to Bert cancelling the proposed next meeting as 'not worthwhile, until I have seen your
successor and found out whom he wants on his staff. (So he
could choose his staff?) We can meet after Christmas and decide
when and how to announce the changes at Corpus Christi.
There will be no dramatic publicity.' Four days later Bert received a copy of the Cardinal's Statement for the Press. It was
carefully worded, praising the staff 'for having given years of
loyal service to Corpus Christ', but making it clear that it was
the staff's decision to resign by selecting only parts of Bert's correspondence: 'There is between us such a divergence of understanding on the nature of religious education that it would be inappropriate for us to remain as a staff in charge of your college
… This means that our resignation would become effective from
July 1972.' On Christmas Eve, Bert and staff prepared their state-

ment for later release, simply stating the disagreement over inviting eminent, international lecturers not approved by the Cardinal.

Bert escaped to Switzerland for a skiing break with priest friends, to clear his head before the new term. But the press embargo was broken, and 'after only 4 days the CCC news broke in all the papers, and I had to do an immediate downhill schuss back.' I was at breakfast listening to BBC 8.00 News, when the staff resignations were announced on air. It was shocking news for Corpus Christi students, past and present – especially for our year. Phones were ringing all day and some of us met up in London. Bert sent an immediate long letter to all former students, explaining the situation, and finishing with hope for the future: 'What fills us finally with joy is the knowledge that in spite of all set-backs the work will go on, both in the widely scattered fields where you work, and here at the college in London, which ought not to be identified with any one group of people. Even if *Pro Fide* were to take over (and I assure you there is no likelihood of that yet!) they would be forced in time to face the issues which you as students forced us to face, and to come up eventually with something like the theological and educational policy which we have tried to follow here. Meanwhile you must pray for the new staff: they have a hard task ahead of them.'

The rest of the Christmas break was taken up with endless newspaper interviews; the diary is thick with cuttings from all Catholic papers and periodicals, and all national newspapers, including readers' letters. Most were sympathetic to the college. 'No one who has experienced the depth of Christian commitment and humanity of those connected with the college can fail to be disturbed by the lack of confidence shown to its staff in official circles. I am sure that many non Roman Catholics share my sentiments when I say that the contacts I have had with Corpus Christi have challenged me and helped me to find a faith and spirituality which is attuned to the age in which we live. I should like to place on record my personal debt to Hubert Richards, Peter De Rosa, and those others who have been concerned with the college over the past years.' (Christopher Colven in *The Times*.) Some statements were very critical of the Cardinal, including the Open Letter from the Catholic Renewal

Movement Executive to him: 'You are putting Christ's message
in a glass case, and you are labelling it, "Do not touch." You are
turning yourself and our bishops and clergy into curators, au-
thorised to evict anybody who reaches out. In this sort of
church, there will be no catechetical problems, because there
will be no catechetics. It seems to us that what is happening at
Corpus Christi represents a very serious blow against the
catholicity and legitimate diversity of the church.'

It was Sister Romain who was perhaps in the best position to
write of what was happening. She wrote to the *Guardian*:

> Since 1958, after a year at the Lumen Vitae International
> Centre for Religious Education, in Brussels, I have worked in
> the field of religious education in this country, with the
> National Catechetical Centre, and for four years on the
> Corpus Christi staff. Having read the statement made by the
> Cardinal on the nature and role of the college, I just wonder
> what has happened ... I have worked four happy years with
> the staff, but never understood the aim of the college was "to
> teach Catholic theology to future catechists" or "akin to that
> of a Catholic training college giving an extra year of divini-
> ty". Would we need a new college for that? I understood
> Corpus Christi to be an international centre for studies and
> research in the field of religious education for English-speak-
> ing countries. This implies that those who attend have had
> some years of pastoral experience in parishes, or colleges and
> schools; have been faced with many problems concerning
> the communication of the Christian message, faith, its
> growth and development and the obstacles it meets.
> Theology, on its own, is not sufficient. To know is one thing;
> to be able to communicate is another ...
>
> If Christ were born today he would not mention sheep
> and vineyards. How do we translate the message, remaining
> faithful to it, in a rapidly changing world? Students have to
> bring their problems, their experiences, listen, discuss, pray
> and meditate, study and go through experiments. Nobody is
> more ready to admit that mistakes can be made than the staff
> and students. Perhaps there should be more sympathy for
> those who take risks for the benefit of the community. The

hierarchy is always invited but seldom attends any religious education enterprise. We were probably the only delegation at the International Congress in Rome who had not one bishop in their company. When have we seen our bishops at Corpus Christi College or Leicester Square lectures? ...

After knowing Fr Richards for so many years, I have never heard him complain about anything or anybody. I believe in miracles, here is one! Such a united, faithful, hard working, pleasant, holy staff, will be missed at national as well as international level.

Sister Romain's description of life and study at Corpus Christi was exactly my experience. The community spirit between staff and students of sharing experiences, of listening to one another, of prayer and study, always inspired by the enthusiasm of the staff, and the quality of lectures, made my faith deeper and gave me a determination to share it, faithful to the church, with those in my future care. My outstanding memories are of Bert's scripture lectures, which came to life on the unforgettable Pilgrimage to the Holy Land, and the lectures on Prayer by Archbishop Anthony Bloom. Past students I have met can all point to life-changing experiences during their year at the college. It was a time of extraordinary grace and happiness.

There was no joy, however, when on the second day of the new term the Cardinal came to speak to the student body. His read address to us was six A4 pages of close type! In it he justified his decision to start afresh with a new college by putting the failure of the present one squarely on the shoulders of the staff. He gave a detailed description of the founding and development of Corpus Christi over the years, frequently supporting the staff, especially Bert: 'A great deal of criticism has been made of the teaching of religion at Corpus Christi. I trust and have always trusted Fr Richards as a theologian. I have never thought that he would permit unsound theology to be taught here. I know how new ideas can be wrongly assumed to be false ideas. My chief reserve, of which I have often spoken to Fr Richards, is the advisability of giving the same course of speculative theology to priests with years of philosophy and theology behind them and to nuns and laity virtually untrained in either.'

It was this patronising statement that infuriated so many of the students. Some of the nuns and laity had theology and philosophy degrees, as well as other qualifications. The average age of the students in my year was 38, therefore rather more experienced than school leavers in their first college studies. It led to a very heated discussion with Heenan after his paper. One student questioned the Cardinal's competency in the field of catechetics. Heenan said that he should not presume catechetics was only ten years old, and that he and the bishops had considerable theological backgrounds. 'I myself wrote two text books and edited a third.' The student wrote later: 'He also forgot to add that he had recently re-issued the famous *Penny Catechism*, complete with his *imprimatur*, dated 1971 ... still widely used in Great Britain, with question and answers, like: 'Q. After your night prayers what should you do? A. I should observe due modesty in going to bed; occupy myself with the thoughts of death, and endeavour to compose myself at the foot of the cross.'

Cardinal Heenan was being honest in his own mind in everything that he criticised, but we were angry that he quoted snippets from Bert's private correspondence to him, in order to lay the blame at his feet. We did not know at the time that he completely ignored the memorandum he had accepted, stating there was always the possibility that the offer of resignation could be reconsidered. This was dishonest, because by doing so he came out of the situation as simply doing what the staff wanted. It implied he had not wanted them to go.

It was hardly surprising that two weeks later the stress was again taking its toll. Bert experienced chest pains and was back in hospital. We were shaken, as were many others. On the first day he was visited by his family, all of the staff, three priests and the Cardinal. During his two-week stay he had little rest, visited often by his family, many priests – mostly his former students and including one of the staff at St Edmund's, Bishop Guazelli, the Vicar General, the staff daily, some of the college students, and even one of his parishioners (then a child) from Much Hadham. We students cheered him up with our cards and messages. He left hospital to arrive back to an almost empty half term college, surprised to find Fr Keegan staying overnight for a 'once over' of the place.

Over the next two months, articles and letters in the press continued to analyse the 'Corpus Christi muddle' as the *Month* magazine called it. The long article by Fr Hebblethwaite SJ was a very fair assessment of the seven years, accurately researched, with his conclusion that the disagreement 'is about the understanding of religious education today: on that both the Cardinal and Fr Hubert Richards are agreed. The agreement, and the difference, can be measured in the concluding words of their two addresses:

> I end by expressing the hope that Corpus Christi will continue to enjoy the loyal support of its past students. I pray that it will always be distinguished for its love of the Holy Eucharist from which it takes its name. (Cardinal Heenan, 11 January 1972)

> I pray that the Corpus Christi of the past and the Corpus Christi of the future will, through a suffering to which its founder the Cardinal is no stranger, continue to build up the Body of Christ from which the college takes its name.
> (Fr Richards, to past students, 15 January 1972)

A final disagreement came in May, when the Cardinal offered to come again to the college to speak with the staff and students. Bert replied: 'It was generous of you to make the offer, but on reflection I am not sure that such a meeting would serve any good purpose, and may simple cause embarrassment to all concerned. The turmoil has died down. The meeting of past students scheduled for June promises to take place in a spirit of cooperation rather than acrimony – Fr Keegan has been invited.' Heenan replied: 'I am sorry that you don't want me to come to Corpus Christi but, of course, I appreciate your motive. I think you are wrong to allow the students to leave Corpus Christi with a sense of grievance against me. Make sure they know that I wished to take leave of them ... I intend to give the Sisters a personal memento before they leave. They have always shown me great affection.' No word about the male staff.

Sister Ruth was clearly unhappy at the Cardinals' presumption. She chose to mention it when she wrote to Cardinal Heenan about her own position. 'In your last letter to Fr

Richards you seem concerned lest some kind of grievance towards you might be kept alive by students. You need have no
fear, whatever their feelings may be, Fr Richards is the last person to foster any kind of resentment. Not once in this long se-
quence – not even in private conversation – have I heard him
speak of you in any spirit of criticism or recrimination. If you
knew how steadfast he has been in his determination to understand your position and place the most favourable construction
upon it, you would be as consoled by his loyalty and deep
Christian spirit as I am edified. There cannot be many superiors
who have such loyalty served in so difficult a situation; and to
know it will surely make you very happy.' In his reply to this
letter the Cardinal simply complained that her understanding of
catechetics could have been shared by humanists, Buddhists or
Protestants, and was full of the current 'jargon' which he found
'very depressing'. 'It would be sad if you locked yourself in a little
catechists' world out of touch with the church.' He mentioned
that small packages would be delivered to her and Sister Rena.
'They are a token of my gratitude to both of you. You were a
great consolation on the day the men wanted a showdown.' He
made no mention of her praise of Bert's loyalty.

On our sad last day at the college Bert gave us a final word of
advice – typical of him, always respectful for others. He made
his usual notes:

> At this moment you can't assess what the year means to you,
> therefore there is a danger to shock or scandalise others who
> did not have such a year. Danger too you can discourage
> those who have other loyalties.
>
> So be prudent, take it easy.
>
> Here you've had freedom and fullness which perhaps is
> impossible in other settings.
>
> Be gentle with people, and moderate, and tolerant.
>
> This is a responsibility you owe to the catechetical move-
> ment, and to the communities to which you return.
>
> Help them positively, not negatively by criticism, or
> odious comparisons. Don't fret, the future is yours!

We had our final Mass together, followed by a social
evening. Fr Jim Hawes composed *A Valediction in Elegiac Mood*:

The party's almost done at Notting Hill,
And those who study there are soon to scatter.
The halls of Corpus Christi will be still,
And the silence shall succeed its cheeky chatter.

But for the generations yet to spring
Some echo of the past must needs be made;
'Tis only right to utter and to sing
The worth of those whose labours were ill paid.

So, therefore, let us praise our famous men
And women too, of learning and renown.
We gladly summon parchment and the pen
To write up all and set the record down.

Of Hubert first the muse must boldly tell,
Who bore the heat and burden of the day,
Who showed us what the scriptures meant so well,
And lived in full that Pauline 'better way'.

In lecture, liturgy or seminar
His words were measured and his thoughts were clear,
With him we sought for God not from afar,
But in the present, now and here.

In Sister Ruth we found an able guide
To help us chart the seas of teenage quest.
Her ways of catechesis opened wide
New insights on their restlessness and zest.

And Rena, too, with adults most in mind,
Did animate her own professional set.
Her lively manner fully underlined
What good from group dynamics one can get.

With Peter Wetz the kids took pride of place.
For them another book will soon appear.
Hid notions of their nature and their grace
Make prelates shake their heads in wrath and fear.

From Farm Street, straight, a Jesuit came each day
To add some tone and polish to our name.
Frank's writings in *The Sower* point the way
For those in search of catechetics fame.

From Desmond too, the audio man,
This fact we've learnt – our message cannot hide –
No lecture, talk or project dare we plan,
Without recourse to photo, disc or slide.

Last, but not least, dear Kathleen must be thanked;
With books she furnished us throughout the year.
In pilgrim parts among the young she ranked,
And solved all crossword puzzles without peer.

Good friends, the roll is called, our course is run:
But this look back is only half the tale;
The future heralds yet another sun,
Faith, hope and love build up what now seems frail.

To those that follow us we say *shalom*.
Find in this place the blessings we have found;
Know here, as well, the kindness we have known
And go from here with good news as your sound.

A student from our final year, recalling the Holy Land visit, wrote: 'Bert was one of my heroes. I have to say that he changed my life and increased my faith and indeed set me free. My undying vision of him will always be seeing him sitting with us in Gethsemane. I can see him there with the city in the background and knowing that he was leading us to truth and was being, like his master before him, persecuted by the authorities. On a lighter note I remember being filled with spiritual thoughts in the church of the Holy Sepulchre and Bert breaking into my meditation by saying "Barney, just time for a swift half".'

Later a student wrote to Bert, 'Your serenity and non-critical reaction at the time of the CCC crisis is the greatest lecture you ever gave me'.

The legacy that Bert left to us, his Corpus Christi students, was the last words of his final lecture. 'Remember the truth of the gospel is something you *live*, not put down in statements.' We all loved him because he lived it, and showed us the way.

CHAPTER TWELVE

A Kind of Exile
July 1972-August 1973

Bert began his diary for July 1972 to August 1973, with a title *Exiled to the Antipodes*. This is how it must have felt. He was no longer part of a permanent community, a way of life he had always known and loved.

> *1 July* Michael Keegan arrived at CCC to take over.
> I went to Cambridge to arrange my move there in September.
> *7 July-18 Aug* 6 weeks in New Zealand & Australia
> Flew to Nairobi and Johannesberg (13 hours) where I stayed 2 nights to give talks at Cathedral House.
> Then 16 hours via Mauritius and Perth to Sydney, where I had to wait 4 hours for an onward flight to Auckland.
> At the invitation of Bishop Delargy, I stayed with Ewan Derrick's team at the Catechetical Centre.

Ewan Derrick had been a student at Corpus Christi and was appreciated by his bishop, who invited Bert to New Zealand. Bishop Delargy had come over to England to visit his student at the college, so he knew what to expect. In May he wrote to Fr Derrick:

> Thank you for the programme outlining the work to be done by Father Hubert Richards. I look forward to his coming very much because I believe he is in the top class of those concerned with catechetics. Over and above this, his learning and scholastic background will quickly commend themselves to all who meet him. When I met him in London he impressed me very much indeed. I intend to participate personally in the Auckland Course. Thank you for all you and your staff have been doing in the cause of Religious Education. May God support these important courses with abundant blessings.

With such hierarchical support the lectures looked promising. It was hard work, 'A very heavy programme'. In the three weeks in North Island Bert addressed four groups of teachers, and two groups of diocesan priests, with four full days with each group. 'Only at the end were we allowed a celebratory meal at Fisherman's Wharf. The next day I flew to South Island for a week's skiing near Mt Cook – a welcome break.'

10-13 *Aug* Three days with the priests and teachers of Christchurch. Bishop Ashby very supportive, as Delargy had been. But then the storm broke!

At the beginning of the lecture tour the New Zealand press had been supportive, with large photographs of 'The Roving Priest', and with welcoming words. 'A fifty-year-old Catholic priest who arrived in Auckland last week from London, smokes a pipe, smiles a lot, strums his guitar and sings his own gospel songs. Father Hubert Richards looks like a friendly parish priest. In fact he is a leading theologian and specialist in religious education.' (*Auckland Star*, 17 July 1972)

After the first talks in Wellington the New Zealand *Tablet* was reporting strong criticism from two outspoken priests, Fr Durning OP and Fr Duggan SM. 'Fr Durning, a man not given to over-statement, writes that he came away reeling from the lectures and that "his God is not my God ..." Fr Duggan, after carefully setting out Fr Richards' views, concludes that they are not in accord with what the church teaches, and says: "It is a matter of some concern that he has been lecturing to teachers of Christian doctrine." He can say that again. It certainly is. Indeed *The Tablet* (NZ edition) is surprised that some of our bishops have given Fr Richards permission to advance the views that he is advancing. It would be interesting to know what Cardinal Heenan thinks about it.' The paper continued to give entire pages to the two priests, to outline 'Fr Richards' "heresies", agreeing with their conclusions: "One does not have to be a theological expert to realise that his teaching is completely destructive of the faith as taught by the magisterium of the Catholic Church".' Interesting that the writer did not mention that half of New Zealand's 'magisterium' (four bishops) actually supported Bert's teaching. The other two remained silent.

There was immediate pressure put on Bert as letter pages were full of criticism, with only one letter of support. He received hurtful personal letters. 'Father, go back to the Christ you knew and loved when you offered your First Holy Mass, the Christ your mother loved before you. I'm just a very ordinary nun in the ranks with no authority to advise any priest, but I feel it a matter of conscience to try to stop this tragedy. Your sister in Christ …' Bishop Delargy, upset by this turn of events, wrote to Fr Duggan, sending a copy to Bert.

Dear Father Duggan,
Thank you for sending me a copy of your reflections on Father Richards' lectures. While I appreciate the compliment, I am horrified at the contents. You have had a reputation as a sincere scholar and objective teacher. These notes belie that entirely. I heard Father Richards. We have the complete text on tape of all his lectures and question periods (including your questions and mine), and the report you give of the lectures shows that however many words you took down, you simply did not listen … You completely distort his thought on the Resurrection and the Eucharist … I find myself forced to say you are talking a lot of rubbish. I am certain that the church today needs to be saved as much from its friends as from its enemies. Being more Catholic than the Pope is an ancient form of heresy.

Bad press for Bert went on and on, even after he had left New Zealand, with Bishop Ashby joining Bishop Delargy in taking *The Tablet* to task for their ongoing criticism. Bishop Delargy issued a 'Memorandum' to the priests, religious and laity of Auckland that *The Tablet* published in full. The bishop wrote of the 'Way of the Christian prophet is the way of the Cross.' He outlined the spirit of the Vatican Council; how a consensus was reached on the need to go out to the modern world and meet it on its own ground. 'God's people were freed from the paralysing human traditions that bound them down like mummies in a museum. But triumphalism, legalism and clericalism were not entirely dead. The backlash from the prophets of doom continues to plague the post-conciliar period with relentless zeal.' The bishop wrote of the dangers that will always result from change, especially in the secularist and scientific age, but 'our model must be the delicacy and sensitivity of Christ as he revealed himself to the Jews.' He continued: 'Recently the full force of the backlash descended on Father Richards, whom I had invited to the Auckland Diocese because he had so much to tell about post-conciliar catechetical experiments. Some of his critics went so far as to attack his personal integrity and to denounce him as heretical.' The bishop explained that he did not agree with him always: 'I would humbly take issue with him on the validity of methods of literary criticism which he inclines to, and even on some of his views on teaching methods. I also believe Fr Richards overrated the theological knowledge and background reading of his audience. He paid us a compliment we didn't deserve. But I am convinced his arch-critics simply didn't listen. They had already fixed him in a category of their own making before his arrival and they were not prepared to hear even him deny it.'

Bert flew out to Australia for a few days lectures at Christ's College, in Melbourne; and then on to Canada for many more lectures in Victoria, Vancouver, Calgary and Toronto, receiving much more of a general welcome there. He met up with former students and his family, which must have been a great relief. On return to England in late September he took up residence in St Edmund's House, Cambridge for three months. He returned to find the English Catholic press reporting the New Zealand lectures with large headlines. 'Bishops back 'heretical' Fr Richards.' He was called to Archbishop's House in order to explain himself to Cardinal Heenan. Although the reporting was quite objective, the word 'heretical' in the headline was unwise and insensitive, as Fr John Coghlan and Joan Robson pointed out in letters to the paper. The latter wrote: 'The word "heretical" has insidious overtones, however fair and unprejudiced the article may be, the headline "sticks".' It certainly did with a few members of my own religious community. I found cuttings from the papers in my pigeon hole, with the word underlined, and other underlinings, pointing out to me that I was now as unsafe as Bert was. He was not a stranger to them because my superior had invited him, only the week before, to start a series of gospel lectures to the community, staying over to say Mass for us the next morning. The majority of my sisters were delighted.

Once again Bert was in trouble with Cardinal Heenan. Following the visit he received a letter from him on 4 November.

'I think I know how you feel about the letters you have been receiving. You probably do not realise that your lectures in New Zealand have also considerably swollen my post. Your recent broadcasts have also brought me a number of letters. I enclose a copy of one that is fairly typical.' (A very critical attack – 'I am increasingly concerned by the devastation and havoc brought about by Fr Richards and others like him...'). Heenan then states, for the first time, that he no longer could accept that 'you still believe the same Creed as I do... It seems clear to me that you have completely altered your religious beliefs. We shall have to give a good deal of thought to your future. I cannot imagine that you will be acceptable as a lecturer in theology in this country unless you undergo another change of view.'

It is interesting that the 4 November issue of the English *Tablet* published the following comment about the broadcasts that Heenan had been told, were bringing 'devastation and havoc':

However reluctant listeners may feel to face the day at 7.45 am, the series of talks 'Thought for the Day' given last week by Fr Hubert Richards on the childhood of Jesus must surely have brought them wide awake. This short programme on Radio 4 is often rewarding, but Fr Richards' contribution was outstanding. For one thing he is a consummate broadcaster, speaking without condescension as if he were talking to a friend or two across a table, and for another he is so sure of his faith and his facts that the listener immediately capitulates to the sheer conviction and fluency of the speaker. Listening to him talking about the angels who amazed the shepherds in their meteoric appearance in the sky or the star which led the three kings made us feel that, come Christmas, we would hear those incomparable gospels with a quite new attention.

Cardinals perhaps, don't listen to 'Thought for the Day'.

Only five months earlier the Cardinal had declared that he had never had any difficulty with Bert's teaching. The contrast between the English cardinal and the New Zealand bishop is surprising. Both had been at the Vatican Council. Delargy could write publicly that: 'The objective norm of truth is not a philosophy but a magisterium, and at the Council Pope John, Pope Paul and the bishops made it quite clear that theological pluralism is eminently Catholic ... Unlike his critics, Fr Richards is quite happy with theological pluralism.' It was Cardinal Heenan who could not accept the Council message that theological pluralism was 'eminently Catholic'. A December issue of the *Times Literary Supplement*, in a series 'Doers and Thinkers' published a long article by the Cardinal on 'Modern theology and the care of souls.' It was a damning analysis of all modern theologians, especially John Robinson, Tillich, Bonhoeffer who 'has an influence out of all proportion to his theological weight because of the manner of his death', but especially Bultmann. 'Most Christians, whether clerical or lay, reject Bultmann while contemporary theologians tend to accept him uncritically as a prophet ... He describes his demolition work (of the gospels) as demythologising. In his view the story of Christ is no more historical than the story of creation in Genesis is scientific.'

It is not unreasonable to suppose that Heenan had Bert in mind when continuing: 'It will be seen that some contemporary theologians take for granted that the twentieth century man must not be asked to believe that Jesus is God. To avoid any assertion of divinity the usual device is to say that Jesus is fully human.' Bert has in his diary a scribbled page of his thoughts on the article. He asks if it is so disastrous, as Heenan thought, that clergy are spending more time now on exploring dogmatic theology rather than moral theology. They are asking questions on:

> Who Christ is, how he related to God, how we related? Now no longer content to simply retell something in which they had no hand (the 'magisterium') but feel responsible to ask what it means and to what extent where repetition of it could be deep unfaithfulness to the past? ... Is it naïve to say 'Christ is God', and stop there, as if that solves all problems, and answers all questions? The question is precisely, what is God? He is the mystery! Why presume theological 'tampering' with dogma is to dilute, to make no demand on faith?

There is no admirer of Bultmann who accepts all his ideas

uncritically. But to refuse to see that he made a break-through after which things can't be the same again – is wilful blindness! Heenan says 'Theologians and pastors have ceased to speak the same language!' Is *this* not the real disaster? This chasm. How bridge? By destroying one side: Bultmann, Tillich, Loisy, Tyrrell, Bonhoeffer, de Chardin?

Bert hardly comments on the three months in Cambridge, where he had hoped to have time to write. He mentions all the other activities he had undertaken: student seminars in Homerton College, work at the BBC with Peter De Rosa, meetings with the Council of Christians & Jews, lectures given for past Corpus Christi students, convent visits, including the 'Weekly visits to Sr Clare's school in N. Finchley to hold discussions and say Mass next day.' On 1 January 1973 he left for two weeks skiing in Sölden, followed by a 10-day visit to Rome, giving a series of lectures to the Sacred Heart Sisters. 'Then spent a few days at the Beda College, to decide whether or not I would join the staff there.' It is interesting that the Roman College could ask Bert to join them to teach New Testament Studies, when they were aware of the criticisms in the press. He did not accept the job, anticipating that the Cardinal would object to sending Westminster students there. He returned to St Edmund's House, Cambridge for a further two months, lecturing again at Homerton College. He wrote to the Cardinal:

> I imagined when I came here that I would have months and months to reflect on my future work ... I have in fact been far busier than I anticipated. Lectures, courses, and teaching locally, have taken me away from my desk more than I had hoped. The copious writing I had looked forward to doing in the quietness of my room has so far produced only three chapters. And I expected to produce three books!

He asked Heenan if he could extend his stay until he had completed the writings he had promised so many people, funding himself through his lectures. The answer was quick and brief:

> My dear Bert,
> The answer to your request is NO. We must have a long talk.

Having heard the tapes of your New Zealand talks (sent to
me by an indignant bishop) I don't think you have any future
in teaching.

Bert immediately had another tussle with Heenan, this time
over a New Testament post at Heythrop College, to which he
had been invited to apply, by the Jesuits. It seemed the answer
to his problems if he were selected. He lived in hope. In 1972 he
had been offered the job, which was deferred until 1974, and this
time advertised. He talked it over with Cardinal Heenan, asking
for permission to apply. The Cardinal was not happy, saying he
wanted Bert to go to a parish and stop teaching altogether, but
that he could not stop him applying to Heythrop. 'I have no
power to stop Heythrop taking you, and no wish to stop you
doing what you feel you ought.' Bert had spoken of the 'sense of
waste' if he could not continue the academic work he was sent
to the Biblicum to study and teach. There were very few others
to do this. He wrote to thank the Cardinal for the frank talk and
expressed his gratitude 'that you did not disapprove of my suggestion that I apply for it.'

The reply came back immediately, with Heenan putting
down on paper how he recalled the meeting. Bert had asked
why could he be entrusted for a parish but not for seminarians
and teachers. The reply: 'You may consider it your duty to make
teachers and seminarians question their whole understanding
of the faith but you would not disturb ordinary Catholics ... I
doubt if you could be shown to teach heresy. My dilemma is
that I think it would be wrong to put our students in your care
again. Rightly or wrongly it was generally thought that the influence that you, Charles Davis and Peter De Rosa had on the
students was undesirable.' He continued: 'Father Copleston
(Master of Heythrop) knows that I would regard your appointment as undesirable because I spoke to him when you told me
that Bob Murray (the Jesuit Scripture Professor at Heythrop)
had approached you. My position at Heythrop does not entitle
me to interfere in the appointment of staff. The only action I
could take would be to withdraw Westminster students.' At this
point Bert seemed to lose patience and even hope for his future.
He replied immediately to his superior:

My dear Cardinal,

At times I almost give up hope of ever understanding you. Perhaps I am just naïve in always wanting to think the best of people, but I came back from my visit to you really encouraged by your apparent understanding of my position, and by your apparent sympathy. I never seem to be able to learn by past experience.

Time and again we have met to talk together, and arrived at what any neutral witness of the conversation could only describe as an amicable solution, even if it is a compromise. A day or so later there has followed, time and again, a letter in which you have slanted the things that have been said, and gone back to the retrenched position you occupied before the meeting.

Bert concluded his letter: 'The question remains whether you wish to make it virtually impossible for me to apply to Heythrop, or for Heythrop to accept me.' He did consider withdrawing his application. Father Ashton SJ wrote back that there were over twenty enquiries about the lectureship, mostly from Protestants. 'How ironical it would be if the Cardinal were seen to prefer his students to be taught by, say, a Belfast minister than by yourself. But please do continue with your application.' In the event the successful candidate was a woman Baptist minister, with a Jewish background. The Cardinal told Bert that he was 'very relieved to know that you are not joining the staff at Heythrop. I am quite satisfied that the appointment would have reopened all the unpleasantness we had over Corpus Christi.' In a later letter he wrote: 'Father Copleston came to lunch yesterday and told me that Dr Isaacs was easily the best of a long list of applicants. Apart from her scholarship in languages and scripture she is also a PhD of Oxford.'

I am left to wonder that had Bert been given that opportunity to teach within a Catholic Jesuit College he would have remained a priest? I think it is quite possible, especially if Cardinal Heenan was no longer his superior. The pages of scribbled notes show the anxiety and almost self-doubt that these events had produced. His diary over these months report frequent visits from members of his family and former students, myself included. I think we all felt his loneliness at this time, and a very heavy pressure on him. At the end of February he received a letter from Bishop Butler, who had just heard the New Zealand tapes. He wrote: 'I am filled with admiration not only for your scriptural scholarship and theological alertness, but also for the mastery with which you play the role of pedagogue. It is absurd to say it, but I have never heard you lecture, so I have had a new experience, if only by proxy.' It seems absurd that, given all the public criticism, the bishop most able as a theologian had never actually listened to Bert, (except on the Corpus Christi occasion). He did not agree with everything he heard on the tape, but was most agreeable in discussing the issues. He finished: 'Sorry if it sounds as though I were merely disagreeing with you: what happened was, I noted points of disagreement rather than those where I agreed. And I don't profess to have meditated the NT material at the same depth as you have. So forgive these superficial reflections.'

They corresponded again, and the next letter from Bishop Butler is surprisingly open about the problem Cardinal Heenan had with the theology and scripture scholars of the day. He writes kindly of him, explaining why he says one thing and writes another. 'I honestly think this may be partly due to the fact he doesn't enjoy personal confrontations, coupled with the undoubted fact that he genuinely likes you and therefore may find it difficult to bring himself to wound you over the tea-cups, so to speak. Then afterwards he gets what in a lesser mortal would be described as a scruple! ... I am sure that H. is as conscientiously in earnest as you, and that he takes his responsibilities as a member of the teaching body very seriously (it's a pity you are not an auxiliary bishop; he would have to move more cautiously if you were!).'

Bishop Butler was very outspoken about the Cardinal's patronising attitude towards the laity. 'It is a tragedy that you and he are thrown into the relations which link you. You hardly need me to tell you that he thinks (almost unconsciously) of the faithful as a crowd of uneducated East Londoners of the first decade of this century; and any lay person who shows more than purely passive acceptance of the penny catechism is, for him, a tiresome person who does not understand his proper position in the church. I am of course caricaturing, but you will get my meaning. He thinks that the faithful should not be "disturbed" by theologians, and finds it extremely difficult to accept that they are disturbed before the theologians open their mouths.' He concluded: 'Dare I add one thing more? Bishops grow old and die. Climates of opinion subtly change. I personally think that Vatican II was one of the great things in history, and almost a moral miracle (knowing what I do of the prelates composing it).'

At the end of March Bert left Cambridge for three months at the Dominican École Biblique in Jerusalem. He had always wanted to spend time there, and described the whole experience in detail in a number of long letters home. They were full of strange, humorous episodes or descriptions, much like the gita diaries of old. He was back in a community who recognised his biblical mind and understood his work. Jerome Murphy O'Connor, Spud's cousin, was a lecturer there, and he invited Bert to join the expeditions to biblical sites being examined, Qumran, the Herodium, Sinai, and the new excavations on Temple Mount. Bert was able to go to places not open to ordinary visitors, travelling in either UNO cars, or USA Consulate vehicles. The first 'adventure' was the loss of his luggage. He travelled via Venice, and 'There discovered that my registered luggage had not arrived, and it didn't catch up with me until more than three weeks' later. Worse, had to wait four days in Venice because of industrial action by sailors.' Assured that his two cases were not to be found and were sitting in The Alps somewhere 'and would be held there for twelve days, and I would be charged for storage! I asked to see the customs man. "He is on strike too." So there I was. I had my pyjamas and toothbrush, and my typewriter (but you can't wear that) and my guitar (but you can't clean your shoes with that). But all the things I really wanted for the journey (let alone once in Jerusalem), like a change of socks, hair cream, books, papers, handkerchiefs, even stupid things like nail clippers – and (noch) my pills ... these were all in my heavy, registered, guaranteed-to-get-it-there-for-£10 luggage.' The rest of the journey was equally catastrophic, and amusingly narrated. He was relieved to reach Jerusalem and settle in.

There are small vignettes that anyone who has visited Jerusalem will recognise.

At this moment my window is open, there is a cock crowing announcing it is midday with enormous pride down below somewhere. He also announces at 3 am, 4 am, and 5 am with equal gusto. Being in the Holy Land I don't mind. It has gospel overtones here with which one doesn't associate cocks elsewhere. It has allowed me to check the guitar music I composed to accompany my gospel song 'Cockcrow'. I am glad to find the cock down there has got the notes absolutely right.

One of Bert's deeper reflections described the extraordinary 'goings on' in the Holy Sepulchre.

The kind of tension in Jerusalem of which I wrote, is of course, always precariously near the surface here, especially at Passover/Easter. The goings on of the various Christian communities are bad enough (the Syrian Patriarch was nearly brained when he jumped the queue on Easter Saturday and got the 'Holy Fire' before he should have); but when Jews are involved as well, tempers really fly. We had three incidents this year, all due to the fact that a fanatical group of ultra-evangelicals has started a campaign of 'Jews for Jesus', which has caused a counter-group to spring up, calling itself 'Christians for Moses', intent on proving that Jesus was a Jewish heretic and appealing to Christians to return to the pre-Jesus truth. This group got into the Holy Sepulchre just before Easter, and began splashing red paint around, not easy to get off the magnificent new stonework in which the whole historical building is being restored. Next a couple of them slipped in overnight, not realising that reveille is at about 3.30 am for the Franciscans, one of whom caught them trying to pinch the INRI sign off the crucifix in the Calvary chapel. He's still in hospital with a broken jaw. On Good Friday itself a bunch of them were handing out anti-Christian leaflets to pilgrims arriving at the Holy Sepulchre, and an idiotic Franciscan, instead of fetching the police, began to manhandle the Jew. A fight ensued, in which a

Muslim came to the rescue of the Franciscan, and a fellow Jew to the rescue of the pamphleteer. An Armenian priest tried to intervene to get peace, but the Franciscan was not to be deterred from throttling the Jew he had on the ground. When the police arrived everyone had scarpered except the Muslim, the Franciscan and the intervening and half-throttled Jew. It turned out he was a Jewish policeman in plain clothes. With extraordinary difficulty the Franciscan was not gaoled. The Muslim was, of course, poor bloke. If I was here another year, I would seriously propose that we Christians made a massive procession to the Western Wall to mark our respect for the Jews, and invite the Jews to form a massive procession to the Holy Sepulchre. As it is, we go on year after year venerating our own little places, imagining this somehow pleases God!

It was clearly a refreshing three months for Bert, although he missed the pilgrim groups he usually led, finding it strange to visit special places on his own. He met up with friends, the Sion sisters, the Grail, and a group of Corpus Christi past students who 'arrived with 18 tins of tobacco'. Besides his research and writing, he preached at the École, gave seminars and lectures, was interviewed by Radio Éireann about Holy Week, had a fine evening reception at the Russian Orthodox, celebrated the Queen's birthday at the British Embassy, sang songs to the orphan children in Bethlehem, and finally 'made some recordings for the BBC, on a very dodgy machine of Michael Elkins'. Then he flew back to London for three days before flying to Canada and the USA for six weeks of lectures. These were mainly on the infancy gospels and miracles, and were to be published later. He went to Edmonton, Washington and British Colombia, before meeting up with the family and with former Corpus Christi students in Toronto.

Bert returned to London on 14 August and four days later was off on a gita with Spud, to Moscow, Leningrad, Tashkent, and Samarkand. The amazing journey he called 'To Russia With Spud', and was eventually typed and recorded in a separate diary.

Ye veritable chronyckle of ye fantastycalle wanderynges of

ye Rvds Patrycke Mary Josephe Murphyo Connore ande
Huberte Rychardes in ye Kingdomes of ye Russyas ande ye
Borderes of Cathay, undere ye bienveillant watchfulnesse of
Yntouryst ande Balckan Holydayes Packayge Toures in ye
Yere of our Lorde nyneteen hundrede ande seventie three.

Bert began by giving a 'vignette' of the 29 in the group. He
described this as the most difficult part of the account, as how he
saw them on Day 1 'such a hilariously strange mixture of odd
human beings' would violently change by day 7, 'when one
began to realise that they were viewing us with exactly the same
amused benevolence as we were eying them,' and by day 14,
'when we saw quite clearly that we were all perfectly normal
people.' In fact, he was delighted that they formed a very united
and well-knit group, with a 'clear mind of its own, mixing freely
and easily, all on personal name terms, and completely inter-
changeable at table (quite a thing when it happens to husbands
and wives).'

It turned out to be one of the most fascinating, enjoyable holidays the two friends would recall. Their favourite (because
amusing) family regularly ordered a suite for themselves, be-
having like 'the typical upper class English family abroad, with
no time for anything in Russia that dated after the Revolution,
which tended to be dismissed with "Har tarsum". The father, a
QC with a practice "within a stone's throw of Mob Lodge", was
difficult to draw on any subject, unless one happened to enquire
about his slipped disc, when he would happily go on for hours.'
Bert's fond memory of the holiday was Spud's mimicking of the
different members of the party, with his usual sense of fun. But
the most striking, and unexpected revelation, was the 'courtesy,
kindness, patience and gentleness of the Russian people. There
was a helpfulness and even a generosity which I have not experienced even among Arab people. The Woods twice went to an
after dinner show (opera and ballet) where seats were all sold,
and were invited to come free while people squeezed together
to make room for them; an itinerant shoe mender outside the
hotel moved aside a student whose shoe he was patching to fix
my sandal for me, and refused to take payment. A boy of ten
asked me for chewing gum (unobtainable in Russia), and when

he found I hadn't any, gave me a cigarette instead. I was very deeply impressed by such gentleness.'

Bert wrote that he wanted to record his admiration for 'the very real achievements of the Revolution, working against extraordinary odds. Although we rather had it rammed down our throats, it is quite remarkable that a country with almost nothing in the way of general education in 1920 should have achieved universal literacy up to university standard in such a short time.' The group were delighted to find that the heavy restrictions on their movements, that they had been warned would happen, was quite untrue. They visited, as a group, the monuments, the ballet, the circus, including an animal circus on ice, and all the places of historical and cultural interest in the four cities. They had free time to go where they liked. On one occasion, hearing that the American Embassy ran a bar for expatriates, they joined Kevin, Sandra and Pat on the trip for cheap drinks. They were served by a marine, off guard duty, 'with a handshake like a vice, but with a deft hand at the gin, whisky and beer he lined up on the bar. The conversation was a little desultory: "Do you like Moscow?" "You can keep it, Sir." "Do you ever get into contact with any of the Russian people?" "No, Sir. No commie is ever gonna get through these doors, Sir. My President wouldn't like it, Sir. Have another drink, Sir." We shifted a fair amount of their drink, free. They were glad the Australian Kevin admired their Australian canned beer, since none of them could stand it, and asked us to take a carton of 24 back to the hotel. Which we did. "Have the Embassy car, Sir".'

At the hotel it was shared with the band and some of the group. This included 'Svetlana, green with envy that we were getting free drinks from *her* embassy!' 'Svetlana' was Spud and Bert's name for Iva, 'the loudmouthed US matron of fifty plus, the eternal tourist, always in high humour, a bit much for the staid English; and clearly out to get her man and monopolise him, which she did from day two onwards.'

The priestly pair amazed their companions with their ability to find countless occasions for laughter, vodka and wine, and initiating musical evenings into which other groups were drawn. Once it was 'with a dozen Italians from another table. Spud grabbed a guitar from the band, and we entertained the assembled company to a selection of Italian mountain songs in full six-part harmony for a full half hour. A final rendering of Zorba, from the band, got everyone on to the floor, arms linked and legs akimbo. And suddenly it was 2 am.' During a long delay at Tashkent airport the group were organised into a song-session over cups of tea, 'It included an hilarious imitation of Louis Armstrong by Nick, and of Vera Lynn by Pat, and as the hours wore on, our cosy circle of 30 poured forth harmonised Gilbert and Sullivan by the yard. Other English groups, embarrassed by this most un-English display of emotion, tried to disassociate themselves from us.' Spud and Bert mixed easily with the Russians they met, and surprised them too. At a restaurant they shared a table with a young couple, graduate economists. When they explained (in German) that they were Catholic priests, there was shock! 'Vatican?' 'Yes' 'But we are atheists' 'That is alright by us'. They shook their heads in disbelief. It was the couple's wedding anniversary, so Spud sent for a bottle of champagne. They parted with much laughter.

A highlight for Bert was the long discussions he had with others of the group over religion, usually on bus journeys. He was amazed at the ignorance of many of them. One lasting memory was the single ikon room in the Tretyakov Gallery, 'which housed all those Rublevs which so far I had seen only in reproduction. The warmth, tenderness, compassion and sheer humanity of this artist have always attracted me to him, and I was glad to see that this was made the theme of the Russian film *Andrei Rublev* which I saw on my return to London. His 'Trinity', which the film spent its last shots lovingly exploring, was in the Tretyakov.' He and Spud sought out a *zerkov russka* (Russian Church) to attend one day. They were taken by taxi to a vast monastic establishment with an ornate nineteenth-century church. They were surprised to find it packed with about 400 people, 'most of them young, all deeply concentrating on the sanctuary, where a bearded priest was holding them enthralled with his singing, and a choir responding in full-throated harmony. The sense of mystery could almost be touched and it was this, no doubt above all, that the youngsters were attracted by, living (as who doesn't?) their largely three-dimensional lives. We were deeply moved. Only the approach of dinner hour tore us away.'

CHAPTER THIRTEEN

A Turbulent Time Ahead
September 1973-1974

Bert and Spud flew back from Kiev to Gatwick on 1 September. Bert was ready for the next round with the Cardinal. He took up residence in the chaplain's flat of the Sion Convent, Chepstow. He had nowhere else to go, and there he was always welcome. He had reflected deeply on his future over the summer, and made decisions. He was going to refuse a parish, knowing he would give all his time to his parishioners. He would share their joys, sorrows and worries, the latter involving anxieties about birth control, and other practices or even beliefs. He would soon be in trouble again with his bishop. He also knew that his preaching at Mass would have to be his own convictions, not Heenan's. It was never going to work. Bert had to act with intellectual honesty, this having been nurtured in the early days of his studies and priesthood, especially at the Biblicum. He was going to be obedient to Pius XII's call to return to scripture exegesis, and to that Pope's blessing on his future work as teacher. He could no longer show similar respect for his bishop, who believed that 'ordinary parishioners' could not understand new thinking, needing to be told what to believe, without question. He was going to ask to take up an earlier suggestion of becoming a convent chaplain, giving him time to write.

Then, out of the blue, Bert was notified by Kings College, London, that he had been offered a bursary for a Senior Research Fellowship. He had no idea, at first, how that had happened. It was a godsend! He had to make a quick decision, but the Cardinal was away. He wrote for him to receive the news on his return to Westminster: 'I have gladly accepted this, and Kings College has gladly accepted me as a Senior Visiting Fellow in New Testament Studies. This will give me the time to do the writing which I feel I owe to many people.' An unhappy Heenan replied, hoping that Bert had made it clear to Kings College that his acceptance had only been provisional. They needed to speak as soon as possible. Bert recorded the conversation at that frosty meeting.

Heenan: You are too old to be a student.

Bert: *I am to be a tutor.*

But that would involve Westminster priests who go there.

I would only accept to tutor non-Catholics.

I cannot be seen to support your unorthodox teaching.

Many wild things are being said – isn't it good to have a moderate and scholarly presentation for confused people?

Butler says that it is your philosophy that is at fault.

All his kind of philosophy is being questioned today.

You will be too old to take a parish in two years.

I confess that it is teaching that I prefer.

Why not go where you *are* appreciated. Canada?

I prefer London.

Who is this burse anyway. Bob Murray SJ?

Adrian Hastings. (Former priest).

Is he working for the good of the diocese?

For the church.

I doubt it.

Don't you see that three out of four CCC staff laicised?

That is unfair. Without pressure they would have stayed. (Another attempt to push me out?)

One thing is clear. Residence in Chepstow is intolerable. An acute embarrassment to M.Keegan.

Asked him?

Don't need to.

The Cardinal would not have understood that Bert had made every effort to be on completely good terms with Fr Keegan and Fr Lavery at the new CCC. The latter had spent that last summer term at the college, on Bert's invitation, so that there could be an amicable takeover. The chaplain's flat was not even part of the college buildings, and the Cardinal had not provided any accommodation for Bert. More letters, and another meeting followed, with Heenan insisting that: 'You quite clearly no longer believe in Trinity, Divinity of Christ, the Virgin Birth.' Bert replied: 'Nor do thousands of others *in those terms*. You accuse me of unorthodoxy on Divinity. I accuse you of unorthodoxy on Humanity of Jesus.' Bert described one New Zealand complaint about his 'disbelief in the Divinity of Christ' – 'because I did not bow my head at the name of Jesus!' The Cardinal said it was his pastoral duty to prevent Bert lecturing on views that were 'incompatible with Catholic Doctrine', but to suspend him was unthinkable. Why was this? Bert presumed that Heenan did not want to get any blame, preferring him to be another Davis and De Rosa. The Cardinal told Bert that he wished him to be examined for his views by theologians, Bishop Butler and Bishop Clark, saying 'but even if objectively you are guilty of heresy, you would never admit it. Charles Davis was more logical to leave.' Heenan *was* thinking in terms of 'heresy', as he added: 'John Robinson is your hero, and his christology is *certainly* heretical.'

Bert wanted to know why he was suggesting then, for him to go abroad to teach 'heretical' theology in another bishop's diocese? He also asked how he could explain that all his audiences clamour for more of the newer teaching? Heenan's reply was that it was for an 'easier Christianity without any mysteries. Mysteries are not meant to be understood.' The examination by the bishops caused another unsolved argument. Bert suggested that it would be fairer if a theologian, like Nicholas Lash who accepted 'theological pluralism', could also join the meeting. Why should he be examined by Butler, who already believed his philosophy was at fault, and Clark who had always criticised Bert, even from student days in Rome? The Cardinal refused. Bert wrote immediately to Heenan with another suggestion.

> You say that diocesan bishops only have the right to pass judgement on orthodoxy of what is being taught in their diocese, and with this I partly agree. But I feel the issue here is a wider one – the truth has a better chance of being served in an atmosphere of academic freedom rather than of heresy hunting. Nor strictly speaking am I asking for permission to teach in the diocese, except to groups who specifically invite me to do so. If it is a question of my right to speak at all as a theologian, then perhaps the matter could be better dealt with by the National Theological Commission, where at least all theological views are represented.

Heenan's reply was immediate.

> Your letter came as a great surprise. I had already told the

bishops of the arrangement we had made. I explained to
them that you were no longer willing to obey me, and that
against my will you have accepted a place in London
University. I told them that I do not intend to suspend you
because I would not like to deprive you of Mass nor do I
want to make you a martyr. Since you are not willing to be
questioned on your theology I cannot allow you to preach or
teach to Catholic students or teachers in this diocese nor
must you act as tutor to any of our seminarians at London
University.

The Cardinal enclosed a bitter poem that had been sent to him,
'To your FRIEND Fr (?) Richards' by Athanatius Gee:

'Why abuse the God who made you?
You – who are a priest – in name?
Why de-mote the God who gave you
That, which brought you worldly fame?
In this weary world now seething
With unrest and disbelief,
By your early morning broadcasts,
You did bring much pain and grief.

Into every home you trespassed,
Aye, e'en in some, 'a light to shine'!
Surely, from a priest, so sacred,
Words would come – inspired – divine!
Judas sold the God Who loved him,
And, in History's name will be
Doomed, demeaned, despised for ever!
Lost-for all Eternity!

So today, and through Mass Media
You denied Him blatantly!
Using all your priestly knowledge,
To reduce Him flagrantly!
In very truth, the 'Smoke of Satan'
Hovers in the air you breathe!
When you use your priestly function,
Not to teach – but to deceive!

The Cardinal wrote alongside the 6-verse poem, 'This came in the same post as yours today. I have never had the honour of being the subject of a poem!' Sending the poem to Bert was unkind. This is the last correspondence Bert had with Heenan until he offered his resignation eighteen months later. Bert moved from Bayswater, gratefully accepting the hospitality of the Grail in Pinner. He finished the year with conferences in Llandudno, with the Sacred Heart Fathers in Clapham Park, and with a study weekend at Park Place, on the 'Miracles of Jesus'. His first of the *What Really Happened?* series, *The First Christmas*, was published in November. Bert received a warm letter from John Robinson praising the book as: 'A little *tour de force* – a brilliant way of opening up the real religious and theological dimension of the thing.' Robinson had been dining with Fr Bob Murray at Heythrop, who passed on Bert's address: 'I did not know whether you were in Jerusalem or Siberia!'

At the end of each year Bert listed the books he had read, month by month. For 1973 there were 90 books, 51 of which were theological or biblical studies. Most of these were by respected and accepted authors of the day, including Rahner, Benoit, Robinson, Wansbrough, Pannenburg, and Raymond Brown. The latter, an eminent Catholic American theologian, never in trouble with the authorities, could write openly of biblical literary form that got Bert into constant trouble. Bishop Butler had commented in a letter to him: 'I confess that it was a bit of a shock to me recently to read Raymond Brown's long paper in *Theological Studies*, leaving the virginal conception an open question. I mention this, because compared with the Cardinal (and the generality of his flock) I am really a quite enlightened person, though you might doubt it!'

Bert also read much Waugh, Wodehouse, Hitchcock and T. S. Eliot that year. A great lover of film, he went to 28 of them, including *James Bond, Godspell, Jesus Christ Superstar*, and *Rublev*. He would usually go with his sister, Margaret, with priests or other friends. It was me he took to see the Rublev film, knowing my interest in iconography, and my love of all things Russian Orthodox.

During 1974 I was to see much more of Bert as circumstances brought us together. The year began for him with a relaxed skiing trip in Mürren, with Fr Leo Pyle, until he settled back into King's College for his tutorials, seminars, frequent faculty meetings and college functions. He had rather few external lectures and short courses early in the year, and he could at last get down to more writing. He still kept up his regular talks with the Sion Sisters, and my community in Finchley, and our new one in Holloway. Then came the first 'disturbing gefuffle over Ralph Brown'.

Bert had been asked by a priest friend to make enquiries for him about a dispensation in order to marry. He wanted it to be given quickly. He was a member of a religious order, and wanted to go directly to Rome, not through his superior. Bert enquired through a contact in Rome, and the dispensation came through. In February he received a very distressed letter from Sr Maura, the Sion nun from CCC days, who was now living in Rome. 'Brace yourself to read this. I had a phone call from Margaret in Sidic who had just been told by Michael Brockie that you were married!!! He had been told so by Bishop Brown! Forgive my language, but who the hell is this Bishop Brown?' Bert was aghast. Brown was not a bishop, but Monsignor Ralph Brown of Westminster, who later apologised to Bert, phoning him to express 'gratitude that I took the hullabaloo so cheerfully'. Bert was not cheerful when he had many more upset friends writing to express concern, not that he had 'married', but that he had not told them in advance. He wrote a sharp letter to Ralph Brown about rumours: 'This one is unlike the common and garden ones, being backed up apparently by an authoritative source.' The Cardinal made no comment.

During the year Bert had many visits to and from his family and former CCC students and staff. He enjoyed his annual Holy Land Easter Pilgrimage with many of these friends, returning to London and a serious reflection on his future. He wrote down his thoughts:

What do I really want out of life? Never mind the expectations of others.
Viz. What do I have going for me at the moment which I would be loth to lose?
? Peace first of all (Margaret says!) less involvement?

? Companionship to counter loneliness (But am I usually lonely?)

Opportunity to teach, orally or by writing.

? Helping people.

? Leadership of some kind (a name, respect, love, gratitude).

? To influence the coming society (church or otherwise).

? Sufficient freedom from pressures to be 'myself'.

To know one is (roughly) on the right lines.

A certain degree of comfort, ease, time, leisure, uncramped.

The disposal of my own time.

Opportunity for doing something creative.

? Community living?

? A circle of easily accessible friends

To what extent are these threatened by present? Future?

This is perhaps the first indication in the diaries that Bert was thinking about his priesthood. The note is not dated, but it is stuck into his typed diary next to the Ammerdown leaflet of the 5-day course he led on 'Growing in Faith'. It was, as usual, highly appreciated by those attending, but an unfortunate article in the *Catholic Herald* resulted in more trouble, and was perhaps the cause for his serious thought. Dr Celia Wokey, an Anglican, writing under the name 'Kay Moss', described the week as a 'unique spiritual experience. No theologian ever spoke like this one. For once I was hearing not abstractions, but truths which applied to everyday life.' Her long article led to letters showing 'horror' and 'alarm' at what was 'being taught'. The Bishop of Clifton (Ammerdown was in his diocese) wrote to Bert of his concern, '... although your reply in the *Catholic Herald* is reasonable'. Bert had written: '... She may not realise that she does me little service in quoting only the more startling things she heard (or thought she heard) me say. Nor do you, Sir, show much judgement in accepting an article consisting largely of statements attributed to me which, taken out of context, can only appear as provocative ... Miss Moss made a clear distinction between the views she thought I held and even more startling views (on Eucharist, divorce, confession, authority and celibacy), which she attributes to members of the audience.' The bishop later wrote again to Bert thanking him for his clear and reassuring explanation of the 'unfortunate report'. There was no reaction from the Cardinal.

The summer of 1974 was a busy one. In May and June he did weekend supply work in the Pinner parish, and over the next two months gave summer schools at Belmont, Spode, Bellinter in Ireland and Ammerdown again. In the autumn he was in Malpas with Liverpool teachers, with Sr Ruth's sisters at Clapham Park, and with his final course at Park Place, with Spud Murphy O'Connor. Bert had meetings with the Council of Christians and Jews; talks with several publishers; broadcasts with ATV in Birmingham, and took part in two very successful ecumenical events. He followed this up with an article in *The Month*, edited by John Harriot SJ. Fr Harriot wrote to Bert: 'I need to write personally, and not just as editor, to say how deeply moved I was by your article on ecumenism. I thought it was quite the finest and most penetrating reflection on the subject that I have read in years and am genuinely proud that *The Month* will be carrying it. It drives straight to the heart of the matter and its honesty is so refreshing on a subject which seems to attract tergivesations and hedging bets. I do congratulate you.'

It is terribly sad that (with a few exceptions) the hierarchy, led by Cardinal Heenan, never found anything to praise in Bert during his lifetime. He gave everything he could to the life of the church as a priest who had been educated at the Gregorian University and the Pontifical Biblical Institute, with the intention he should teach the Word of God. So many others, priests, religious and laity, recognised that he also lived the gospel even as he preached it, and all loved him for it.

I find that many of Bert's friends want to know more about me. I have been asked: 'Did you fall in love together at Corpus Christi?' 'Did you leave your convent to marry Bert?' 'Did he leave the priesthood to marry you?' The simple answer to all three questions is 'No.' To come to the decisions we did was not easy. We both had months of anguish and soul searching, first quite separately, on our vocations to priesthood and religious life, and then on our decision later to marry. We wondered just how much we had influenced the other, without meaning to, and especially at this time. Since the ending of the Corpus

Christi era, I was in touch regularly with Bert through the welcome my community gave him. He met up with many past
students, but I was the one who lived in London, and how lucky
I felt.

When Bert was the seventeen-year-old sixth-former at
Finchley Boys' Grammar School, I was a young toddler living
only 200 yards down the road! I grew up to know Canon
Parsons, his headmaster, and Fr (Doc) Ward, his Latin and
Greek teacher. Sometimes we would go with Mum to Mass at
the school chapel – when we were running late for the parish
Mass. I knew Fr Ward's dad, who lived in our road, and would
stop and talk at the gate when he caught me practising netball
shots through the ring Dad had put up over the garage door.
This was when I was in the netball team at St Michael's
(Finchley) Girl's Catholic School. While reading these diaries
with extra attention, I have discovered many things that Bert
and I had in common, although we had quite different tempera-
ments. I never had his academic brilliance, but did well enough
to love school, become Head Girl and later achieve, at Endsleigh
Catholic Teacher Training College, the 'Double Distinction'
(Theory and Practice) – a very minor *Summa Cum Laude*! I did
well in my education simply because, like Bert, I was into everything going, determined to enjoy work, leisure and sport. I was
busy all the time at College, especially when I was elected onto
the 'Student Council'. Bert and I liked to be at the heart of things.
One small coincidence makes me smile. Bert was favoured by
his lecturer, Fr Robert Dyson, known as 'Old Bob'. I was
favoured by a lecturer, Sr Mary Robert, known as 'Black Bob'.
She took me aside before final exams to give me tips on 'putting
that little extra into your essays, as "You are on course to get the
Double Distinction".'

Just like Bert, I had a loving and totally supportive family
who gave us everything they could, in spite of little money, for a
stable, happy, confident life. It was only different in that my
Dad was not a Catholic, and I was one of three, an older sister
and a younger brother. I was influenced by Sister Teresa. She
was a fine geography teacher, but her religious education
lessons were distinctly pre-Vatican II theology. She told us that
to be a 'fully committed Catholic' we should consider the religious

life, in order to follow the gospel completely. I was quick to take note. Her 'Congregation of the Poor Child Jesus' was founded by Clare Fey in Aachen, Germany, during the Industrial Revolution in 1844, to care for vulnerable children, orphaned or abandoned, in children's homes, and 'poor schools'. The work was funded by fee-paying schools for the rich, usually one in each country where the sisters worked. In the past our school funded the childrens' homes in England. As a fourteen-year-old I was immediately attracted to join the convent with these sisters. It was to mean that I would eventually learn to speak German.

I went to college first to please my Dad; we enjoyed sport together, especially football. I trained as a PE teacher, with geography as a minor subject, in order to have a final sporting fling. I also thought it would ensure that in the convent I could not teach with such a qualification. I had one year teaching PE in St Thomas More's Secondary Modern School, Tottenham, before I entered the convent in 1959. My Provincial Superior understood that I wanted to work in the children's homes. It never happened. Within months of making my final profession, the Vatican Council issued a document on Religious Life, and Congregations began to review their work. We asked whether Clare Fey's work for vulnerable children in care homes was still appropriate in the 1960s. We (belatedly) realised it was better that our children should be adopted or fostered into loving families.

Before long I was teaching the younger children in my old school in Finchley. I did enjoy it, but I was uncomfortable, teaching privileged scholarship girls, without a degree you would expect of a Grammar School teacher. One special joy was the opportunity to go to the Leicester Square lectures with others of my community. Bert, more than any of the other lecturers, impressed me. I had a new, exciting introduction to the scriptures. Faith became more real, more demanding, not less. It was very comfortable being a nun, especially as I was near my family,teaching at an excellent girl's Grammar School, with everything being done for me by others in the community – cooking, laundry, and managing the finances. I thought of Mum, working hard as a secretary just down the road, fitting in the shopping, the cooking, the washing – and worrying about how they would pay off the mortgage, and whether they could afford a holiday. The vow of poverty always baffled me. I wrote to my Superior General abroad, and asked if I could go to our sisters in South America. There I would be able to work with the poor and feel some deprivation, in order to make sense of the vow. The answer was negative, as my superiors had decided to have no more European nuns in such a Catholic country. Instead I raised money with my pupils to send parcels for the children in Colombia and Java. Unhappily, that eventually fell through, as both countries had trouble at the docks and airports, with goods stolen and not reaching the convents.

I was grateful when Sister Clare Dominic, my Provincial Superior, suggested that I should go to Corpus Christi College to be better qualified to specialise in religious teaching back at St Michael's. She would love to have gone herself, and even though I could have travelled to Notting Hill each day, she insisted that I should live in at the college, and also book in for the Easter Holy Land Pilgrimage. It was a life-changing, wonderful year. I have forgotten many of the details of earlier and later years, but the Corpus Christi experience of living in a totally committed Christian community is quite different. I can recall all of it – its richness day by day: the lectures, the seminars, the social life, the joyfulness, the excitement for the future, the warmth and love within the community, the deep respect for one another, whatever our views. Some experiences were outstanding, and my life changed because of them. Holy Week and Easter in the Holy Land is almost indescribable, as it had a profound affect on me. Bert was not a tour guide; he seemed to lead us in prayerful meditation around the life of Christ. Bethlehem, Nazareth, the Mount of Beatitudes, the Sea of Galilee, Jerusalem and Emmaus. Evenings were happy social gatherings, usually with Bert leading us in song with the guitar, and often drawing in other pilgrims. There were hours of free time, and my favourite place to visit was the Holy Sepulchre Church.

In college we had a 'long essay' to prepare, on a topic of our own choice. I loved art and was fascinated to look at the death of Jesus through the eyes of artists over the centuries, and I researched this for my essay. The Calvary Chapel in the Holy Sepulchre Church seemed the place for me to spend some time. I even got locked in there early one morning as I attended a Mass and found the Latin Patriarch celebrating. He was not to be disturbed by visitors. Later I had a wonderful time at the Victoria & Albert Museum, and art galleries in London, looking for examples to illustrate my reflections on the theology of the Cross. Bert was very interested in my topic, and he would often give me a postcard, or picture of another cross he discovered. Jerusalem had introduced me to the Eastern Rite, and to iconography. My essay got longer and longer as I compared the different 'theologies', looking through the eyes of artists and icon painters. The Russian Archbishop Anthony Bloom was a visiting lecturer at the college, and his church at Ennismore Gardens was near enough for me to visit, at first to learn more about the icons. But it was the liturgy that attracted me; the dignity, the singing, the stillness that drew you into quiet meditation. It was a surprising discovery and I began to go every Sunday morning, after our own Mass, to join the Orthodox congregation. Bert put my dinner in the oven when I was late back. I didn't know then that he too was attracted to the Russian Liturgy.

My other outstanding memory of Corpus Christi was the opportunity we had to take part in unusual activities outside the college. Some of us joined with the St Mungo's Community to go out on night runs delivering soup to the homeless. During my year in London, Mother Teresa was setting up a house in Notting Hill. Two of us went to help the sisters, and found ourselves very involved. We made curtains, cleaned the house, and went out begging for the sisters. I found this hard, asking shops for food, and when Mother Teresa was expected to arrive, to ask in a second-hand shop for a free coat for her to wear over her habit. My Finchley community lent me the car to drive to Heathrow to collect her. All the way back to Notting Hill she said the rosary, 'for our safe arrival', making me nervous. On our night soup runs we were able to persuade a few women to go to Mother Teresa's house for shelter. It was a strange experience as the sisters, putting prayer first, would answer the bell for the Office or Rosary immediately, dropping everything and occasionally leaving a distressed woman to be helped later. I had breakfast one morning with Mother Teresa, and was surprised that she talked only of her sisters, and her need to found many more convents 'to bring Jesus into places without him'. She had come to London from Ireland, saying that she did not feel welcomed there. I asked about her work with the poor, but she never answered me, nor asked about my sisters. I could not make her out. Her sisters seemed more important than the poor. My foundress was different. Mother Clare invited us to 'Walk in God's Presence', so our work with poor children was to be with them, seeing Christ in them. It meant that some sisters could not always attend community prayers because the needs of the children always came first.

It was devastating for our year to be present to hear the Cardinal criticise what had been so important to us – an experience that increased our faith, our love of Christ, and gave us a renewed enthusiasm for service in the church. How could he want a different sort of college, one that returned to the old ways of instruction? It did not surprise us that the new 'Corpus Christi' only lasted two years, when it failed to attract students. I returned to our Grammar School in Finchley and for a short time taught religious education.

Early in 1973 a small group of us moved to Holloway, to work in the local parish. I was happy when it was agreed that I would work part-time in Holloway Prison, to assist the chaplain, Fr David Evans. I loved my work there. I could visit prisoners in their cells, where Fr David couldn't; and listening to their troubles, their fears, their tragic experiences, and the problems they would face on release, was an eye-opener to the struggles that vulnerable people face. There were few 'criminals' in this women's prison – the vast majority were victims of brutality, extreme poverty, social deprivation and low self esteem. Dr Bull, the governor, understood the prisoners and was helpful whenever I asked her advice. One woman, bullied by her husband who drank away the housekeeping money and demanded the children's allowance, was forced to steal small items from the shops. She did not know where her children were. I asked if I may find out for her, and Dr Bull agreed, telling me that she trusted me to make decisions for myself, without asking her. Better that way, she said.

I was astonished when some of my sisters complained to our General Superior that I was not doing the work of the

Congregation, as we were founded to help children in need.
There were sixteen-year-old girls in Holloway, and I spent much
time with them. There was no room for them in more appropriate institutions as they had severe problems. Our Superior
General came over from Holland to see for herself what I was
doing. She was quite moved by what she saw, not least when
one of the women, quite by chance, asked if I had a rosary for
her. She immediately gave the girl her own. I did not tell her that
it would perhaps be confiscated. On Sunday mornings I was at
the prison to unlock Myra Hindley from her cell (she was always in solitary confinement), to take her to the chapel for Mass,
where she was often greeted with boos and hisses. I met so
many good people there, especially Father David, who was appreciated by all the prisoners because he dressed smartly, and
wore a pleasant after-shave. The women were always made to
feel that he respected them, both by his warm manner and his
appearance. One said to me: 'He dresses up so posh to come and
see us; it makes you feel he cares.' There was a motherly warder
in the baby unit, who would sit and talk with the new mothers,
teaching them to love their babies and respect themselves. They
loved her. Many of the prisoners were kind to one another, pro-
tecting the most vulnerable; unselfish women who were victims
of circumstance.

I continued to work in the prison, but was uneasy about the
reservations my sisters had. At this same time, an appeal went
out from the Westminster Diocese for a nun to work part-time in
the Catholic Information (Media) Office. As I was used to writing up reports and enjoyed designing information sheets for cir-
culation, it was suggested that I should apply for the post, giving up my part-time teaching. By sheer chance the Office was in
Pinner, very close to Bert's cottage at the Grail. Every week I
would call on him to collect notes for his forthcoming talks to
our community, in order to make copies for everyone. Over a
cup of coffee we talked about everything. Work in the Media
Office was interesting but it soon became another anxious situation, when Monsignor George Leonard, my boss, began to
make critical remarks about Corpus Christi, and about Bert. Our
reports were often about the consequences of Vatican II, and
clearly I was open and enthusiastic about change; I quickly

learned that I was in a firing line. On reflection later, it was obvious that Monsignor Leonard would have to be loyal to Cardinal Heenan's line of thinking. I began to have a hard time defending Corpus Christi. I had to attend the priests' conferences as a reporter, and travelling with several diocesan information officers, I listened to both praise of, and bitter criticism of Bert and his theology. I wonder if it was this that made me feel so much closer to Bert; I wanted to defend him but remained silent – as I had to be neutral in reports.

I was invited to have lunch with Monsignor Leonard and the editor of the *Universe*, Terence Wynn, at the London Press Club. I was delighted to go with them, until I realised that I had been set up to give Terence Wynn subject matter to write about. After small talk, Mgr Leonard asked my views on the resurrection accounts in the gospels, pressing me to agree that it was a 'bodily' resurrection. Remembering Bert's accusation about that very wording by Bishop Holland, I was thrown. I did not have Bishop Butler to give me the words of defence. I replied that bodily, or not, made no difference to me. 'Does it matter?' I asked, 'what is important to me is to believe in Christ's resurrection as it is in my life today. He lives on in me, if I live a life of love, forgiveness and compassion, as he did.' The words 'Does it matter?' were to be quoted against me twice in the press by Terence Wynn, once as late as 1996. Following that lunch I began to share my frustrations with Bert, and to seek his advice. Within months I was in trouble again with some of my community, this time with a superior leading the doubts about me. The 'World Council of Churches' was holding a meeting in Jakarta, Indonesia, and Catholics were to be invited. We had sisters in Jakarta, and it was suggested at the Media Office that it would be really helpful if I could go out there, stay with my community, and act as a guide to English Catholic journalists, perhaps as a car driver for them; my sisters could help us too. At first the idea was accepted, until a community meeting was called, and I was firmly put in my place for 'always wanting to be different', not content to be like the rest. As the main criticism came from a superior I was totally disheartened, and felt 'out of place' in my religious life. As it happened the Jakarta WCC meeting never took place because of strained relations between the Christians and Muslims.

I notice in the diaries that Bert went to 'have a long talk with Sr Clare Dominic', my superior, at this time. I had shared with him my worries about religious life, so perhaps he talked with her about this. Perhaps not, as months later she left the convent herself. I was devastated. She was our Provincial Superior whom I admired, and had been my headmistress when I was a pupil at St Michael's. She had supported everything I did, and encouraged me to be myself. Bert, the most 'correct person' I have ever known, never spoke to me about that meeting. We both kept contact with her and would visit her together in Oxford. In the autumn of 1974, with the listening ear of Bert, and long talks with Archbishop Anthony Bloom, I made the decision to leave religious life myself. I found it very hard, but my Holloway community were kind and supportive, and Sr Ursula advised me to stay on until I found a job. I was surprised that I was soon accepted at a London school for 'maladjusted children', and felt quite at home with my small group of teenage boys, all excluded from their former schools. I taught them the basics of literacy and numeracy through the sports pages of the *Sun* and the *Mirror* – a forerunner of today's study centre at Norwich City and other clubs! My love of football was a godsend.

I missed my work in the prison most of all, but never had any doubts that I had made a mistake in leaving religious life. Archbishop Anthony had impressed on me the importance of living just one day at a time in God's presence, 'and he does have a way of leading us where we never thought we might go'. How true that was.

CHAPTER FOURTEEN

An End and a Beginning
1975-1978

Bert called summer 1975 'Operation sinking ship'. The year began with doubts about his future in the priesthood, which he shared with me. When he jotted down his thoughts on what he really wanted out of life a year earlier, one was 'A circle of easily accessible friends?' By the time I had left religious life, towards the end of 1974, we had certainly become close friends. Earlier in the year, with so many similar interests, we had gone together to icon exhibitions at the Temple Gallery, to exhibitions at the National Gallery, and to the Russian Church. I was introduced to Gilbert & Sullivan with a performance of *HMS Pinafore*. This was at the time I was working in Pinner and sharing my worries with him. In retrospect I realise that Bert was lonely and needed company with special friends, and I was one of them.

After a January skiing holiday, Bert was back at King's College and into the busy schedule of life there, with the extra meetings and lectures for nuns, for the Jewish Community, and other groups. He chaired the Cardinal Bea Lectures, and was broadcasting with the BBC and ITV. There was little time to get down to writing. A large group, including many friends, booked in for the Easter Holy Land pilgrimage. I was able to join it too. It was such a joy to see Bert back in the places he loved and with the warm greetings of his Arab friends, especially Hani, our coach driver, and Mohammed the 'camel man'. Bert took me to have meals with them. Being in the 'cave' chapel at Bethlehem, celebrating Mass outdoors overlooking the Sea of Galilee, and being in the Holy Sepulchre Church was, strangely, like being back home at last. I doubt if it would have felt like that if Bert was not the leader of our group. I perhaps, unconsciously, realised then that I was completely 'at home' with him.

The diary records that at this time Bert was sharing his thoughts of resigning from the priesthood with Spud, and a little later with Sr Maura and Archbishop Anthony Bloom. (I discovered from his diary that earlier he had considered going to

South America as I had.) We had talked about his thoughts on resignation, but I was earnestly encouraging him to stay a priest for the sake of all of us who needed him. But now I could understand his frustration at the pressure the Cardinal, bishops, and the insensitive press were putting upon him. It was clear that he had little hope of a future teaching ministry in the English Catholic Church. The last straw was the knowledge that he was not even allowed to preach at Masses he celebrated with teachers and students. Bert applied for a teaching post at an Anglican Training College in Norwich. Keswick Hall was looking for a 'New Testament' lecturer for their teachers in training, not for a specialist in teaching the 'catechism'. Things moved quickly once Bert was accepted for the post in Norwich, and in early June he wrote his Press Statement about resigning from the priesthood.

> I am announcing my resignation from the Roman Catholic priesthood because it has been made progressively clearer to me over the past three years that as a priest I am not free to teach theology in any Roman Catholic establishment in this country.
>
> During my twenty-nine years in the priesthood, I have tried sincerely to follow what I regard as my vocation – to make the results of theological scholarship available to teachers and students, by lecturing and writing, in as moderate and constructive a way as possible. I regret that this is no longer acceptable to my superiors.
>
> I have been very happy in the priesthood, which has given me countless opportunities for helping people, and in so doing of receiving help myself. It is my loss that the present choice has been, as I see it, forced on me. I intend to remain a Catholic, and I am confident that my future work in a non-Catholic College of Education will offer me opportunities at present denied me in my own church.

Bert wrote a covering letter, *Strictly Private and Confidential. Not for Publication*, to nearly 500 family, friends, and past students, along with the Press Statement. 'I am writing this because, out of my love for you, I feel I owe you a fuller explanation than may appear in the press.' Bert explained more fully the pressures and restrictions put on him by the Cardinal and bishops. He was sparing Heenan from that publicity. He concluded his letter: 'I do not want you to think that this marks the end of my work for the church. The Body of Christ is not as restricted as some people would like to think. It exists in wider areas too. I hope to minister to the *Corpus Christi* there as wholeheartedly as I have done until now in a more restricted circle. I am only "resigning my priesthood" in inverted commas. I regard my future ministry of the Word of God as "priestly". My hope remains that all of us who share in the body and blood of Christ will be brought together in unity by the Holy Spirit.'

The Press Release was on 9 June. Bert met the Cardinal at 11.00 am. The Statement was embargoed until Midday. Heenan expressed surprise at the announcement: 'The last thing I expected, yet quite logical.' He noted that the Cardinal was grateful that 'both of us' had done this without rancour. He was 'Fatherly, gentle, calm, sympathetic. Showed no distress or anger.' He read the Press Statement 'and admired its moderation & gentleness, and was glad I was not going to stress publicity.' When asked if he was going to get married, Bert replied 'possibly'. On leaving Archbishop's House, the Vicar General asked Bert could he not have waited, 'until the old man dies'.

There follows in the diary pages of press articles. The headlines describe him as a, 'Controversial priest, Heenan clash priest, Leading Catholic theologian.' One of the first to write to Bert was Canon Parsons who had encouraged him for the priesthood, and arranged for him to go to Rome. He was deeply sad, but gracious in his disappointment, describing his former pupil as one 'who outstripped me in academic learning'. He assured Bert of his friendship and would pray for him daily at Mass. He signed himself, 'With my esteem and every blessing, affectionately ...' Bert received over 400 more letters, all except seven of them were as understanding as Canon Parsons. Bert did not keep them, which was a pity because they were such a testimony to the good he had done for the church. He did, however, write out a few sentences from some of them, which clearly gave him comfort. They so clearly express what he meant to those who sat at his feet, and enjoyed his friendship. A few need recording here.

For me you are living your priesthood when you reach out as you do towards the mystery of God, and by preaching and teaching allow others to follow. *Mrs M. M. Watford*

You have chosen the way in which you can serve most people – as I should have expected. It has been a joy and inspiration, in the midst of sorrow, to see you so truly living out what you taught us at CCC. *S. R.*

There are lots of ways you could have compromised. I admire you for not doing this. *M.McD OLS*

The cross is said to be a mark of divine approval, but I trust the good Lord will find more kindly ways to bless your future work. *A.B.*

Wherever your path leads, the love of those you have related to in Christ, will be with you. You are very much loved. *M.I.*

I feel an impotent rage that yet again the body of the church is suffering the loss of a major academic talent and a prophetic voice, a loss that is self-inflicted. *J.McN*

I weep for you and for us – and for our poor church. It was not the authority of the priesthood that made your teaching valid for me, but your obvious deep commitment as a fellow human being. *M.E.*

You are the person I most admired in the archdiocese. I hope you won't feel in any way ill at ease with your former colleagues; there are so many of us who respect you for your personhood that changing from the priesthood is not all that concial ... You seem to collect crosses the way other people collect stamps. *Fr K.M.*

I really hate the church's cruelty, its talent for creating manmade suffering ... If you should marry, I for one, should dance at your wedding. *B.C.*

I feel a deep sense of personal loss at your news. More than anyone else in my life, you have been the greatest single influence in opening up new visions and new ways of looking at Christ. *B.J.*

Not one bit of your 29 years of the priesthood now loses any of its value. One can say without exaggerating, that all the lights you lit during that time are spread far across the world. *S.H.*

I don't see this as a tragedy for you, but as a conviction

carried out in faith. And if you ever chose to marry I shall say 'God bless him', and thank him again for having given me the privilege of sharing in the richness of your life. *Sr.A.P.*

I am trying to put aside anger and frustration, and to look into a future where the Holy Spirit will be using you to bring a divided world into a fuller unity. *Sr. M.K.R.*

In these dark moments I find myself repeating St Augustine's dictum, 'God has many the church does not have; the church has many God does not have.' Though the pain you suffer is great, it is shared and, I hope, diminished by that one pearl of great price – the love of friends. You have more than any priest I know. *Fr Hugh Lavery*

As an Anglican I can only imagine the position you find yourself in with your hierarchy ... You were more help to me, dealing with a handful of essays, than the rest of King's College staff put together ... You helped me to find an approach to theology which treated the gospel as something living, and not dependent on clichés or outmoded language. *L.T. student at KCL*

Your vision and careful scholarship, I feel certain, will be the future church's pride. *D.P. Canada*

Maybe it is you who have the courage and the rest of us who have not. *Fr.T.McG*

Many are very grateful for the stand you have taken. Our hierarchy must feel very uncomfortable. *Sr.A.D.*

Your serenity and non-critical reaction at the time of the CCC crisis is the greatest lecture you ever gave me. *Sr.M.B.*

I don't like to be identified with a church that can be so cruel – and also so bloody stupid and shortsighted.But if you can stay in the church I suppose I can! *M.H.*

Being the kind of man you are, Bert, you will never cease to be a Christ-bearer. *SR.M O'*

Please keep in close contact. Some of us put blinkers on or hide ourselves away at SEC, and we need help from men like you. *FR.PdM*

These words, and similar, were repeated over and over in almost every letter in his vast post. The handful that disagreed with his decision were from contemplative nuns, and from lay women, two of whom had already criticised Bert in the press. A contemplative nun wrote:

> Your news came as a great shock. I still feel quite stunned. I feel it is not the answer. I cannot see what good can come out of it, least of all to yourself. Sr.B.

The priest who dealt with laicisation was away until July, which delayed Bert's application to the Holy Father for a month. It needed the Cardinal's counter signature, and writing to him Bert asked if the application could be speeded up. He had thought about his decision for many months, and now needed to feel free from 'being betwixt and between'. People were asking if he could still say Mass for them, and it was unsettling. He also felt embarrassed to ask Heenan if there was any financial arrangement in such cases, to help him with immediate expenses for his move. It should have ended there with no more strain between the two men. Bert wanted his parting from Westminster to end peacefully, with each showing respect for the other. It was spoilt when a past student sent the Cardinal a copy of the letter Bert had sent to his family and friends, the one marked *Private and Confidential*. It was not meant for Heenan because Bert knew that it would renew all their differences of opinion. Which it did, with the Cardinal eventually replying to Bert, first assuring him that he would 'ask the Holy See to grant your dispensation with the least possible delay'. He enclosed a personal gift 'from the royalties on my books. There is no rule about these things. If a man has saved no money I give him what he needs until he gets a job.' Bert felt like sending the cheque back. Once again Heenan told him that he no longer believed in the doctrine of the Blessed Trinity, yet in another part of the letter he claimed, 'On one occasion I said that though I regarded you as unorthodox it could be that I was just old-fashioned.' Bert had not heard that; perhaps Heenan just thought it. He absolutely denied ever suggesting, by insinuation, that Bert should leave the priesthood 'like your friends.' He was upset that Bert should think so. 'I thought that you were so deeply devoted to the Mass that you would never give up the right to celebrate.'

It seems to me, reading all the correspondence between the two, that the Cardinal was never able to understand how his con-

stant niggling at everything Bert did in line with Vatican II thinking, and with his biblical approach to expressing doctrine, would
eventually make Bert lose heart. It had begun on the day Heenan
was appointed Archbishop of Westminster, when Bert was acting
President at the seminary, and continued right up to this point.
The tragedy is that both were being true to what they believed.

A clash between the Cardinal and Bert was inevitable, given
Heenan's mindset. He joined the seminary in 1924 when theological manuals were in the mould of Trent, affirming the need
of a teaching church while denigrating the role of scripture. It is
likely he studied manuals like J. P. Herve's four volumes of
Dogmatic Theology (each 500 pages) that, for example, reduced
the resurrection to a scholion at the foot of one page. Heenan's
presence at the Vatican Council, where the Pontifical Biblical
Institute came under such fire from the Holy Office, would have
undermined his confidence in Bert. The insight that Bert explored all his life is well described by Gregory Baum who wrote
of the 'Believing Community', who finding themselves in new
situations 're-read the scriptures addressing that situation, and
so hears what its ancestors did not hear'. Cardinal Heenen
would never have accepted this, and perhaps, as a busy parish
priest in 1943, never even read *Divino Afflante Spiritu*.

The Cardinal could only see things from his position of
power and unbending church law; Bert could only act from his
understanding of the humanity of Christ, and the implication of
this for the Christian community. I see the differences poignant-
ly expressed in the last paragraph of the letter. Bert's sister,
Bertha, died on 30 June, and her funeral Mass was on 2 July. Bert
only wrote for laicisation to Rome on 6 July, having simply announced that he was resigning in June. The Cardinal wrote of
'my deep sympathy on the loss of your sister. It must have been
hard for you and the family that you were unable to offer the requiem. I shall say Mass for the repose of her soul.' But Bert was
still a priest, and this was a private family Mass, away from
London. Could he not have been the celebrant? Bert perhaps
thought so, as he underlined the words, 'you were unable'.

Bert had been very upset, on the day Bertha died, by a meeting requested by a close friend of the Cardinal. 'This evening,
confusion and anger over a four-hour session with her.' She told

Bert everything that Heenan had said to her over his resignation. 'What appalled me was the evidence of rumour-monger-
ing and scandal-mongering on a scale I had rarely imagined,
and the ease with which the most sacred confidences are broken
right and left, no doubt with the thought it is all *Ad Majorem Dei
Gloriam*.' What strikes me as quite bizarre was the report that the
Cardinal believed Bert was in the 'class of Teilhard, de Lubac
and others who had been silenced, but who were proved right
eventually'. That meant, even as he was silencing him, Heenan
believed Bert would one day 'be proved right'. No wonder Bert
was so upset. His reply to the letter on 9 July was the last time
they corresponded. Referring to the Cardinal's reference to
rumours that he was going to marry, 'I thought it would be kind
to let you know what is being said.' Bert wrote: 'I had already
heard about the rumpus over my future. If people wish to gos-
sip in this unChristian way I don't want to add fuel to the fire by
issuing further statements or denials. I resigned from priesthood solely on the grounds which I presented to you, the press
and to my friends. What I may or may not do in the future is
surely my private concern.'

This was a sad ending to his 29 years of priesthood, sad for
him and the church; sad for his family and so many friends. It
was family and friends who enabled Bert to look towards a
happy future, predicting that it was not really the end of a
'priestly' life, but the beginning of a blessed new way of living it.
One former colleague wrote: 'I have been praying for a long
time for you to have the freedom to teach, particularly scripture
... The Catholic Biblical Association is not an association of
priests but of lovers of the Bible, and as the excitement cools
down we shall value your help in the future.' A past Corpus
Christi student wrote: 'There are some people who are a bit bigger than any "institution". You are one of them, and your person and all the wonder of you can't be held back or contained in
anything little.' She could not have put it better. It was the 'person and wonder' of him that I had grown to appreciate and love,
and I was the privileged one who was there to understand and
share his struggles. Little wonder, therefore, that we did grow
even closer at this particular time, and were married at the end
of the year.

Bert was accepted at Keswick Hall College, Norwich, to teach Anglican student teachers: 'I will be teaching NT Introduction to 1st Years, NT Ethics to third years, St Mark and later Modern Theologians to specialist students, and supervising Teaching Practice.' I learnt recently that one of those female students, so impressed by 'a wonderful, inspiring teacher, Bert Richards, who gave me an overwhelming love of Christ in the gospels, which completely changed my life,' is now a priest in Norfolk. The principal at the time, Bill Etherington, told me that agreeing to his appointment – over Anglican applicants – was the best decision he ever made in his educational career.

It was a very busy Summer. In September Bert moved into his rooms at the college, and we could arrange our marriage for the end of the year. Amazingly, I was able to apply, at a late stage, for a job in a Norwich Special School for children with emotional problems. Even more amazing that I was given the post, when the other interviewees had far better qualifications. We bought a house and I moved in there until Bert finished his first term at the college. We arranged the wedding at St John's, our parish church, for 22 December. The exciting preparations were interrupted by anxiety. Bert's laicisation papers should have been ready, so he had been told, in eight weeks. By October we were worried, by November we were very worried. At the beginning of November Bert sent a letter to the Cardinal to enquire about the delay. On the BBC news the next day we heard that he had died. What a shock. Bishop Butler taking over at Archbishop's House, found Bert's original letter of application for laicisation still sitting in the Cardinal's desk drawer. He had never sent it on to Rome. Bishop Butler promised to do his best to rush it through, by proxy. He immediately contacted Rome, where Monsignor Coughlan at the English College passed the application on to Cardinal Seper.

Bert's account of the wedding and honeymoon in Tenerife was written with his usual humour. It was almost like a gita, especially as it was Spud who came to marry us. The account begins:

> The wedding was a mad rush, of the kind of which one afterwards says 'never again', except that in this case that would be ungracious. Bert's term ended two weeks earlier, but then

had to move all his clobber from Keswick Hall, finish an article for Mr Aronsfeld, and get the bedroom painted, attend
endless Christmas parties, and chase the plumber to get the
bathroom hot water flowing – so that in the long run he
wasn't any better off than Clare, whose term ended literally
only two days before the wedding. How we filled in the
spring cleaning of the house, the flower arrangements, the
Christmas decorations, the shopping *et hoc genus omne* is now
irrecoverable. The rescript from Rome, after countless phone
calls to Westminster, St Edmund's, bishop's house in
Northampton, and the local presbytery, finally came
through with only hours to spare.

Mum and Dad arrived on 20 December to take over
household chores while Bert and Clare grew slowly more
dazed. Sunday a flurry of nicking holly off the bushes in
country lanes, delivering the two-tiered cake to the Tatler
restaurant, and avoiding the Mass crowds to decorate the Bl.
Sacrament chapel for the wedding. Dad sat up patiently for
hours making rose buttonholes. Frank and Teresa phoned
from Canada bursting with the news (the mail strike had delayed things) and wanting to talk. Spud arrived late on
Sunday 21st, and we celebrated with gin, wine and brandy,
ate an enormous roast, and sang Italian songs to the guitar.
Spud then announced that he too had just received a Roman
rescript, appointing him a *monsignore*. I translated the Italian
document for him, and he (in good form by now) replied in
Soho English, promising the Pope that he would not wear his
'pooorplel sockes' except when ... etc. He and Bert then retired, still rocking with laughter, to the Heathcote Hotel up
the road to finish off a bottle of whisky, solemnly given us
the day before by kind old mother Pond next door, 'to ward
off the chill Norfolk wind.' I had told my parents about Spud
and Bert's 'get togethers', and we all enjoyed that evening as
much as any part of the wedding weekend.

It was a small wedding party of twenty, as a laicised priest
was required to keep it rather quiet. The diary account describes
the chaotic morning and evening departures, and in between
the calm of the Mass, celebrated by Spud, and the charm of the

log-fired restaurant room and fine meal. Peter De Rosa was best man. 'The Mass put everyone at their ease. Spud spoke beauti-fully *ex corde*, the rose flower arrangement looked exquisite, we sang four full-throated hymns (in spite of the canon's qualms about whether we were even allowed to have a Mass!) and filled the mighty church more convincingly than the usual full Sunday congregation. Spud invited everyone to communion, and we finally processed to the Lady Chapel (our original choice but too cluttered this week with the intestines of an organ hav-ing a hysterectomy) to sing a fine *Salve Regina*.'

Amongst the wedding photos stuck in the diary, Bert put these words of Khalil Gibran. He had chosen them for me to read at the wedding service. It is as though he chooses them for me now:

You, the married, were born together,
and together you shall be for evermore.
You shall be together
When the white wings of death scatter your days.
Aye, you shall be together
Even in the silent memory of God.
But let there be spaces in your togetherness.
And let the winds of heaven dance between you.

Amongst the greetings telegrams, read out at the reception, was one from Bishop Butler sending his 'warmest good wishes and prayers. Christopher Butler'. That meant a great deal to us.

Bert's 1 January 1976 diary entry begins: 'Difficulty of com-ing down to earth after wedding and honeymoon.' It certainly was. What a wonderful wedding and lovely Tenerife honey-moon, full of sunshine and ten-foot-high poinsettias around our hotel on the hillside. Ever since, the Christmas poinsettia plant has a special place by our Christmas crib, to celebrate Jesus and Bert's birthdays. The holiday was a taste of all the travels we were to take over the years. Easter was celebrated in the Holy Land, with a delightful group of pilgrims, and Bert's Arab, Christian and Muslim friends greeting us with great warmth. Hani, our Nazareth bus driver friend, exclaiming: 'Father Richards, you were "father" that way, now you can be a father the other way!' Summer intro-duced me to the families in Canada. Christmas week was in the West Country, celebrating on the way with both families, and meeting up with many of Bert's past students and friends. The holiday finished in London, at Ennismore Gardens, for the Russian Liturgy.

We had already met up with many of those past students, friends and family in March, when we held a Wedding Celebration Party at the Sherlock Holmes Hotel in Baker Street. It was a joyful occasion, well described by my former Superior:

> Saturday was such a wonderfully memorable day, filled as it was with warmth, happiness and laughter and above all with deep human love. I have been to many parties and receptions in my lifetime, but yours was a truly Christian gathering. I have never experienced such love as I felt last Saturday.

1976 set the stage for our future 35 years of wonderfully happy and fulfilled married life. Some people had wondered if Bert had been wise to move into a new way of life at the age of 54, with a none too healthy heart, and the possibility that his books would never be written, or accepted, and that his teaching would be only to those outside the church he loved. They need not have worried. He blossomed with the new challenges and was to write 55 more books, teach in many Christian communities, including some of the Catholic groups that had invited him in the past.

On our first wedding anniversary Bert wrote:

> *First Wedding Anniversary:* Meal at Maxim, Panto at Theatre Royal, Letter from Spud, Present from me, Hospital for miscarriage.

This was the first of several early miscarriages, but our disappointment and sadness was to turn into complete and lasting joy when we eventually adopted our twins, Pedro and Blanca, from Colombia. The journeys there, in 1980 and again in 1989, were the best 'gitas' of our lives.

The main memory of our first three years of married life is of visitors, and more visitors. It seemed that everyone wanted to see how we were, and where we were. Bert settled easily into the college life, with a warm welcome from the Chaplain, Fr Phillip McFadyen who became a life-long friend and colleague.

The religious education department was run by a delightful Welsh priest, Ron Jones, with Brian Turner. The trio became known as the 'Trinity', in an excellent department where all got on well together. I was told recently that Bert quickly established himself as the 'community-maker'. Soon after he arrived he bought a large urn for the Senior Common Room. This lovely room, overlooking the grounds, was hardly ever used, with staff staying in their departments to boil a kettle for their own drinks at the 4.00 pm break. Before long everyone met together for coffee and cakes, resulting in a new spirit among the staff.

Meanwhile I loved my work at the special school, often having to rush home to prepare for all those visitors. One even arrived on the first day of my school term. Some came from abroad, including an Indian priest, once Bert's student, but now taking over as 'in charge'. Bert noted in the diary – with exclamation marks – 'Fr L. announced, "I will now say Mass for you," and later "This is what I will have for breakfast", now we will say night prayers.' We could not believe it when, in the morning, he knocked on our bedroom door, saying 'It is gone 7.00 am!' He asked Bert why he wasn't still saying the Divine Office, before announcing that he had to phone Rome – it was a 20 minute conversation. Bert noted that 'he then scrounged the new book I had just bought and the pair of pyjamas we had lent him, before leaving us saying "Now I will give you my priestly blessing".' We were left dumbstruck having felt like guests in our own home.

We were invited all over the country for happy gatherings, over much wine and good food, with Bert leading the singing with his guitar. We never lost touch with our past, appreciating the great friendships developed over the years, including, for Bert, some of his priest friends from the English College and from St Edmund's College; also Bishop Butler, and Bishop Konstant. He remained in contact with Bishop John Robinson, Rabbi Lionel Blue and Rabbi Hugo Gryn. Bert and I did so much together, yet as Khahil Gibran recommended, we 'let there be spaces in "our" togetherness, and the wind of heaven danced between us.'

Bert did find time to sit at his desk to continue the writing he had promised himself and others. In 1975 he had published *The*

Miracles of Jesus. What Really Happened?, and the third in this series, *The First Easter. What Really Happened?* was published in
1976. Invitations to lecture, lead seminars, give Days of
Recollection, and run workshops grew rapidly. It is surprising
that he found time to write so many books. A list of engagements in 1976 outside of his college work, show how much he
was appreciated by the Norfolk Christian churches (less so the
Catholic Church in Norfolk), and by Catholic groups who already knew him, and by the education authorities:

> Regular seminars at the London Rainbow Group (Xtns &
> Jews)
> The Norfolk Theological Society. (Become Chair, in 1977)
> Summer Renewal Courses at Spode
> CCC Association meetings, with talks by Bert and others
> RE Education conferences in London
> Study days for Anglican clergy
> Preaching at Keswick Hall services
> Preaching at past students weddings
> In-Service Training Days for Norfolk RE teachers
> Study weekends, with Damian Lundy at Kintbury
> Lent lectures in Norwich Cathedral
> Seminars at the Anglican Cathedral Centre on Vatican II
> Seminars at Westminster on Biblical Interpretation
> Norfolk Mothers' Union
> University Chi Rho Society (on Resurrection)
> Preached in Anglican, and United Reform Churches
> 4 Day Session at Ammerdown
> Summer School, Durham (with A. Weston OP & J. Harriott)
> Leading morning prayers in college chapel
> Leading music group at children's Mass
> Broadcasts with BBC & ATV
> Preached at Nottingham University's student Mass

Many of these became annual events, and over the years
other groups and organisations were added to his diary. We set
up a Discussion Group ourselves with a few parish friends. Bert
was able to publish his book *St Paul & His Epistles* in 1979. It is
surprising to recall, on reading the diaries, that we found time to
explore Norfolk, visiting old churches, different pubs, and

much of the coast line. Every year there was the visit to Walsingham, visits to our Norwich Theatre Royal, especially for every Gilbert & Sullivan production. We enjoyed the cinema, not least the James Bonds, and continued to visit art exhibitions and galleries, both local and in London. Between the longer diary entries are little snippets on homely tasks, as we enjoyed these early days of settling in. 'Planted flowers in the front garden, and carrots in the back.' Meanwhile I was able to resume my love of football, with matches at Norwich City FC, and was delighted when the Catholic Prison Chaplain invited me to join him on visits to our Norwich prison. My prison work, in London, had introduced me to Lord Longford, and Bert and I had several visits to the Houses of Lords and Commons, at his invitation. I later became part of the catechetical team in the parish. Our welcome to St John's Church was somewhat muted, as some clearly found it difficult to accept an ex-nun married to an ex-priest, especially one who had made media headlines. It was Sister Monica and Sister Mary Cluderay, Notre Dame sisters, who gave us the warmest welcome. Bert gave many talks and song sessions to the community in the early years.

In March 1976 our parish church was elevated to Cathedral status, when the new Diocese of East Anglia was established. Bert was rather taken back when we heard that Bishop Alan Clark was appointed to the diocese. They had studied together; Bert had taught him to ski; they had appeared in the English College drama productions together; but they were very different people. Bert was the fun-loving, yet serious student who chose to study scripture, while Alan was a serious, rather 'correct' student, who went on to become a Doctor of Divinity, and to be quickly chosen as a church figure of authority. He was Cardinal Heenan's 'theologian' and, as such, critical of Bert's approach to doctrine and his interpretation of scripture. However, we had an easy relationship with him in Norwich, sharing an occasional meal together, when the two of them enjoyed after dinner pipe-smoking over pleasant chat. When Bishop Alan retired, at the parish farewell occasion, Bert presented him with a copy of some of the English College diaries, complete with photographs of the years they studied together.

Sadly, it was during his retirement that there was an unfortunate disagreement between them. Sister Mary retired as head-mistress at Notre Dame High School in 1997, when I was 'Head of RE' at the school. It was my task to organise the Celebration Mass, and she had requested specifically that Bert would say a few words on the scripture readings, perhaps after the bishop's sermon. After first agreeing, the bishop changed his mind at the last minute saying Bert could add 'a paeon of praise for Sr Mary, but you may not sermonise, as there are irresponsible folk around and I fear for your reputation and Fr John Drury's. I would be in trouble with the rightful authorities, and I think Sister Mary would be embarrassed if we did otherwise than speak informally.' Bert was upset, thinking that things had moved on, and wrote his reply: '... You may think the homily only a minor detail, but it was to be (at Mary's request) the cen-tre of the celebration of the Word, she being particularly anxious that what you called "paeans of praise" should be deferred to the reception and meal later, as being out of place in the liturgy. Yes, I know that the homily is regarded as part of the task of ordained ministers, but I would have thought that in a week where we are inviting all and sundry to preach in our churches (and they inviting us to preach in theirs) a bit of discretion could have been exercised, *humano modo* ... You refer to your fear for trouble arising from "irresponsible folk" and "rightful authori-ties'. I remain gobsmacked that even in your retirement you feel unable to stand up to them.'

Bert put aside his hurt, and later regularly visited Bishop Alan when he eventually moved to the local Bupa Nursing Home.

CHAPTER FIFTEEN

Family Life
1978-2005

In those early years we had memorable holidays. I am reminded of them as they stare out at me from the bookshelves – separate small 'diary' volumes all labelled. I am reminded of the Amsterdam Rijks Museum, the Van Gogh Museum and the fine old houses of the religious Begijnhof. A year later, 1978, it was a glorious two weeks in Capri, with many of our sketches in the diary to recall the lazy, sunny days. The pasta at the hotel was the best we have ever enjoyed. In 1979 I was introduced to skiing when we joined the SEC annual trip to Switzerland. There was the short, brilliant canal holiday in the Midlands, shared with my parents and sister, Bert's sister Margaret, and friend Nadine, on a colourful barge drawn along by George, the patient horse. That was pure relaxation.

Quite the opposite for Bert was the annual Holy Land Easter pilgrimage. How hard he always worked to make them prayerful, historical and scriptural experiences for the group. He always succeeded, even by the second day, in bringing strangers together to form a joyful community. His evening pre-supper sessions with drinks purchased by all at 'Duty Free', probably had much to do with this, as well as evening guitar singing on the balcony. On returning home he would write a 'Memory of the Group' for all the pilgrims. In April 1979 he wrote the following, along with £6 refund to each, 'which I happily found on the credit side after doing my final sums. *Ah que le bon Dieu est bon!'*

Clare and I will always remember with affection the gracious courtesy with which *Eleanor, Janet* and *Jenny* put up with our queer Roman Catholic goings on; the extra-ordinary sensitivity with which *Richie, Daisy* and *Joan* were able to unearth bottles of beer even during the prohibited Passover season; the elegant abandon with which *Magdalen* was willing to dance for us; *Maria's* evident satisfaction in getting the real gen on her second visit to the Holy Places; the calm aplomb with which *Pamela* was able to deal with all the eyes that gravitated in the direction of our 'pretty lady'; the true British fortitude with which *Barbara* pressed on regardless in spite of a half-severed leg; *Fr Joe's* triptych, indelibly imprinted in our minds; *Fr Jim's* irrepressible and infectious laugh from the back of the bus; the infinite variety of *Sr Dominic's* head-scarfs; the endless good humour of *Ahilya* even when she was streaming with cold, and the delightfully enigmatic wisecracks of *Paul*; the passionate camel ride on Shushu shared by *Mary R* and *Mary O*; the words of Pilate spoken for us by judge *Patrick*, which we will never hear in the same way again; the solicitude and skill with which *Helen* looked after everyone's nursing needs; the cryptic assignations which periodically prevented *Pat* and *Ann* from joining the walking tours; the clandestine pre-breakfast tea-bar run by the *Quirke sisters*; the tale of derring-do proclaimed to all Jerusalem by *Sylvia*; *Mary T's* disastrous imitation of Christ at the ninth Station, which did not prevent her singing a fine *Magnificat* at En Karem; and the mosquito-ravaged legs of *Lucy* dancing gaily in the Dead Sea.

We awoke to 1980 unaware that this was to be a most re-markable year; one which was to change our lives forever. We had enquired about adoption earlier but Norfolk had turned us down as being 'too old'. A television programme on overseas adoptions from Colombia made us sit up, as it was where, in my nun days, I had wanted to go. The sisters agreed to help us, and we were accepted by Norwich Social Services to go ahead. In February our medical examinations revealed that Bert had early cancer of the colon. The operation was successful, but it meant he could not lead the Holy Land Pilgrims. I had a phonecall from Mahomet, the camel man on the Mount of Olives, dis-tressed and asking if he 'could pay the hospital fees, because he is my brother'. Bert recovered well, and we were able to spend a restful, charmed holiday in Venice instead. We had already booked a half-term May holiday in Rome and Assisi, where I could be introduced to his beloved Italy. Our visit to San Damiano and St Clare's in Assisi was special, and I note that Bert wrote in his part of our diary that 'Clare was almost tempted to revert to the religious life if it meant living here.' Well, not quite! He took me to his favourite places, especially the churches in Rome, and I had to inspect those Egyptian obelisks and hear the translations from hieroglyphs. 'A visit to the English College to revive memories of 1939/49: chapel, refectory, garden, swimming bath (tank), library. The present rector Mgr George Hay received us most graciously and gave us coffee in the Salone, quizzed us on Liverpool, and invited us to join the students on Thursday for lunch at the Villa. Wandered into the Campo dei Fiori, and so on to the Biblicum and Gregorian, and a Papal audience.'

The reference to Liverpool was the 'National Pastoral Conference' held there three weeks earlier. Bert had been invited by Archbishop Worlock to attend, and in preparation asked Notre Dame 6th Form what he should say on their behalf. The diary records the event :

> The central Congress experience was of a practical piece of adult on-going formation, all listening, all sharing their insights, all recognising each other's talents, all catechising each other ('even the *monsignori*'). This basic reality was of far greater importance than individual resolutions or structures (even though without carefully thought-out structures the experience could not have taken place). A sense of freedom, openness, shared responsibility, the laity 'come of age'. A sense not of newness (everything had been said before), but of it being said by ordinary people. It is this (rather than simply talking about the Congress, or trying to communicate its spirit) which must continue, nationally and regionally. The repetition of the experience itself is the only thing that can disseminate the Congress.

Bert added that the bishop spoke well, saying that the progress made at the Congress leaves 'us vulnerable. The years ahead are dangerous ones, as we preach a gospel that for many of us is strange and new. This is preferable to a false sense of reassurance, demanded by some laity and clergy. They too have need of evangelisation.' Later I was present at our diocesan 'Lay Congress', it was less successful. We speakers had about three minutes each, one following the other, with no time for questions, or debate. We just had time to make a statement. What upset many of us was that the large platform was full of priests, no laity at all. During Mass we sang a hymn that referred only to 'brothers', and a nun next to me sang 'sisters', rather loudly, every verse. I joined her.

Leaving the house for school (now at Notre Dame), on 10 July, the postman handed me a letter from Colombia. It announced:

> Here the news. Your twins arrived! A boy and a girl ... So we will be happy to see us, to know us, and to love us from the bottom of our hearts, and we pray to Our Lord that the children will be your happiness and his Glory.
> *Sr Maria Virgilia PCJ in 1934 in Finchley, London etc.*

After school I was in Mothercare, almost skipping with joy. The school staff raided their lofts, to provide us with cots, baby baths, and high chairs. My class made mobiles for the babies, and by the end of the term had set up Saving Accounts for them. The Governors gave me permission to leave school without the term's notice, but I had to promise to visit often. On 4 August we flew to Bogotá, not knowing what to expect. Bert made an enormous diary of the whole adoption process. I am still shaken, reading it again now, on the poverty of our son and daughter's birth and struggle to survive in the mountains. I am in admiration of the welcome we received and the love and care my sisters gave Pedro and Blanca. It even extended to their breaking the 'rule of enclosure' by giving us the comfortable infirmary in the convent. Bert was entrusted with the convent key! Pedro would not have survived but for the sisters' quick action and gentle care. I treasure the days we spent with them as we awaited court decisions, helped by the convent solicitor. We visited the convents, schools and clinics in the shanty towns where I would have been very happy indeed. Mother Teresina simply hugged me and said: 'You are still part of us. It was simply that Blanca and Pedro were going to need you and Bert to care for them and love them.'

From the moment we saw the tiny babies in the sisters' arms, we fell in love with them. As I took tiny Pedro in my arms for a first hug, (with contented sighs from the gathered large community), Bert reached out for Blanca. She looked at him, took his sunglasses from his shirt pocket and dropped them on the floor. 'That's my girl', he said. Thirty years later I still see him in her; both quietly determined, both outspoken when needed, never hiding behind half-truths; and both great lovers of art. Blanca's collection of art books is several times the size of Bert's big collection. Pedro too is like his Dad, but in a different way. He could sing 'babble' in tune before he could walk or talk. Before too long, both of them went off for drum lessons, Bert learning the paradiddle from his son. Pedro, just like Bert, never needs to be surrounded by material goods, both always content with very little. From these first moments it was clear that Bert was going to be a wonderful father. He had endless time for them. I have lovely memories of him recording their first words, of reading bedtime stories, composing his own stories, and playing his guitar to them as I prepared their bottles. He came on all the clinic visits and the doctor appointments, changing lecture times if needs be.

His children's diary has wonderful letters Bert composed, 'from the children' to the Colombian sisters. He wrote first in English and had some help to translate into Spanish. Pedro's first letter began:

Dear Sisters,

Now that I am two years old I think I am old enough to write to you in Spanish. I am getting a big boy (Mummy calls me 'Gordito'). I wonder if you would recognise your little Pedro. Here are my favourite things: food, playing with cars, swimming, singing, being full of mischief and learning to talk. First about food. I *love* mealtimes. My mummy cooks me lovely dinners and I eat very quickly. In fact, I always finish first and then get Blanca or Daddy to give me some of theirs. When we are very good Daddy gives us a sip of wine.

Most of the day I play with my cars or ride on the motorbike which I had at Christmas. I say 'Brr, brr, brr,' as I make my cars crash or disappear under the table. I get rather cross when Blanca spoils my game as she does sometimes. But we always kiss each other better after an argument, and we are really good friends. By the way, I have my own little girl friend, Olga Lucia. She is only three weeks old and her parents come from Neiva. She calls me her 'awfully handsome boy-friend, Pepe.' I have discovered how to sing. I love it. I make a very big noise and it always makes people laugh. I start at 6.00 am and I sing to myself for an hour. Blanca sleeps through it and Mummy and Daddy pretend to sleep. I sing when I play. I sing when we go in the car. I sing in between eating. I sing with my Dad when he plays his guitar. On Sundays in church he plays his guitar and I always shout out and then clap when the song finishes. Blanca yells out 'Daddy' and people all look at her. People call me a little rascal. I do have lots of fun. I am discovering all the things that make Mummy and Daddy say 'No.' I pull books of the study shelves. I hide things in secret places. I open cupboards (I have discovered the wine cupboard!). I will have a little cuddle now and go to bed. I forgot to say that being cuddled is another one of my favourite things. Sometimes I have a dream of Sr Marta Lucia cuddling me. She taught me how to cuddle, and now I get a lot every day. I wish Bogotá were nearer Norwich. Then I could come and give you all a big cuddle and I would sing for you because I love you very much.

Love and kisses,
Pedro

Of course Blanca sent a letter too.

Dear Sisters,
Christmas is past and our birthday is gone, so I have a little more time to write to you. We have had a lovely time with our family and friends. The days were full of laughter. I am now Mummy's best help. Pedro plays all day with his cars, but I put on my apron and help. I love to wash the dishes and the kitchen floor at the same time. Last week I baked some biscuits. Pedro loved them. He is a nice brother and we have lots of fun together. But he is an untidy boy and unlike me, he hates to be clean. I like to look neat and tidy. I have some lovely clothes. My favourite colour is blue. I like to wear hats even indoors.

I do like to walk everywhere. I prefer to push my pram,

even with Pedro still in it, and I get cross when Mummy says I have to sit in it. I often try to get my own way but I don't always succeed. I have five dolls and I carry them everywhere. I sleep with them and with two teddy bears. Occasionally I sleep with Mummy. I wake up sometimes and feel a bit lonely and it is so warm and cosy next to Mummy. She doesn't seem to mind. She says I am like a hot-water bottle.

My favourite things are gymnastics, dressing up and reading. Daddy is full of fun and ideas. After tea we have our Neiva South American music and we all dance. Pedro dances with Mummy and I dance with Daddy. Then we play 'hide and seek' with Daddy and make a lot of noise. Then we have ten minutes of gymnastics on Mummy and Daddy's bed. It is such fun. After this we have our bath and when we are ready for bed we sit quietly with our books while Mummy makes us a drink. Sometimes Daddy plays us the guitar or he tells us a story.

I do wish I could come and see you. I want to see my Sr Claudia again, and I would be so helpful to Sr Teresina. Mummy has just said I would be most helpful to her if I went to bed now, so I must say goodbye. With lots of kisses and cuddles (that I like as much as Pedro),

your *Blanca*

It seems surprising that Bert, already busy at college and out visiting students on teaching practice, was still able to have two books published in 1980: *Death and After. What will really happen?* and *What happens when you pray?* In 1982, alongside composing the children's letters to Bogotá, Bert was preparing for publication his popular *Pilgrim to the Holy Land*, which has since gone into five editions. This was a lovely shared task, as I drew the illustrations. We moved my desk next to his, and I recall hours of gentle music as we worked away sharing ideas occasionally, or just being together, with the children tucked up in bed. A year later he put together 50 of his songs based on biblical texts, each introduced in its context, into a book, *The Gospel in Song*. He wrote songs too about the children, his first being a lullaby, followed immediately by 'You have turned my life upside down'. His diaries include one liner notes recording their development,

handwritten between the longer typed entries. They recorded
the first teeth, first sitting up, in fact, first of everything. On our
first Christmas we had a lovely moment at Mass. Pedro, sitting
on Bert's knee, burbled what sounded like his first word, and it
was loud enough for all to hear: 'Abba'. Probably most babies
say that, but for us it was special as we celebrated the birth of
Jesus who would later address God as his 'Abba' – Father.

Bert's notes recall lovely memories of those days: 'Pedro
prefers watching the washing machine to TV.' 'Blanca insists on
wearing rosaries around her neck.' 'Blanca crawls forward,
Pedro backwards.'

As they grew older Bert noted that 'Pedro sings Happy
Birthcake to me'. 'Blanca wants to share her food with starving
people on television.' My favourites are: 'After pre-breakfast
milk, we all went up to wake Clare with three mouth organs',
and 'We built a snowman in the garden before breakfast.' In
spring of 1983, after Bert had made a sand pit, he wrote: 'We
drove to Eccles to nick sand for our sand pit. Pedro acted as
map-reader.' Then 'Work on the roof. Blanca (age 4) wants to
marry all the workmen', and when Frank died in 1984, Pedro's
comment as he was playing near me in the kitchen, 'Daddy is
sad, because you can't buy a new brother.' At Easter that year
there was trouble in Jerusalem during the time of Bert's
Pilgrimage. Bert wrote in the diary: 'When Clare expressed worries about me, Pedro answered her: "I expect God will look after
him." Blanca asked, "Why, does he live in Jerusalem?"'

When not at College, or at his desk, Bert was making the children new toys: a wheelbarrow, a garden swing, a trailer for
Pedro's bike and a doll's house for Blanca. One of his best cre-
ations was an engine made out of old pieces of wood and pram
wheels. Painted it looked grand, with room for both of them to
sit in the driver's cabin. He made the garden shed into a play-
house for them and their friends. He made up games for their
parties, leading the children round the garden as a Pied Piper
with a guitar. There are records of our visits to pleasure parks,
zoos, the puppet theatre, the annual pantomime, the circus, the
Norfolk Show, banger racing at Yarmouth, and weekly swimming lessons. We were fortunate enough to have a London base,
at Margaret's Hampstead flat, for an annual stay to visit the

museums and children's shows. Favourites were the Natural History Museum and the Children's Museum. When they were young, these days had to include a ride in the car, on the top of a bus, on the underground and in a taxi. Bert never missed any of this, always encouraging the children to explore the world around them, and making it fun. Bedtime reading was always a joy for us. As a toddler Blanca would take *The Truth of God Incarnate* off the shelf for her book (attracted by the purple cover). We would hide the Little Miss book inside. Pedro and Bert's favourite was the *HA Ha Bonk Book*.

As the children got older and moved into St Thomas More Middle School, Bert began his 'poetry teaching' with them. As he walked them to school they made up clever, amusing poems, each composing alternate lines. As a six year old, Pedro and Dad produced this:

> As I was going to school one day
> I met my God upon the way.
> He said to me, 'Hello my dear'.
> I said to him, 'Speak up. Can't hear.'

And one of Blanca's:

> Dad played his guitar at Brownies tonight
> and half way through we all had a fright,
> 'cos Dad's guitar broke completely in two –
> and what Dad said made Brown Owl turn blue.

These early days of parenthood taught us to look carefully at the religious language usually presented to children. When our two were preparing for First Communion, with a very good teacher, it was a remark of a school-friend that made us sit up. We were horrified when Pedro said, 'Mummy, Matthew said that Fr Robin had blood in the cup. He wouldn't drink that, would he? Yuk.' We were just as disturbed when Blanca told Bert a very odd bedtime story, a few weeks later. 'Daddy what do you think of this? Supposing you turned into a biscuit or bread; no into an apple pie? And somebody ate you up. Then you suddenly turned back into you. And that very big, enormous person you were inside, ate a strawberry, but you were struggling to get out so he bit your fingers or your toes.' We laughed about her strange story, but was it a six-year-old's vivid imagination trying to make sense of the notion of 'receiving Jesus' in Communion Bread? I shared these thoughts at a diocesan meeting and was shot down for being 'critical and unhelpful.' Bert's response was to write a series of booklets for children. The first two were a *Carol Service for Children*, and the *Our Father for Children*. There were 13 titles in all; the most popular with parents and parishes were *A Way of the Cross for Children* and *A Maundy Service for Children*. We still hear of parishes and schools using these texts. We spent hours in photo libraries finding appropriate photographs to illustrate each page. Equally popular in parishes was, and still is, a booklet Bert wrote, *The Passover Meal*. He consulted with Rabbi Hugo Gryn over it, and only published it with his approval. For several years Bert would lead this 'Passover' service with a group of parishioner friends in one of their homes.

The highlight of 1989 was our extraordinary return to South America. The short diary entry reads: '1-26 August we were all in South America. We had arranged to go in any case to introduce the children (now 9) to their roots. A local BBC producer, Dick Meadows, parent of Blanca's schoolfriend, asked to bring a team of five to record the visit, pay some of the expenses, and enable us to visit the childen's remote birthplace which we would not otherwise have been able to reach. I kept a full account of the month in a separate diary. Neighbours, Srs M. Paul and Teresa, and Sr Oswin looked after cat.' The visit was highly successful in every way, especially in giving our children a renewed love for their own people. Dick Meadows had wanted to show, at a time when overseas adoptions were having a bad press, that it was possible for them to be good news for everyone involved. The BBC *Everyman* programme was sensitively produced and voted the best of that series. It resulted in about two hundred letters of delight and approval. Only one was unhappy about the 'long-term damage' that could be done to our children. We were sad that the only negative press report was in the Catholic *Universe*, reporting the view of Mgr Michael Connelly, secretary of the Catholic Child Welfare Council. 'He has urged children's agencies not to offer help to people wishing to adopt outside the UK. We believe that it is in the long-term interests of children to grow up within their families of origin ... We feel sure that the people in developing countries who make children available for adoption do so with good motives, but they do not appreciate the consequences for the children and the fact that this traffic in children is illegal.' How strange to call approved overseas adoptions 'illegal traffic in children'. Perhaps I should have sent these words of eight-year-old Blanca to Fr Connelly to reassure him that not much damage had been done to her self-esteem by our 'child trafficking'! Asked to describe herself, she once wrote:

> Intelligent, adorable, kind, clever, pretty. Mum is the same, plus cooking. Dad, is the same plus, powerful, clever at mending. Pedro, is the same, plus cheeky and funny. But *all* the family are very loving.

The local Norwich papers were enthusiastic about the visit, pointing out that the 'BBC was interested in showing how an inter-racial adoption can work. It is a means of bringing cultures together and uniting people.' These positive reports resulted in wonderful support, especially from Norwich schools, for our appeal to raise money for the children's impoverished town. When the water filter tanks were repaired there was enough money left to build two schools in the mountains, named after Pedro and Blanca. Unicef oversaw the work for us, and later our schools became the training centres for an education project for rural areas. Today the project has grown to about 30 schools in the mountains. I treasure one special photograph of our town, L'Argentina. Our first distant view of it, a small huddle of little white washed houses around the church square and market place, nestling in the hillside, was surprising. A rainbow broke out and one end rested exactly over the houses. In retrospect, I like to think in a dreamy way, that we were able eventually to bring the Pot of Gold to our 'family' of Chibcha Indians in the Andes Mountains. They are 'our' family as Bert and I were made 'honorary citizens' of the town in a moving ceremony before we left. A few years later the priest of L'Argentina was killed, like Archbishop Oscar Romero, for supporting the rights of the poor.

I returned to part-time teaching in September 1989, at Notre

Dame High School. Later Bert was to join us to teach scripture in
the Sixth Form. He continued to write on scripture over the next
years, and to compile a series of *Worship Anthologies*. Many will
probably consider that one of his best publications is *An
Anthology for the Church Year*. It is a collection of biblical texts
(some in Bert's own translation), readings, reflections, poems
and prayers drawn from different countries, centuries and religious traditions. It is a book to return to again and again. I return
to Bert's own powerful reflection on the Trinity, wondering how
Cardinal Heenan could have accused him of not believing in
this great mystery:

> The reality to which people give the name 'God'
> is an unfathomable mystery,
> so far beyond human reach that if he didn't breathe a word,
> no one would ever know anything about him.
> Christians acknowledge that there has never been a time
> when *God* did not breathe a word:
>> He has always made himself known.
> But, they claim, that Word of God
>> was never breathed more clearly
> than in the life and death of *Jesus*.
> And that Breath (or *Spirit*) is still felt in the inspiration
> that Jesus is able to give, even after his death.
> Christians claim to know the *Father* through the *Spirit* of *Jesus*.
> That is what the word 'Trinity' is trying to express.

The tortured language used in the church's formulation of
dogma points to the obvious difficulty in finding words to describe the mystery of God. The fifth Century Chalcedon answer
to the question, 'Who is Jesus?', for example, is not inspiring.
'We are all agreed in teaching ... one and the same Christ, the
Son, the Lord, only begotten, in two natures unconfused, unchangeable, undivided, inseparable. The difference of natures
will never be abolished by their being united but rather the
properties of each remain unimpaired, both coming together in
one person and substance, not parted or divided among two
persons but in one and the same only begotten Son, the divine
Word, the Lord Jesus.' (*Enchiridion Symbolorum*, Denziger 148)
Bert's life work was an attempt to present a Jesus who could be

understood in a better way than through puzzling dogmatic formulas.

In 1991 we took the children on the Easter Holy Land Pilgrimage, keen that they should understand why dad loved his annual visit. I was anxious to go again because I had written three GCSE resource-books, *According to Mark*, *According to Matthew* and *According to Luke*. Teaching had made me quite 'homesick' to walk once more in the footsteps of Jesus and the apostles. Later in that year Bert had the great sadness of Pat Murphy O'Connor's death. He would miss Spud more than anyone.

In the 1990s Bert continued to write, lead teacher conferences, and train Anglican lay readers. He was examiner at Endsleigh College in Hull, and Christ's College, Liverpool, and he increased his hours at Notre Dame when numbers taking A-level Philosophy and Ethics grew rapidly. He taught Philosophy of Religion, producing a popular Heinemann resource-book of this name, while I taught the Ethics. Two other teachers shared a second group of students. Bert's students were always enthusiastic about his lessons, resulting in five students going on to study theology at university, at Oxford, Durham, King's College, London, and Manchester. Many more chose to study philosophy at university. One of his students went on to ordination as an Augustinian priest.

The mid 1990s were the busiest times in our family life. We were both teaching and writing, and I was now Head of RE in our eight-form entry school. The children were preparing for their GCSEs and holidays were important. Bert recorded in July 1994: 'Up North to catch up on Pedro and Blanca's geography projects.' We retraced their school trips to take good photographs and to sketch. From our B&B in Whitby: 'We went via Filey to the Ravenscar cliffs and Robin Hood Bay to re-inspect Pedro's project, climbing cliffs and collecting fossils. Back into Whitby where the children wanted to shop, and Clare and I drove up to St Hilda's Abbey and the brilliant exhibition of its history. Whatever happened to Christianity in England?' Later 'Then via Thirsk, Northallerton and A684 through Wensleydale to Blanca's project in Grisedale. Impossible remoteness and lengthy walks. We found an ideal B&B near Kendal (totally dead), Windermere (impossibly crowded) to Bowness, found a brilliant pizzeria, and drowned much Orvieto ... Back next day to Sedburg for Blanca's project charting a stream near Kirby Stephen. Pedro and I sketched.' The next year was a relaxing holiday in the Greek Islands, with a memorable boat trip, accompanied by dolphins, from Samos to Patmos. There we climbed the hill to the small church over the cave where tradition says St John wrote his gospel. Strangely Bert never recorded this holiday in words, but with delightful sketches and striking photographs.

In June 1996 as the children completed their exams, Bert retired from teaching at Notre Dame. To celebrate his life's work the two of us had a magnificent few days in Venice at the Danieli Hotel, travelling outward on the Orient Express, and returning first class, with a victorious 'Heineken Cup' Bath Rugby team (Jeremy Guscott and Mike Catt). We were, as Bert wrote, 'Bedazzled as ever by Venice.' He continued giving lectures across the country for a number of years, but enjoyed more leisure in his writings and in communication with friends. A letter to Anna, a friend of forty years, from his Hadham days, is typical of his warmth and understanding that endeared him to so many:

> I was thinking today that, years (no, millennia) before we invented telegraph, telephones, internet, worldwide webs, the good Lord had already, in his wisdom, provided us with the means to stay closely and unbrokenly in touch with each other. It is called prayer. When we stand in the presence of God, and hold up before him those whom we love, how can we imagine we are distant from them, or they from us? ... Juliet has been in touch to tell us of your recent painful history. Our hearts go out to you, and we pray that your recovery will be long-lasting ... I know how wretched it is to feel unwell, and how aggravating it is when people jolly you along with a 'There, there.' Suffering is suffering, as even Jesus knew, and there is no wishing it away. What is reassuring is that friends are thinking of you, and we write this to let you know that we are. And a big kiss to Katherine too.

The following year Bert and I had our last visit to the Holy

Land, just the two of us, to revise his popular guide book. While there we visited an extraordinary Catholic Melchite priest, a Palestinian born in Galilee. Fr Elias Chacour learnt from his parents to love and accept everyone. In 1947 his father had celebrated on hearing that Jews could return to Palestine. 'We must be especially kind and make them feel at home,' he said. 'This year we will celebrate the resurrection early – for our Jewish brothers who were threatened with death, and who are alive.' The later suffering of the family, and his parents' patient acceptance of the pain, led young Elias to the priesthood. We visited him in Ibillin, a small Galilean town, where he devoted his life to education, building a school and college where thousands of young Christian and Muslim Palestinians and Jewish youth have been educated together. Strangely, he is funded by American Evangelical Christians, as he had no support from the Catholic Church, or others. It was ten years since I had been to Jerusalem, but I was spotted at the Damascus Gate by a stall holder, shouting out, 'Clare, Clare, come, I make you special felafel.' It had always been a favourite stopping place of mine.

The visit was a welcome relief from a disruption in our peaceful lives that I had caused. I had been invited by Heinemann to contribute to a series of GCSE books, 'Examining Religions'. My title was *Roman Catholic Christianity*. The publisher asked for the Nihil Obstat and Imprimatur, for assurance that it was free from doctrinal and moral error, knowing that Catholic schools were a big market. Each author had to follow the same double-page spread format, which included discussion points, good photographs, reflections, and essay suggestions. The book, published January 1995, was received well, with good sales. About 16 months later I was called from the classroom to answer a phone call from America! It was Joanna Bogle of the *Catholic Times* informing me that my book was not teaching the Catholic faith and the Vatican had been told. The next day it was a *Daily Telegraph* headline by the Churches' Correspondent: 'Catholics accuse textbook of heresy'. This was my first experience of journalists embellishing statements. I was supposed to have said that 'half the Catholics in my classes have divorced parents and usually one girl had had an abortion.' The examples of my 'heresies' were pieces taken out of context. I now knew just how bad Bert must have felt when he was the subject of distorted press criticism. By midday we had journalists from the local press, BBC *Look East*, and Anglia Television arriving at my school.

That weekend it was the *Catholic Herald*'s main headline: 'RE text outrages Catholics', with several articles criticising the 'ex-nun' Clare Richards. According to William Oddie, 'This book is clearly and deliberately subversive not only of specifically Catholic doctrine, but of the central articles of mainstream Christianity.' According to Christine Odone, the Director of the Catholic Education Service wanted it stressed that I was a free-lance writer whose book was not commissioned by the Bishop's Conference, so she had not been shown 'any of the work-in-progress'. In other newspapers she seemed to blame my diocese for not overseeing my work. Yet I had two theologians appointed to read the text carefully for the 'Nihil Obstat', and the approval of Bishop Alan Clark. The *Catholic Herald*'s editorial was also critical of the book. 'The Church must strike back, quickly remove this textbook from our classrooms and its teachings from our children's minds.' Heinemann told me that they had received only six complaints in nearly two years.

For months the paper published articles and letters about the book, with only three letters supportive, two from my school, one a letter signed by the majority of the staff, and one from my sixth-formers, who also gave me a huge bouquet of flowers. They wrote: 'We can hardly believe what we are reading about our Head of RE, Mrs Clare Richards. In our school she is known as one of the best teachers who makes every lesson interesting and helps us to understand our faith without forcing it on us. The nastiness in some of the letters is exactly how she teaches us *not* to behave. In fact the type of cold Catholicism expressed by the correspondents is what puts us off going to church.' I was moved by being told by a sixteen-year-old, 'You have been an inspiration and taught me how to think hard about many issues, and I now have strong beliefs. "LFC" will always stick in my mind as being in the forefront of your lessons and your personality.' LFC referred to my summing up of Luke's gospel, 'Love, Forgiveness and Compassion'. We remembered it by Liverpool Football Club's initials.

I was receiving letters of support from Diocesan Education Centres and from teachers across the country, and grateful to Mark Stanford, writing in the *Universe* in response to the criticism that I 'doubted' the resurrection. He pointed out that the GCSE examination 'demands that pupils investigate all possible reasons for belief and arguments in support of beliefs. Clare Richards has done an excellent job throughout the book ...' David Torevell, a Senior Lecturer at Liverpool Hope University College, wrote a letter to the *Tablet* also giving a clear analysis of GCSE requirements, using the resurrection page as his example. 'Nowhere does the author state the historical way of understanding the resurrection is either intellectually inferior to or mutually exclusive from other ways.' He wrote that the book's 'proposed methodology in helping pupils to grasp the issues and complexities of Catholicism is second to none.' I was very grateful for such support.

It was hard to feel that I had caused such a bitter debate, which inevitably resurrected the past problems others had experienced. Bishop David Konstant was criticised again, as were the earlier school programmes like *Here I am* and *Weaving the Web*, not to mention the closing of Corpus Christi College. Correspondents in the press loved to describe me as the 'ex-nun who was married to the ex-priest, Hubert Richards.' I was most annoyed by Terence Wynne, of the *Universe*, repeating the conversation he and Mgr Leonard had with me 20 years previously, where I supposedly denied belief in the resurrection. He was surprised that a book by me would be given 'the Nihil Obstat – so cheaply. The book makes my blood run cold. No book with Catholic in the title should represent someone's heretical views.' He wrote to me: 'Your book was in tatters even before I put the paper in my typewriter ... Reputable Catholic booksellers refuse to stock it. You should concentrate on holding on to your job at Notre Dame and keep your head down. If you go, Bert will be sure to follow and money in the bank is important! I have just returned from the press briefing after the Low Week Hierarchy meeting and soundings I took would make my advice well worth your attention.'

The most hurtful letters came from Norwich parishioners. One blamed my mother saying 'she probably remained a

Catholic only because it was the "done thing" to do'. It was unfortunate that at this time in 1996 I had accepted, on Sr Mary's
recommendation, the invitation of the Local Education
Authority to take early retirement, and be re-employed part-
time, while remaining Head of Department. It saved the school
money. It evoked another large, sensational headline in the
Universe: 'Row Teacher Shock': 'A Catholic teacher whose RE textbook has caused protests from parents has decided to step
down.'

How grateful I was for the sensitive and understanding support I had from my bishop, Peter Smith. No sooner had he been
welcomed to our diocese in May 1995 than he was confronted
publicly with the controversy. He received more hassle than I
did. He discussed the weaknesses in the book with me, suggesting that a revision would be useful as some of the material could
have been 'expressed more clearly', and a mistake over contraception needed omitting. His July statement pointed out that the
book was a resource or support for pupils who were encouraged to express their own opinions and not a manual of Catholic
dogma. He also accused critics of using the book as a catalyst for
making sweeping and unjust attacks on the whole system of
religious education in Catholic schools. We hoped that it would
end there, with some changes made to the text. Cardinal Hume
had also written to me that I should try to ignore the bitter press.
He would have expressed some of the content differently, but it
was certainly not heretical. The Cardinal had been present at the
May 'Faith of Our Fathers Conference' in London, when a famous
American nun, Mother Angelica, had criticised the present 'dis-
tortion' of Vatican II Documents. She was supported by Daphne
McCloud of the *Pro Fide* group, who were behind much of the
criticism of me. I'm told she took a copy of my book to the
Conference to denounce it. Most of the Press did not report that
Cardinal Hume warned *Pro Fide* not to sit in judgement on
teachers, telling the audience that teaching was not only impart-
ing knowledge of the faith, 'minds and hearts had to be won'.

Complaints rumbled on well into 1997. I was denounced in
most Catholic newspapers and magazines, as Bert had once been.
Fr John Redmund, in his *Universe* columns agreed 'basically',
with Daphne Mcleod's *Pro fide* judgement on the book, referring

to a long critique made by Fr Rochford and Peter Grace in a 96 page booklet, *Roman Catholic Christianity: The Facts They Don't Want You To Know*. It had been distributed to the governors of every Catholic school in the country, and to Rome. Letters and phone calls started all over again. Apparently the booklet contained 118 errors, most it would seem, 'heretical'. We managed to obtain a copy, and Bert, to 'cheer me up' pointed out that it would appear I was a world record-breaker as it implied I was 'a crypto-atheist, humanist, rationalist, materialist, pantheist, syncretist, determinist, liberalist, evolutionist, pelagian, arian, nestorian, deist, marxist, Freudian and protestant heretic.'

Bert was sent, anonymously, a paper written by Canon Telford years earlier. It was another criticism of Bert and Peter De Rosa and Corpus Christi College. On the back of the paper was typed the following:

> Your 'ex-nun turned mum' *married to her priestly-husband* is continuing the work this sad man began in the sixties. Ever since Our Blessed Lord, Jesus Christ, began his church he has had the doubting-Thomases and the Judases. The sad fools.

In August 1997 the *Catholic Herald* was the first to report that Rome had banned my book. I had not been told. Heinemann's were furious and considered libel action, only withdrawing because of cost. They feared that the name 'Richards' would harm Bert's philosophy book, and further writing they had suggested for me was withdrawn. Cardinal Ratzinger called Bishop Peter Smith to Rome. He told us that he would have to respond to Ratzinger's command to withdraw the 'Imprimatur'. He honestly wanted to support me and in his careful press statement made it clear that it was Rome's action, not his. 'At the request of the Sacred Congregation of the Clergy I am withdrawing the *Imprimatur* accorded to the book *Roman Catholic Christianity* on 6 October 1994 ... Consequently, in accordance with c.827.2 of the Code of Canon Law, this book may no longer be used as a textbook in Catholic Schools.' In the rest of his long statement Bishop Peter wrote with great understanding of the difficult role of those engaged in religious education, and wrote of me as a faithful, practising Catholic, regarded as an extremely good teacher ... 'in good standing in the church, and highly respected

amongst Catholic teachers who are engaged in educating children in the faith.' Bert and I were moved by our bishop's support,
which would inevitably put him into conflict with our 'oppon-
ents'. Bert had been supported by the laity, and opposed by the
bishops. For me it was the reverse. I was saddened that Bishop
Peter Smith, now Archbishop of Southwark, had to be drawn
into this. It is no surprise to me that today he is greatly loved
and respected as a thoughtful, understanding church leader.

Bert relaxed after all the stress by putting together the wise
and humorous sayings that he had collected over a lifetime, in a
new book *Quips and Quotes*. Meanwhile I enjoyed my last few
months of teaching as I prepared for retirement at the end of the
summer term. We immediately flew out to Florence and Rome,
where we stayed in Palazzola, the Venerabile summer retreat.
Over the next few years Bert could begin to slow down, with
fewer lectures away from home, spending more time at his desk
reading and writing. He wrote four books on biblical themes,
and he remained as Chairman of the Norfolk Theological
Society until 2001, when approaching his 80th birthday. He was
greatly appreciated in this role, which he held for over twenty
years. The new chairman wrote of him later: 'Bert was always an
inspirational figure whose agile mind never concealed his warm
heart. He was one of those people with whom an encounter always left you feeling more alive than you were previously. I
know so many of his erstwhile students for whom he opened
doors, which proved to be life-changing … I could never aspire
to emulate his style of chairmanship which, with its blend of
humour and scholarship, was always in a league of its own.'

I was invited by Bishop Peter to organise the national
Catholic Certificate of Religious Studies (CCRS) for teachers and
parish workers, and I set up several small groups across the diocese. Bert contributed to the scripture modules and, as always,
was greatly appreciated. Sitting at his desk, with his diaries
sometimes open, his thoughts often returned to Rome and he
kept up correspondence with the few fellow students still alive.
He wrote to Fr Michael Killeen in Sheffield:

'Mick Killeeen, dost thou remember
Days of young frivolity?

Dost thou still in Life's November
Think of 1943?'
'Hubert, my emotion quells me
Molto con sospirio;
Careful calculation tells me
That's near sixty years ago.'
Refrain: *Fugit Bossus, fugit Hossus, Fugit Tyler et Farrow,*
           Tempus fugit, fugiamus, anno octogesimo.
(Sung to Beethoven's *Ode to Joy*)

In October 2002 Bert attended the symposium 'Abbot Butler and The Council' at Heythrop College. 'With few exceptions', he wrote, 'a dry and wasted day, with an ageing audience (no priests at all!) Not only is Vatican II a dead duck, but its concerns are not the issue of 2002 … Lonely journey home, via a walk along Portobello Road.' It summed up Bert's increasing sadness that nothing seemed to reflect his vision of what could have been.

Another sadness was his visit to Rome in 2003, when he went out to check details for a revision of his pilgrimage guidebook to that city. He stayed at the English College, expecting to meet up with lively students and staff. He wrote: 'I returned from Rome, highly confused by the experience, and even more bizarre journey home. I wrote to the rector: "I write because I feel a sense of shame in abandoning the VEC the way I did, especially after the trouble you went to find room for me. The fact is I suffered from loneliness, with all common rooms deserted at all times, and everyone hard at their laptops. I say this not in criticism but in admiration. I approve of your regime of seriousness and purpose. But though I kept busy in my daily walks to update my guidebook, I felt as a family man the need to relax in company, and never got the opportunity. So I decided to cut my losses and run. Forgive me".' How I wish I could have gone with him, but my CCRS work and frequent talks for UNICEF prevented this.

Later, our participation in a conference at London Colney on 'Scripture in Education', attended by 27 Heads of RE and chaplains, left both of us wondering which way things were moving in schools. Bert gave a lecture on 'Scripture', and mine was on 'Scripture in the Classroom.' We were very well received, but the problem was the GCSE syllabuses on offer. Catholic schools seemed to want the 'Catholic syllabus', which offered doctrine, with no scripture option. Our worst fears were to come. With the appearance of school league tables, it seemed that heads were willing to choose the easiest syllabus to gain high marks. Was knowing Jesus of the gospels less important than academic high success? In my own school very high grades are now achieved by learning doctrine by heart and, I am told, scripture barely features. A Catholic Ofsted inspector tells me that this is now common across the country, with little serious study of the gospels. How deeply depressing. We were not surprised when, in 2005, our new bishop asked me to step down from running the CCRS, on the grounds that it was 'not professional enough'. He did not want small group discussions that followed the lectures (given by priests, teachers, and Bert); it must be taught, he said by 'real professionals, the theologians'. This means that it was taken over by the Dominicans in Cambridge, where all participants attend lectures without, I am told, time for discussion.

The joy and the great expectations that Bert had in his study days and early priesthood was now ending in disappointment, disillusionment, and overwhelming sadness. It was a good thing that we had our families, especially Pedro and Blanca, to keep us more than content in this precious side of our lives.

CHAPTER SIXTEEN

The End Time
2005-2010

From 2005 the diaries tell very little of Bert's life and thoughts, except in the press cuttings he included. His entries are little more than jottings of daily activities, with most about *my* busy life. We had a short holiday in Barcelona enjoying the Gaudi landmarks, and dining in the 'Four Cats' artists' restaurant, where Picasso had designed the menu cards. We even got to a Barcelona Football Club training session, with Ronaldino entertaining us with his skills and smiles. We returned home just as the Pope died.

> Fri 1 April. Death of Pope John Paul II. Astonishing cover from all the press. The only criticism comes from RC reporters and writers!

Bert kept several press cuttings with his underlinings, clearly appreciating Clifford Longley's reflections in *The Guardian*. It was a balance between praise and criticism, commending, for example, the Pope's commitment to 'genuine brotherhood with the people of the covenant', but criticising his 'weeding out by the Vatican's thought police under Cardinal Joseph Ratzinger, those theologians who dared to challenge him. Longley's greatest criticism was the Vatican's preference for "safe yes men" to fill the top jobs in archdiocese and diocese across the world.' Bert had been upset by this over the years, and strongly underlined Longley's words: 'He therefore deprived the church of the sort of imaginative risk-taking leadership it badly needed. Better men, meanwhile found their career paths inexplicably blocked.' A later *Guardian* article described John Paul II's papacy as 'one of the most punitive, centralising Vatican regimes in recent history'. In another hard hitting article Bert underlined the words of Terry Eagleton: 'John Paul II set about rolling back the liberal achievements of Vatican II.' I recall a perceptive comment Bishop Butler made to us when Bert and I had lunch at St Edmund's with him very soon after the papal election in 1978.

Bert had said it was good to have a non-Italian pope. Butler said that he was worried about having a Polish pope. The communist restrictions imposed on Catholic Poland meant that Karol Wojtyla would not have moved forward with the 'thinking' church, nor been prepared to move with the Vatican Council.

We were not enthusiastic when Cardinal Ratzinger was elected the new Pope. A Spanish Jesuit theologian, Jose Ignacio Gonzalez Faus, writing in *The Tablet*, urged him to explore the meaning of the 'Petrine ministry'. The cutting has red underlinings from Bert, who wrote on it 'Brilliant!'

By the end of this year Bert's hearing was deteriorating; he could no longer play his guitar, nor listen to the classical music that was always a background to his work at the desk. He was also reading fewer books. In January 2006 we had a delightful overnight stay at a Millennium Hotel in London, where Pedro was a chef. 'Booked into poshest floor, Kingsize bed. Bar downstairs, where everyone smoked. Enormous and expensive snack, but very tasty. Short nap, then walk to V&A Museum. Watched the ice-skating, and back to the hotel for a gin. Pedro came to meet us at 7.00. Brilliant lasagne and wine. I went outside for a smoke, and got utterly lost … A very comfortable night followed by 9.00 breakfast (full works) in fine restaurant. Left Pedro and walked to Westminster Cathedral for v. nostalgic Latin Mass and Communion.' The signs were probably there that Bert was slipping, slowly, into alzheimers. He was still able to enjoy Blanca's graduation with a good Fine Arts degree later in the year.

The 2007 diary was his last. It is short, with one-line entries, and with no book list. It also records the deaths of several close friends, especially that of the Anglican priest, Alan Webster, 'the boldly innovative Dean who brought a welcome openness to Norwich Cathedral and St Paul's'. He had warmly welcomed us to Norwich and became a dear friend, sharing a great deal with Bert over the years. For some time, Bert had been preparing a book on *The Four Gospels*, a simple introduction to the evangelists' writings and to the understanding of 'literary form'. Published by McCrimmons, it was launched at St Paul's bookshop in Westminster on 30 October, by Cardinal Cormac Murphy O'Connor, who wrote: 'Hubert Richards is a scripture scholar of the highest repute. He is a marvellous teacher and has a wonderful gift of clarity and simplicity in his writings. His book, *The Four Gospels*, is an example of erudition and learning but communicated in the simplest style.' This is a perfect description of what Bert had achieved in his biblical writing. At last he was recognised publicly by a Westminster Cardinal. We had a celebratory meal over the road at the Spaghetti House, with family and a few friends.

The final diary entries are 'Late meal with Pedro and Blanca. Football. Bins out front.' Pasted in is a letter from Margaret and Nadine praising the book, and a typical note from his nephew Brian, which accompanied a parcel with a wooden pipe rack. 'Stroud, Friday: This belonged to your father. I think you are old enough to have it now. Puff puff. Brian.' Bert scribbled underneath:

> Ich bin uberwhelmed not to mention uber der moon and feelen Dank. H.

In spring 2008 Bert was diagnosed with alzheimers and prescribed the drug that could slow down its progression. Happily, in October he was able, accompanied by Pedro, to give Blanca away at her Cathedral wedding to Neil, whose family and friends flew over from Galway to make it a wonderful, Irish, English, Colombian celebration. Delia Smith's Norwich City 'Top of the Terrace' was the setting for a magnificent reception. Bert's confusion and isolation by deafness slowly increased, but he was aware when our little grandson, Cian George, arrived the following summer. Eventually the cruelty of alzheimers had the last word, and a weary, struggling Bert finally seemed to give in. Physically he weakened, and following a fall, needed to be admitted into hospital. For five weeks the Norfolk and Norwich Hospital gave him wonderful care. The doctor and nurses were surprised that Bert was so quiet and patient, given the advancement of his dementia. They asked to know more about him, and remarked again and again that he was very special, and it was a privilege to care for him. It was, they said, unusual that he recognised me to the end.

When it was apparent that Bert was near to death, and on a palliative care programme, we were able to bring him home. He

was peaceful during the daytime as he was sleeping or unconscious, but surprised us when he opened his eyes and concentrated when the priest gave him the Last Rites. It appeared Bert
knew then what was happening. I hope he recognised that he
was anointed as a priest, 'Because that was what he always was',
Fr Dick White told me. Blanca had the inspiration to play
Gregorian Chant by his bedside. I willed him to hear it.

At night Bert was restless and deeply disturbed. His last
words to me were heartbreaking: 'I don't know anymore who I
am, where I am, or what I am. And I don't know anymore if God
even exists.' Born on Christmas Day, he died like Christ on the
Cross: 'My God, my God, why have you forsaken me?' On 24
March 2010, the eve of the Feast of the Annunciation, Blanca,
Pedro and my sister were in the room when Bert died; I was out
answering the door-bell.

Reading through the diaries, I was struck by an entry, fifty-four
years earlier, where he was thinking about death. He was re-
flecting on the burial of Archbishop Myers at St Edmund's
College, Ware.

> Never so impressed as by the whole clergy taking up the
> Requiem *aeternum dona eis*, softly and melodiously, a deep
> moan of great sorrow and beauty. The polyphony from the
> choir was also most moving ...
>
> Is the Church wrong in making funeral music sad and
> nostalgic? I used to think so, and held that our faith in an
> after life demands that we go to our death singing with joy
> and exultation. I have also frequently said that I was quite
> willing to die at any time – what is there to lose? But today,
> with the immense coffin right in front of me, the Mass, the
> procession here, the empty grave in the Galilee chapel – the
> deep loneliness of death hit me. We all die utterly alone. And
> one needs colossal faith because faith itself is a kind of death
> to oneself, a venture into the dark, alone.
>
> The sadness of the music seems fitting for such a medit-
> ation. We're not frightened of going ourselves – as long as it
> is not yet! And subconsciously, but really, we're afraid that
> what appears to be a strong faith now will, when it's put to
> the iron test, falter. We really have to take the plunge into the

abyss and darkness. The true light lies beyond.

I played sad and haunting music on my guitar all evening.

The Requiem Mass was in our Cathedral, celebrated by a Corpus Christi priest, Canon George Browne. A Notre Dame student of Bert's who went on to study theology, gave the eulogy, and Phillip, our Anglican priest friend, spoke movingly of Bert's influence amongst the other churches: 'Bert was a remarkable person, one of the few who was as close to an embodiment of "The good man, Jesus" as you will get … One last memory. Returning to his bedside when I last saw him looking gaunt but still with that twinkle in his eye, "What's God up to?" he asks me. "I don't know, Bert, but I know one thing. You had better go on bothering him for that's what you're best at and you've done it all your life".'

Bert's burial was in the bright spring sunshine of Easter Week. He used to speak of death as 'Dying into the Love of God', (whatever that means.) I trust that he now knows the embrace of God's love. After all he spent his whole life studying, teaching and living the gospel, which he summed up in the words: 'Jesus says, God is love, so go and be like him.'

On 30 October 2010 we held his Memorial Service at St Aloysius' Church, Euston, London. Cardinal Cormac was present, with the Mass celebrated by Archbishop Peter Smith, with Bishop David Konstant, Bishop Rawsthorne and 14 priests concelebrating. I was grateful that Fr Brendan Callaghan SJ gave the homely. Bert would have approved that it was a Jesuit priest who had almost the last word about him. Many other priests, nuns and laity, most his former students, even parishioners from Hadham days, were there to join with our families and many friends, to celebrate Bert's life, and his love that we all shared. It was the Cardinal who sent us from the church to the reception with laughter, not tears. He reminded us of the fun-loving student Bert, friend of his brother Pat (Spud), who together kept the Venerabile on its toes with their pranks and endless enthusiasm. It was St Thomas More who expected to meet his family and friends 'merrily in heaven'. What a merry reunion Spud and Bert must be having.